The Divine Romance

365 Days Meditating on the Song of Songs

BroadStreet
PUBLISHING

BroadStreet Publishing® Group, LLC
Savage, Minnesota, USA
BroadStreetPublishing.com

The Divine Romance: 365 Days Meditating on the Song of Songs

Stock or custom editions of BroadStreet Publishing titles may be purchased in bulk for educational, business, ministry, fundraising, or sales promotional use. For information, please e-mail info@broadstreetpublishing.com.

Cover design by Chris Garborg at garborgdesign.com.
Typesetting by Katherine Lloyd at theDESKonline.com.

Printed in China
19 20 21 5 4 3

Introduction

The Lord is beckoning every believer into a lifestyle of unhindered devotion. Through the Song of Songs, Jesus extends the invitation for a relationship with Him that defies natural understanding. It is mysterious yet tangible, satisfying, and wonderful. Dive into *The Divine Romance* and watch as His love lays a foundation of confidence and identity.

Journey with us as we walk step-by-step through the Song of Songs. Each day, you will find a short encouragement and a prayer, but most of all, you will discover Jesus' unrelenting love for you. Take time to soak in the devotion of the day. Give yourself an extra moment to let the glory that flows through these words penetrate your heart. Allow the Lord to breathe upon you and awaken places of your soul that have been weary, dry, and asleep.

You are God's masterpiece—beautiful, unique, and priceless. It is our prayer that you will emerge from these devotions understanding just how loved and powerful you are.

January

The Greatest Song

The most amazing song of all, by King Solomon.
—SONG OF SONGS 1:1

Open your heart as you embark upon the journey of a lifetime. This is Jesus' song, which He sings over you, His beautiful bride. Today, allow the greatest song ever composed, the Song of *all* Songs, to lead you into the flaming heart of Jesus Christ. Embrace these truths and they will pierce the deepest places of your being and radically change your relationship with God.

Today the Lord is beckoning you to step into the mysteries of His love. A love that cannot be compared to any love you have ever known on this earth. Just one kiss from Jesus has power to transform your entire life. You have a divine destiny and were created to encounter His tangible presence. Along the way, you will be blessed and broken, cherished and challenged. Yet in the end, you will be consumed with Him and discover your true identity.

❧

Father, I gratefully accept your invitation to divine romance. Let the presence of your Holy Spirit saturate every fiber of my being and teach me things I've never known before. I open my heart to you today without reservation. Transform my relationship with you as I discover the reality of your love in new ways. Speak to me and lead me on this journey. I want to hear your sweet voice as you sing over my soul.

Let Him

Let him smother me with kisses—his Spirit-kiss divine.
So kind are your caresses,
I drink them in like the sweetest wine!
—Song of Songs 1:2

What a wonderful way to begin your journey into God's heart! There is no striving or heavy burden, only a simple cry from your heart for Him to come kiss your life. Yield your heart and simply let Him be your everything.

Let Him be your strength today!

Let Him be the One to hold you fast today!

Let Him carry every burden and care that is unbearable for you!

It's so easy to daily let Him be your all. To go further into Christ's love doesn't mean you struggle or painfully push yourself forward. You simply bring Him a yielded heart and let Him do the rest. Soon, He will become everything to you.

Lord, so many times I thought the burden was on me to advance and grow in love. But in fact, your love is what opens my heart for more! I rest in your love today and calmly yield to you. Smother me with your kisses until I am drawn deeper into your love. I give you every burden of my heart and each passion of my soul.

Lavish

Let him smother me with kisses—his Spirit-kiss divine.
So kind are your caresses,
I drink them in like the sweetest wine!
—SONG OF SONGS 1:2

*J*esus longs to smother every aspect of your life with His love. If you will invite Him to come, His glory will flood the deepest, driest, and most wounded areas of your being. His love is filled with mercy, grace, healing, and wisdom. Nothing remains the same once it's saturated with Him. God wants you to have a good life, and the invitation of divine love is where it all begins.

Expect His love to extinguish every fear. The kisses of His Spirit will smother anxiety, doubt, and unbelief. His hope can heal disappointment. His joy will overwhelm every sorrow. He is the light in the darkest seasons of your soul. The more deeply you receive His love, the more it will overflow into every part of your life. Ask Him to saturate your spirit, soul, and body today. It is time for you to experience a fresh kiss from heaven!

God, meet with me today. Let the kiss of your Spirit smother my life and launch me into a deeper relationship with you. Jesus, I long to experience your love and glory in ways I never have before. Leave no part of my life untouched by your beauty. Lavish me with your love.

Kiss Me

Let him smother *me* with kisses—his Spirit-kiss divine.
So kind are your caresses,
I drink them in like the sweetest wine!
—Song of Songs 1:2

Even the simplest revelations can impact your life forever. This is the revelation of His love for you, personally. It is not about others, it is about Jesus and you. Sermons and rules will never satisfy the longings of your heart, because you were created for so much more. Let this cry come from the depth of your being: "Jesus, come kiss *me*!" When you call for Him to make this relationship personal, He will come running.

You were created with a holy kiss—the very breath of God. Everything about you was created by and for His love. Any walls that you have erected to protect your heart are about to come crashing down! And you will never feel safer. This heavenly kiss will awaken your spirit to His affections and destroy every hindrance to a deeper relationship with Him. Jesus loves you, just the way you are.

❧

Father, I'm asking that your Son, the Son of your splendor, would kiss me with the kisses of His Word. I cry out for the kisses of His affection, the kisses of His mercy, and the kisses of His forgiveness. Thank you for loving me, believing that I am special, and choosing me to walk with you on this journey. Awaken my heart with your kiss.

Kindness

Let him smother me with kisses—his Spirit-kiss divine.
So kind are your caresses,
I drink them in like the sweetest wine!
—Song of Songs 1:2

*N*othing is more pleasurable to the human heart than the love of Jesus. Nothing is more delightful. Nothing can compare to the caresses of His love—it awakens our hearts in the most unexpected ways. It makes us feel alive and fills us with joy. It wipes away the past and reaches out its hands to guide us forward. It stirs up desires we never knew existed and gives us the means to satisfy them.

His kindness is overwhelming. His love is better than wine. Relentlessly He pursues us, knowing that what we desire most in this life is found in Him. Once we taste of this love, we know that nothing else could ever fulfill us. Drink deeply from the passions that flow from His heart. Let the mystery of His presence wash over you as you embrace the reality of His nearness.

Jesus, I want to know you in ways I never have before. Let me feel your touch. Pour your love into my soul and revive me with your sweet caress. I will embrace the mystery of who you are, and I know you will reveal yourself to me anew. Thank you for seeking me out and igniting my heart with a fresh passion to know you more. Your kindness amazes me. I can never get enough of you.

Fragrant Love

Your presence releases a fragrance so pleasing—
over and over poured out.
For your lovely name is "Flowing Oil."
No wonder the brides-to-be adore you.

—Song of Songs 1:3

*G*et close enough to Him to smell the fragrance of His presence. It's so pleasing, so winsome and inviting. It speaks of who He is, what He thinks, and what He feels. This is the fragrance of His beautiful personality—His internal qualities of love and gentleness.

Let the Lord capture you and sweep you off your feet. Look into His eyes and you will see how much He enjoys you. The way He gazes at you will ignite hope and calm all of your worries. His smile is more radiant than a brilliant sunrise—it warms your heart and illuminates your soul.

Allow yourself to get lost in the fragrance of Jesus—carried away by the delight of His love. Take a deep breath and faith will invigorate you. The cologne of His compassion will leave you undone—unable to resist Him. Release every thought about Him that is not true and embrace His generous love.

Father, I love you. I want to experience the fragrance of your presence and the reality of your Son. Surround me with your love. Wrap yourself around me and draw me closer to you than ever before. Breathe upon my life. Exhale the splendor of your majesty upon me. I worship you. You are my delight forever.

Over and Over

Your presence releases a fragrance so pleasing—
over and over poured out.
For your lovely name is "Flowing Oil."
No wonder the brides-to-be adore you.
—SONG OF SONGS 1:3

Over and over again, Jesus will faithfully come woo your heart until you are totally His. Your passion may not be fully awakened to His love, but if it's your desire, He will not disappoint. Jesus knows exactly what you need and precisely how to stir your love. All you have to do is ask.

His love is irresistible when it crashes upon our hearts like unrelenting waves. With one taste of His divine passion, we are addicted. Lovesick ones become even more lovesick, and hardened hearts melt like wax when He comes on the scene. Just to think of Him opens us to the sweetness of true love. Ever so graciously, God pours a continuous stream of love into the deepest caverns of our soul. Though we cannot fathom the depths of His love with our minds, we can experience them in life-changing measure.

Jesus come. Now and always, I want to encounter your love. I want to know you as well as you know me. Quench my thirsty soul with the power of your passion and draw me into the depths of your presence that I've yet to discover. No matter how long it takes, make me fully yours, with no barriers to restrict our love.

The Most Beautiful Name

Your presence releases a fragrance so pleasing—
over and over poured out.
For **your lovely name** is "Flowing Oil."
No wonder the brides-to-be adore you.

—SONG OF SONGS 1:3

Jesus is our true Savior, Friend, and King. His name is like fragrant oil, pouring over us and lingering upon our soul. His name is the power of victory. It heals the sick, unlocks the chains of bondage, and raises the dead. His name is like no other—setting our hearts on fire while extinguishing the fiery darts of hell. It is sweeter to the soul than honey.

When we feel alone and detached from Him, all we have to do is say His name, *Jesus*, and He will flood our longing hearts. Soon, weakness is replaced with strength, fear is conquered by love, and wisdom annihilates confusion. He is enough to satisfy every desire of our soul.

Jesus is all of the lovely and powerful things combined. Dive into the secrets of this name that is above every other name and you will unlock treasures that will cause your heart to soar!

Jesus, your name flows from my lips like soothing oil. It warms my heart and ignites an insatiable desire to know you more. Simply saying your name begins to calm the storms that rage within. Hold me close and whisper secrets that only your beloved may hear. I want to experience the power of your name in my life.

Adore

Your presence releases a fragrance so pleasing—
over and over poured out.
For your lovely name is "Flowing Oil."
No wonder the brides-to-be *adore you*.

—Song of Songs 1:3

There is nothing as soothing as the presence of Jesus. Turn your focus away from temporary distractions and fill your mind with the beauty of your King. Imagine His eyes gazing into yours. Listen for His words to strengthen your faith. Expect His love to flood every fiber of your being. Surrender everything—every hope and dream, each fear and worry. Lay it all at His feet and worship Him. Nothing is too big for Him to handle.

No one deserves your love more than the Lord. No one is as trustworthy. He's already proven His love for you. Invite Him to come meet with you today, then simply believe He is there. Rest in His love as He wraps you in His arms. He who is faithful will take care of everything.

Jesus, you inspire me. You see everyone through the eyes of love. Perfect wisdom dwells within you. You are life, hope, and joy. You are the peace that surpasses all understanding. Everything good and beautiful is found in you. I want to live my life constantly aware of your nearness, love, and power. Let me experience the reality of your love in ways I never knew possible.

Draw Me

Draw me into your heart and lead me out.
We will run away together into the king's cloud-filled chamber.
The Chorus of Friends
We will remember your love, rejoicing and delighting in you,
celebrating your every kiss as better than wine.
No wonder righteousness adores you!
—SONG OF SONGS 1:4

God Himself wants to tell you everything that He loves about you. He wants to whisper secrets to your heart and uncover mysteries that have yet to be revealed. You have resurrection power flowing through your veins. The greatest treasure in all of heaven and earth lives inside of you. Embrace the truth of who you are and your entire life will be transformed.

Perhaps you don't fully understand how to get closer to God, or maybe you feel stuck in your relationship with Him. Well, I've got great news for you—He knows what you need and how to give it to you. It's His desire to bless you with a life of divine encounters. You never have to beg for them, but you do need to ask. Open your heart and He will lead you straight into His. Get ready! This will be the adventure of a lifetime.

God, draw me into your heart—into a life of continuous encounters with your tangible love. Lift me out of complacency and set my heart ablaze for you. Take me from one glorious experience to the next and open your Word to me with fresh revelation. Let me see the world through the reality of perfect love.

Together

Draw me into your heart and lead me out.
We will run away together into the king's cloud-filled chamber.
The Chorus of Friends
We will remember your love, rejoicing and delighting in you,
celebrating your every kiss as better than wine.
No wonder righteousness adores you!

—Song of Songs 1:4

When Jesus draws you, the only proper response is to run with Him with all your heart. Jesus has chosen you to be His partner in ministry. He invites you to run alongside Him, knowing you can keep up. You were created for a purpose, sealed with a divine destiny. Nothing will stop you if you set your eyes on your Beloved. Hurdles of misunderstanding, persecution, and failure will only serve to strengthen you in this race. Together, you will ignite the flames of holy passion in others, breathe life into weary souls, and set the captives free.

Journey with Him and He'll bless you with creativity and wisdom in all you do. Talents and gifts, which have lain dormant within you, will spring to life. All that you need to run this race victoriously is yours through Jesus Christ.

Jesus, with holy resolve, I will run with you. When I'm weak, take me by the hand, so I won't trip and fall. I may not always understand where this journey is headed, but I trust you. Together, we will release your glory into the world!

Holy Chambers

Draw me into your heart and lead me out.
We will run away together into *the king's cloud-filled chamber*.
The Chorus of Friends
We will remember your love, rejoicing and delighting in you,
celebrating your every kiss as better than wine.
No wonder righteousness adores you!
—SONG OF SONGS 1:4

*Y*ou have been granted access into the holy of holies, the chamber of the King—the very presence of God Himself. When you choose to worship the Lord and turn all your attention to Him, you're accepting His invitation for a deeper relationship. You're stepping into His heart.

Here, Jesus will reveal His glory. It is in this place, where deep calls unto deep, that the spiritual and the natural realms collide. You were created to experience heaven on earth. This cloud-filled chamber is not only a place you'll see in heaven; it's the place of His presence here and now, where He discloses Himself to the seeking heart. Unlike the courtyard, where you learn *about* the Lord, the chamber is where you get to know Him personally. This is His desire for every believer—to walk through the chamber doors where He awaits and enjoy Him forever.

❧

Jesus, lead me by the hand into the secret place of your presence. I want to see you, hear you, and experience the beauty of your redeeming grace. I'm not satisfied with glimpses of your glory. I want to dive into its very depths and never resurface. Flood my soul with the substance of your holy love. Thank you for lifting the veil, so I may enter in.

Remember

Draw me into your heart and lead me out.
We will run away together into the king's cloud-filled chamber.
The Chorus of Friends
We will remember your love, rejoicing and delighting in you,
celebrating your every kiss as better than wine.
No wonder righteousness adores you!

—SONG OF SONGS 1:4

All good relationships must be intentionally cultivated. The same is true of our connection with the Lord. Though we are joined with Christ, we must purposefully tend to this first love, so the flames of holy passion never grow dim. We don't strive to show ourselves worthy; we simply fall—repeatedly—back into the arms of the One who gave His all for us.

At the Lord's table, we remember the price He paid for us. His love is greater than any other. Through the participation of the bread and wine, we draw near and enter the realm where symbols become substance. As we drink the cup of communion, we remember His intoxicating sweetness. It is better than wine and more alluring than the pleasures of this life.

Father, I honor you for the perfect gift of love you've given me through your Son. Give me grace to pursue your heart with unrelenting devotion. Our relationship means more to me than any other. Your love satisfies every longing of my heart. Over and over, I will choose you and remember your perfect love that has set me free.

Joy

The Chorus of Friends
We will remember your love, *rejoicing and delighting* in you,
celebrating your every kiss as better than wine.
No wonder righteousness adores you!
—Song of Songs 1:4

*J*oy dwells deep within you because the Holy Spirit inside of you is a well of joy! You may not be happy about what's happening in your life, but joy isn't determined by circumstances—it's the profound result of what you dwell on. Instead of rehearsing your problems, rejoice in the Lord. Remind yourself that with Him, nothing is impossible!

When your faith is in Him, you can be totally at rest regardless of what comes against you. Miracles, breakthrough, blessing, physical and emotional healing, and abundant wisdom come from the Lord. When you focus on truth, instead of facts, faith and joy begin to bubble within. The joy of the Lord will transform your life, when you remember that God is on your side.

Father, fill me with your joy. I shake off worry and release my cares to you. I choose to think about your goodness and faithfulness. I choose to be thankful. Nothing is too hard for you! You can heal the pain of the past in a split second. You can download creative ideas for breakthrough and pour out wisdom without measure. Today marks a new day! From this moment forward, I will rejoice because I know my answer is on its way.

The Light Within

The Shulamite: Jerusalem maidens, in this twilight darkness
I know I am so unworthy—so in need.
The Shepherd-King: Yet you are so lovely!
The Shulamite: *I feel as dark and dry as the desert tents*
of the wandering nomads.

—Song of Songs 1:5

*L*oving Jesus will eventually lead to a revelation of our own condition. When purity and holiness are the cry of our hearts, God, in His great mercy and tender affection, will reveal the areas that need our attention. Nothing is hidden from His sight.

Recognizing our weaknesses isn't a call for guilt and condemnation. Instead, it's an invitation for true repentance—where we come face-to-face with our great need for God. In exchange for the yoke of guilt, fear, and religious duty, Jesus offers us the yoke of holy union. He sets us free from every sin and bondage. No amount of obedience, or adherence to religious law, can make us righteous. To fully yield our lives to Jesus is to be emptied of self-confidence and selfish ambition. We are totally dependent upon Him. There is such freedom in knowing that even in our darkness, He is the light within.

Father, I need you. Even when I try to do everything right, to live with pure motives, and to walk humbly before you, I still mess up. I'm so grateful that you see me through the eyes of mercy and compassion. Let the fire of your love burn away everything that doesn't look like you.

Lovely

The Shulamite: Jerusalem maidens, in this twilight darkness
I know I am so unworthy—so in need.
The Shepherd-King: Yet you are so lovely!
—SONG OF SONGS 1:5

Even when we're confronted by our weaknesses, Jesus calls us lovely. He doesn't point an accusatory finger or constantly bash us because we aren't perfect. He opens His arms, pulls us close, and tells us how beautiful we are. He exchanges our imperfection for His perfection. His love for us will conquer our fear and unbelief, healing every wound that has crippled us and left us feeling ugly.

The Lord speaks to our identity and opens our eyes, so we can embrace it ourselves. Receive these words into your heart today: You are beautiful. You are anointed. God Himself has a purpose for your life. Favor and wisdom are yours. The joy of the Lord is your portion. Righteousness and peace have kissed your soul.

Jesus, thank you for seeing me through the light of your mercy and grace. The way that you encourage me always makes me feel special. Your gentle whispers become gusts of wind for me to soar upon. When I'm with you, I feel beautiful. When I look into your eyes, the dreams of my heart come alive, and I want to praise you forever. I feel as if I can conquer every obstacle when I'm with you!

His Masterpiece

The Shepherd-King
Yet you are so lovely—
like the fine linen tapestry hanging in the Holy Place.
—Song of Songs 1:5

Within the sanctuary of the holy of holies, Solomon hung the finest linen curtains. Only the priests who entered could see them from the inside. You are like this fine tapestry—a work of art placed on display in His private chambers, where He alone admires your beauty. You are God's most magnificent masterpiece; more valued than anything else in this entire world, more precious than the curtains that hung in the holy of holies.

Others may look at what you've done or define you based on your past, but God sees your inner beauty—the real you. Never let anyone make you feel insignificant. Never accept the lie that you have no value. You are worth everything to God. It's the reason He sent His Son to suffer and die on the cross. You move His heart, and He loves you exactly the way you are.

Father, come wrap me in your presence. Let your love wash away anything I've believed about myself that doesn't agree with how you see me. I want to carry myself with humble confidence, remembering who I am and to whom I belong. I am amazing because I was made in your image. Hope is springing up where doubt and confusion had once taken root. I am defined by the price of perfect love. I am your masterpiece.

Perfect

The Shulamite to her friends
*Please don't stare in scorn
because of my dark and sinful ways.*
—SONG OF SONGS 1:6

Our identity in Jesus—who He says we are—isn't always easy to accept. The good news is, He understands our doubt and enjoys reminding us who we are in Him. From the moment we said yes to His invitation to divine romance, He placed a crown on our heads and knew it would take us time to grow into it.

We see the darkness of our own souls more clearly than anyone else. It seems almost impossible that we could be the beautiful creatures Jesus says we are, let alone be worthy of the King's love. Yet this is where deity and humanity merge—perfection poured into vessels of imperfection, making them equally perfect.

Once you embrace the truth of who you are, you won't strive to prove it to anyone. You will be at peace with who you are and be happy with how He made you.

Jesus, you're so good to me. So patient and kind. No matter how many times I mess up, you just keep reminding me who I am and who you've created me to be. I choose to see myself the way that you see me—cherished and loved. When I'm confronted by the darkness inside my soul, flood me with the light of your glory. Transform me into the beautiful bride you've called me to be. Your mercy and grace amaze me.

Accepted

My angry brothers quarreled with me
and appointed me guardian of their ministry vineyards,
yet I've not tended my vineyard within.

—Song of Songs 1:6

*A*t some point, Jesus will address impure motives. Trying to make everyone happy, so they won't think poorly of you, is a motive that stems from a fear of rejection. Doing and saying things in order to honor others is commendable, but it will lead to burnout and eventually, bitterness. It's impossible to please both God and others, and at times, you'll be misunderstood.

Instead of striving to earn others' approval, live with a servant's heart because it is your joy to do so; let it not be out of fear. Never let people bully you into service or force your obedience. Respect yourself, by letting others know how you feel in an honoring way. As you grow in your identity as the bride of Christ, you'll gain confidence in what you are, *or are not*, called to do.

Father I seek to honor you in all I do. If there is any area of my life where I am led by wrong motives, reveal it to me. Help me to never trade your approval for the approval of other people. As I grow and mature, teach me how to carry myself with honor and respect both for myself and others. Let peace and wisdom guide my every decision.

The Garden of Our Heart

My angry brothers quarreled with me
and appointed me guardian of their ministry vineyards,
yet I've not tended my vineyard within.

—SONG OF SONGS 1:6

Nothing matters more to Jesus than the condition of your heart. Your life is a vineyard; a precious garden where He meets with you to share secrets, stories, and love. Garden walks—these moments of devotion, worship, prayer, and simply resting in His presence—aren't only enjoyable, but they're a vital part of your relationship with the Lord. Taking care of your vineyard means nurturing your personal communion with God.

Weeds of sin, distraction, busyness, and lukewarm affection can quickly overtake the garden of your soul. Tend the fires of passion that burn within and never let them grow dim. When you feel the gentle tug of the Holy Spirit, don't ignore it. Delight in the Lord and nourish and protect your relationship with Him. Nothing is more beautiful than spending time with Him!

Jesus, meet with me in our secret garden. I turn my heart to you. Speak to me, lead me, hold me, and laugh with me. Throughout my day, let my thoughts continually land on you. Help me to keep my heart soft and pliable in your hands, so you can mold me into the person you have called me to be. I want to break away from everything that hinders my relationship with you.

Listen

Won't you tell me, Lover of my soul,
where do you feed your flock?
—SONG OF SONGS 1:7

Quiet your soul and listen. Turn from everything else and lean into Him. Release your concerns, put down your list of prayers, and don't say a word. Simply be.

You were created to hear God. He's always speaking, yet often in unexpected ways. A deep sense of peace when you've been heavy and burdened. A sudden burst of joy, for no reason at all. An image that flashes across your mind. A moment of clarity about a situation that has left you stumped. The art of listening takes practice, especially when your mind is used to being in control. If you aren't used to waiting on the Lord and listening for His voice, the important thing is not to give up. Come into His presence with expectancy and listen to what He will say. He longs to speak to you.

Father, I come into your presence today, having so much I could pray about, but instead, I simply want to be with you and to listen. Speak to me. Share what's on your heart. Let me encounter new realms of your glory and love as I wait upon you.

Satisfy

Won't you tell me, Lover of my soul,
where do you feed your flock?
—SONG OF SONGS 1:7

Nothing will satisfy the hungry heart like Jesus. Conferences, worship services, and prayer gatherings all have their place, but only He can give us what we need. Others have fed us from the overflow of what they receive from the Lord, but until we reach out to Him for ourselves, we will never truly be satisfied.

Within all of us is a yearning desire—a deep hunger to know Him. He alone is the Bread of Life who gives us Rivers of Living Water. That's why learning *about* Him is never enough. Filling your brain with facts will never satisfy. You must continually feast upon the Lord and partake of the food He offers. Reach out today and receive all that you need from the heart of God. He's waiting for you.

Lord, my heart cries out for you and you alone. I've enjoyed eating from the hands of others, but I want to eat with you at your banqueting table. I want to feast upon your love and satisfy the true longing of my soul. Fill me, so I will be able to feed others. Everything I've ever needed, I will find in you.

Shepherd

Where do you lead your beloved one
to rest in the heat of the day?

—Song of Songs 1:7

Jesus is our Great Shepherd, Best Friend, and faithful King. He has our best interests at heart and desires to lead us on a beautiful journey. He is the path of wisdom and knows the best and safest route. He knows when we're tired and need to rest and when we must push through to overcome.

Life is filled with hills and valleys. Sometimes, despite our best intentions, it feels as if we've lost our way. Disappointments and failures thrust out their claws to trip us, but Jesus is there to catch us. During the darkest, most painful times, He is there.

God wants you to succeed. He's cheering you on. Go and explore the path that leads to your purpose. He's watching, and when your heart is toward Him, He will never let you wander too far.

Lord, sometimes it feels as if I've aimlessly wandered in the wilderness. My feet are tired, and my faith seems weak. I release my disappointments, fears, and failures to you. I don't want to go my own way—I want you to lead me. You will bless me, provide for me, and open doors that no one else can. You are the Good Shepherd. I trust you.

Unveiled

For I wish to be wrapped all around you,
as I go among the flocks of your under-shepherds.
It is you I long for, with no veil between us!
—Song of Songs 1:7

One touch of His presence, one encounter with His love, and we are never the same. Unexpectedly, our entire lives change, and we begin to yearn for His nearness. The Lord makes Himself so real that we become obsessed with knowing Him more. We are undone by this love that is stronger than death. Nothing on earth can compare.

You weren't created to live a spiritually dull existence. You were designed by God to enjoy Him, hear His voice, and see His face. The veil of separation was torn when Jesus died on the cross. He paid a great price so that nothing could ever separate you from Him. He is as close to you as the air you breathe.

Lord, the way that you love me leaves me totally undone. Nothing matters more than getting to know you and becoming all that you've created me to be. Come unveil my heart, that I may see and hear you more clearly. I want nothing to hinder me from having a more meaningful relationship with you. Love has been awakened within me, and I will never be the same!

Radiant

The Shepherd-King
Listen, *my radiant one*—
if you ever lose sight of me
just follow in my footsteps where I lead my lovers.
—Song of Songs 1:8

Every part of you is beautiful to Jesus. Right now, no matter how you look in the mirror, regardless of what you've done or haven't' done, He calls you radiant. When He looks at you, He sees your beauty, inside and out. He didn't make a mistake when He bled and died on the cross for you, and He didn't make a mistake when He chose you to be His bride. You are not a disappointment to Him. He is thrilled with you!

Jesus is wooing your heart—beckoning you to come closer as He drenches you with affirming words of sacred love. He will remind you of your beauty, over and over, until you believe it. You are His. He loves you. He believes in you. You are worth the price of love. You are His beautiful bride. You are royalty. This is your identity.

Jesus, your mercy and love have washed me and made me beautiful. I am yours. My life has been transformed. I will position myself before you with humble confidence and learn to see myself the way you see me. I want to be all that you say I am. Thank you for believing in me. Thank you for your love.

Closer

The Shepherd-King
Listen, my radiant one—
if you ever lose sight of me
just follow in my footsteps where I lead my lovers.
—Song of Songs 1:8

Everyone goes through occasions when God feels distant. Sometimes life distracts us and we allow our hearts to be drawn away by the whirlwinds of busyness and stress. Our prayers become dry, reading His Word feels like a chore, and it seems His voice is silent. But right there, on the flip side of this wilderness and only a breath away, is the manifest presence of God.

If you've lost sight of Him, reach out again. Allow Him to embrace you. Even if you don't sense it at first, you will. Still your thoughts and begin to remember what His touch was like. Once you've been in His presence, you already know the way. If you've never encountered the profound love of God, ask Him to come near and pour it out. Sing your songs of worship. Let words of praise and gratefulness catapult you right into His love. He is waiting.

Father, I don't want the seasons of hardship and distraction to guide my future. Come meet with me. Lead me by the hand into glorious encounters. Crash upon my heart like a waterfall. Soak every dry place. Whisper words of love that awaken my spirit. I turn my spirit and soul to you.

Embracing Vulnerability

Come with your burdens and cares.
Come to the place near the sanctuary of my shepherds—
there you will find me.
—SONG OF SONGS 1:8

Come with your burdens and cares and lay them at His feet. No trauma is too hard for Him to heal. No memory is so deep that He cannot reach into it and remove the sting. His love and power are unstoppable.

Part of healing the wounds of the past is to become vulnerable with others. God never asks you to wear a mask and pretend that everything is okay when it isn't. God created you with emotions, and those emotions should lead you into freedom, not keep you locked up in pain. Sometimes processing emotions with the Lord in private is enough to set you free. However, sometimes it takes someone you trust, to help walk you through to victory. If you don't have someone you trust, ask Him to bring the right person across your path, and He will.

Father, I want nothing to hinder our relationship—no wrong thought patterns, unhealthy reactions, or walls to keep you or others at a distance. I open my heart to you. Bring wholeness in my life. Every painful memory and trauma, anything that makes me react in a negative way, I bring it all to you. If you want to work through others to help me, I trust you to bring the right person. I'm excited to walk into freedom with you!

Affirming Love

My dearest one ...
Let me tell you how I see you—
you are so thrilling to me.
—Song of Songs 1:9

Nothing unlocks your soul like the revelation of His love. It goes beyond understanding, beyond your performance. It is rooted in what He has done for you, not what you can do for Him. This love is unchanging, never ending, and completely undeserved.

His words of love and affirmation are divine kisses upon your heart. They will sustain you in the wilderness and breathe life into your weary soul. They will captivate you and make you come alive. You are His darling, His favorite one—the one He's called to His side. Let this love grip you. Yield to it completely, and you will be transformed. Every desire, every dream, even your thoughts, words, and actions, will effortlessly begin to reflect His heart. Everything about you and your life will fall beautifully into place when you begin to see yourself the way He sees you.

～

Jesus, I love to hear how much you love me. The way you care for me has unlocked my soul. I lack nothing because your love sustains me. My heart is drawn to yours with yearnings so deep I can scarcely voice them. Though I'm not worthy of such affection, you lavish it upon me like flowing oil. Please, never stop.

Uncovered

My dearest one ...
Let me tell you how I see you—
you are so thrilling to me.
—Song of Songs 1:9

Quiet your soul and be still. The Lord is gazing upon you with unrelenting passion and perfect understanding. He sees you—even the deepest thoughts and intents of your heart. Nothing is hidden. He sees it all and still calls you beautiful.

If you're used to coming to the Lord in prayer, always talking and never listening, you're missing out on a most glorious conversation. Cultivate the art of listening. Let Him tell you how He sees you—it's the healing balm for your soul. Let Him into every crevice and never be afraid of His soothing, searching gaze. You don't need to impress Him with your knowledge, fancy prayers, or memory verses. You cannot cover your sin or imperfections from His sight. Instead, you can invite Him to enflame your heart with a holy passion that will burn away every impurity.

Lord, fill me with the wonder of your love. Let me discover the beauty of your emotions for me that cannot be ignored. I adore you, and as I look into your eyes, I know you feel the same. Countless times, in a myriad of ways, you reach for me with invisible love that is more tangible than any human substance.

Thrilling

My dearest one ...
Let me tell you how I see you—
you are so thrilling to me.
—Song of Songs 1:9

We wonder how our love could thrill the heart of God, as much as His love moves ours, but it does. To hear Him say we're beautiful, strong, and brave encourages us and ignites our faith. His love gives us confidence and removes our insecurities. Even His Word is written to us as a letter of love.

When all you see is what's wrong with you, He swoops in and highlights the beauty you never knew you had. He doesn't just tolerate you; He celebrates you. He'll overwhelm you with favor and cause others to see what He sees. Let Jesus become your deepest delight and source of unrestrained freedom. Let nothing inhibit this love. Give Him all that you have and all that you are. Life with Him is a wonderful privilege—embrace it fully. There's no place to hide from love.

Jesus, your words touch my heart. I'm amazed that in my weakness, my love still moves you. It's beyond my understanding. I've done nothing to deserve such affection, but I gratefully accept it. Thank you for loving me just as I am. You don't base your approval on what I will one day become. You delight in me right now. Because of you, I will never be the same.

Strength

To gaze upon you is like looking
at one of Pharaoh's finest horses—
a **strong**, regal steed pulling his royal chariot.
—SONG OF SONGS 1:9

Jesus has paid the greatest price so you can walk in victory. Even when you're weak, He says you're strong. He becomes the strength within you. With your gaze fixed upon Him, you will overcome every opposition. God Himself will chase away the dark clouds looming on the horizon. Discouragement will not muffle your voice; neither will you freeze with fear. God, who is faithful, will cause you to rise and run, leaping over the walls that once held you back.

With God on your side, nothing is too difficult. Run into His grace, and you will find all that you need. Fill your mouth with praise, and your enemies will be silenced. God sees your potential, especially when you don't. Place all your expectations in Him, and He will never disappoint.

Father, thank you for loving me even in my weakness. Help me to live my life, tethered to the power of your love. Nothing will defeat me when I trust in you. My faith will overcome the enemy and set others free, for you are my source of strength. Empower me today with your love, for I am yours—the place where dust and deity have met.

February

Expressions

> *Your tender cheeks are aglow—*
> your earrings and gem-laden necklaces
> set them ablaze.
> —Song of Songs 1:10

*Y*our deepest emotions and expressions are symbolized by your cheeks. Tears of sorrow are meant to be cried. Joy is meant to be unrestrained and freeing. Righteous anger strengthens you to stand against the enemy. Yet too often, we ignore what stirs inside us, when God gives us permission to acknowledge and walk through every emotion with Him. Never hide behind a mask of pretense. God created you to feel.

Allow your body, soul, and spirit to flow with what you sense. The tender affections of the Lord should warm your heart, build your faith, and cause you to overflow with abandoned worship to Him. Embrace the joy and excitement of life in His Kingdom. Don't allow the way you feel to dominate you, but most certainly do not ignore what you experience. If you feel sad, talk to Him. If you want to laugh, laugh! Let your emotions propel you into His presence.

Father, you created me with beautiful emotions. The more I get to know you, the more comfortable I am expressing my deepest emotions. I won't be afraid to let the impact of your presence be seen upon my face. I will learn to be more vulnerable and embrace what I feel stirring inside of me. I will laugh, worship, feel deeply, and enjoy life with you.

Ears to Hear

Your tender cheeks are aglow—
your earrings and gem-laden necklaces
set them ablaze.
—Song of Songs 1:10

*L*ean in and let the Lord speak to your heart. You have been created to hear. Earrings speak of the voice of God and His words, piercing your ears. You are His sheep. Never doubt that you can hear Him; simply take time to listen. Tune your heart into His presence and welcome His voice. Sometimes it's soothing, at times convicting, and often inspiring. It can be found in His Word, heard in your thoughts, whispered in a sunset, discovered in a movie, or spoken through the voice of a stranger. God is not limited in the ways He speaks.

Treasures of gold are found in His every word. Hearing Him is vital for your daily life, your family, and your ministry of representing Christ to others. *You* can hear Him, for earrings of gold are upon you. His words, more than any other, have the power to transform.

Father, speak to me. I long for your voice to illuminate my mind, strengthen my spirit, and direct my life. I will listen for you in every conversation, expect you to speak to me in my dreams, and even listen for your whispers of love blowing upon the wind. Awaken my heart with the sound of your voice. I am listening.

Beauty of Surrender

Your tender cheeks are aglow—
your earrings and **gem-laden necklaces**
set them ablaze.
—SONG OF SONGS 1:10

The beauty of a surrendered will is like a gem-laden necklace. While it's Jesus' responsibility to make you shine like gold and diamonds, He does ask one thing: a total yielding of your will. This is what the neck symbolizes. As you grow and mature, there comes a time when you must allow Him to govern every aspect of your life—spirit, soul, body, and decisions.

Relinquishing control and letting Him hold the reins can be scary at first, but in this place of complete trust, you'll experience new realms of freedom. This is where your identity and purpose for living are discovered. Hold nothing back from this faithful One who loves you and is fully committed to you. Open your life to Him and let Him fill every crack. Free-fall into love and explore the joys of adventuring with Him.

Jesus, take the reins of my life and steer me in the right direction. I've tried for too long to make things go the way I want them to. Today, I give you full control. Let your love govern and guide my life. Even though I may not always understand the way you lead, I choose to trust you. I surrender my will. I am yours.

You Make Me Beautiful

We will enhance your beauty,
encircling you with our golden reins of love.
You will be marked with our redeeming grace.
—Song of Songs 1:11

The Lord has promised to take you from glory to glory. The good news is that the *starting point* is the place of glory. You aren't starting out as an ugly, cursed, rejected failure. Your beauty was evident from the beginning of time. Now, the fullness of the Trinity lives inside of you. As you spend time daily in His presence, He will saturate every fiber of your being, until you shine and glisten with enhanced beauty.

As you worship and pour out your love to Him, He will envelop you with unimaginable splendor. The beauty of a lovesick worshipper is unparalleled. The flames of sacred love refine you. And eventually, everyone around you will see the beauty of the Father, Son, and Holy Spirit in your life.

Lord, come breathe upon my life with the beauty of your love. You are the very essence of perfection. The definition of love itself. Nothing compares to what I see, feel, and experience when you are near. Saturate me with your glory and let others catch you gazing at them through my eyes. I long for you more than any other. Let your beauty rest upon my heart.

Entwined

We will enhance your beauty,
encircling you with our golden reins of love.
You will be marked with our redeeming grace.
—Song of Songs 1:11

*Y*ou are not just filled with the Holy Spirit; you are one with the Father, Son, and Holy Spirit. They encircle you and reside within you. The very nature of God—the golden glory of His love, mercy, and truth—courses through your being. The fellowship of the Trinity is so unique; it cannot be understood with the mind. It must be embraced and experienced.

God Himself has pulled you into this never-ending, always-connected dance of love. It permeates you and embraces you with perfect harmony. Entwined within His presence, life takes on new meaning. Impossible situations become possible. Faith rises to an entirely new level. Joy overcomes sorrow, confidence replaces self-doubt, and love conquers fear. When you reach out and accept this invitation for holy union with Him, He will reveal Himself in ways you never knew possible. Lean back into His arms today, and let Him embrace you with this perfect love.

Your love tugs at my heart, and all I want is to be cradled in your arms and encircled by your golden reins of love. Strengthen me with your embrace and remove every burden that has weighed me down. Let nothing hold me back from wholehearted devotion. I want you as the center of my life. Seal your purposes within my heart, so nothing will steal them away.

Grace

We will enhance your beauty,
encircling you with our golden reins of love.
You will be marked with our redeeming grace.
—SONG OF SONGS 1:11

There is something about a life of grace that marks us. Not only has God redeemed us by His tender mercy; He strengthens us by the power of grace. This love, this power to rise above difficulty, begins to define us. We carry ourselves differently. We speak differently. We walk with ease through trials that normally would overwhelm us. The surging power of the Spirit lifts us high, so we soar above temporary pain and pressure.

God's grace enables us to do what He's called us to do. As we find pleasure in Him, He gives us the ease, wisdom, and strategy to do what stirs in our hearts. Doors of opportunity open and favor finds us at every turn. His grace is sufficient to overcome every obstacle. Everything you need to walk in victory is already yours. Align your thinking with His promise of grace. This is your portion, and He will not deny you.

Father, let your gift of grace characterize my life. Anoint me with the ease and confidence I need to fulfill my destiny. Cover me with the beauty of grace, so I will flourish in every good work. Strengthen me when I'm weak. Sustain me in trials. Encourage me and fill me with hope. My heart overflows with thankfulness.

The King Has Come

The Shulamite
As the king surrounded me,
the sweet fragrance of my praise perfume
awakened the night.
—Song of Songs 1:12

Think about this for a moment—the King of kings, the Creator of the heavens and the earth, God Almighty Himself, cares about you. He doesn't sit upon His throne thinking of ways to punish you for your sin or lack of faith. Instead, His Spirit fills you on the inside and wraps you with love from the outside. If that isn't enough, He turns to His angels and tells them to keep you safe.

Every blessing that pertains to life and godliness has been granted to you. Life in the Kingdom of God is vibrant and beautiful and filled with gifts from a loving heavenly Father. A banquet has been set before you, and you're invited to eat your fill. Just when you least expect it, He will swoop in and surprise you with His presence. Nothing about the Lord is average or predictable, and the way He loves you is no exception.

Jesus, surround me and draw me into a place of holy intimacy with you that I have never known before. My heart is completely open to you. Your love has torn down the walls of separation. I flourish when I'm with you, becoming someone I never knew I could be, transformed by the power of the cross. Come meet with me as I turn my heart to you.

A Fragrant Life

The Shulamite
As the king surrounded me,
the *sweet fragrance of my praise perfume*
awakened the night.
—Song of Songs 1:12

Jesus' love expands our hearts. What other response could we possibly give when He comes, other than to overflow with praise and worship? Our hearts cry out to know Him, to see Him, and to hear His voice. For lovesick worshippers, it isn't enough to cast an occasional glance in His direction. We want to experience the reality of His presence every moment. We want our lives to reflect what burns within us.

This fragrant life is meant to be lived among those who don't yet know Him. We don't want to become a group of people who are so unapproachable and obscure that others can't stand being around us. Instead, we live like Jesus did—in service to others, our lives spilling over with an attitude that draws all people to Him. A truly fragrant life simply lives in the beauty of His love, releasing His captivating aroma to the world around us.

Father, without hesitation, I lavish you with my praise. May the atmosphere be saturated with the fragrance of extravagant and uninhibited devotion as adoration exudes from every part of my spirit, soul, and body. I want to represent you well and carry the beauty of your love to the world around me. May the aroma of my life rise to bless you.

Awake

The Shulamite
As the king surrounded me,
the sweet fragrance of my praise perfume
awakened the night.
—Song of Songs 1:12

Even in the darkest night of your soul, Jesus is with you. His love will revive your heart and cause you to sing when you'd rather cry. Praise will flow from the depths of your being, even when circumstances merit no joy. His divine love prompts you to speak and believe in a way that contradicts chaos. You live from the position of faith, believing the impossible is possible, and God is able to make every wrong thing right.

No other truth unlocks your soul like the revelation of His love. His touch makes your heart come alive. He strengthens you with His grace and soon you are running after Him with renewed hope. His presence is a fountain of peace that never runs dry. His glory is the brightest light in the darkest hour, and His faithfulness will be seen in your life.

Father, fasten me to your heart and never let me go. You've awakened my heart with a holy kiss and blessed me with the fragrance of your love, but I want to know you more—nothing else will ever satisfy this longing in my soul. Let me feel your breath upon my life. Kiss me with a thousand kisses that enflame my soul with hope and ignite my faith afresh. With you, nothing is impossible.

Suffering Love

A sachet of myrrh is my lover,
like a tied-up bundle of myrrh resting over my heart.
—SONG OF SONGS 1:13

There is no greater love than the love of Jesus. He suffered and died to free you from the snare of the enemy and bring you into the Kingdom of God. This revelation of the beauty and bitterness of the cross must touch every aspect of your life. Though the price for your salvation has been paid, a life of true devotion will cost you. The same is true of all good relationships—love must sacrifice anything that inhibits a healthy connection.

Let nothing hinder your relationship with Him. Live your life with intention and dedication. Be everything He's called you to be and let nothing stop you. Let love rule your heart. It will be tested, but when your heart is aflame with passion, you look beyond the price and to the One you love. Everything you do for love is worth it.

Lord, your atoning love is extravagant and costly—worth more than anything in the entire world. As I meditate on the beauty of the cross, my soul cries, "You are the King of my heart!" You poured out pain and suffering as a sacrifice of pure love, and I gratefully drink from its overflowing cup. I am intoxicated with the joy of knowing you. I willingly release anything that could hinder our connection. Let my life reflect the devotion that floods my heart.

The Power of Love

A sachet of myrrh is my lover,
like *a tied-up bundle* of myrrh resting over my heart.
—Song of Songs 1:13

*J*esus was a tied-up bundle—the Savior who hung on the cross in your place. The revelation of the cross must pierce the deepest place of your soul and catapult you into a life of resurrection power. The cross wasn't the end; it was just the beginning! The power of the cross was the power of pure, unselfish love.

Bitter to the taste but sweet to the smell, myrrh in the spiritual sense speaks of dying to self to become a "sweet-smelling savor" to the Lord. Nothing is as beautiful as a surrendered life. You must believe that even when your love has suffered long, it will lead to victory. You must be willing to hold on, even when it's difficult. Love must persevere.

Jesus, thank you for the cross. Thank you for the price of love you so freely paid. You are a dream come true—altogether lovely, a bundle of gentleness, courage, strength, and compassion. The dimensions of your many virtues are a treasure waiting to be discovered. Remove the veils that inhibit me from seeing you clearly. I choose to abide in you and live in the power and victory of love.

Embrace

A sachet of myrrh is my lover,
like a tied-up bundle of myrrh *resting over my heart*.
—SONG OF SONGS 1:13

Rest in His love today. Embrace the One who loves you with perfect love. Let the knowledge and reality of His holy passion settle deep within your heart. His love has redeemed you from sin and death. His love is real, tangible, and unmatched by any other.

Fall back into the arms of the One who continually reaches to draw you near. All that you need to face the day, is found in His presence. Wisdom, peace, joy, faith, and prosperity are gifts waiting to be exchanged for your baggage. As you look upon His face, doubt and fear melt away. He is the kind and generous Shepherd who leads you on your journey—just take His hand and see where He leads. Your future is safe in His hands.

Jesus, I turn my heart to you. As I rest in your presence and look upon your face, I experience deep peace unlike anything I've ever known. I'm coming closer, Lord—coming with all my burdens and cares, which I will lay at your feet. Wrap me in your arms and seal my heart with a holy kiss. Bathe me in the light of your glory, and I will forever be ruined for anything less.

Beautiful

He is like a bouquet of henna blossoms—
henna plucked near the vines at the fountain of the Lamb.
I will hold him and never let him part.

—Song of Songs 1:14

Jesus is like a beautiful bouquet of redeeming grace. A fragrant flower of redemptive love. When you meditate on the cross, you discover how lovely your King truly is. His beauty is captivating. Once you see by inward revelation how beautiful He truly is, you will never go on the way you were before. You become a lover of God, longing for His beauty to cover your life.

Jesus' beauty comes from every aspect of His character. He is the splendor and glory of God. He is the majestic King who rules in perfect judgment and undeserved mercy. God's wisdom and creativity brought the world and everything in it into existence. His power has no end. He loved you before you were conceived, and He is with you every moment of your life. Hungry hearts delve into the mystery of His presence every day, yet it will take an eternity to discover all that He is.

Lord, nothing compares to your presence. Come fill every aspect of my life with your beauty. As I gaze upon your face, I'm ruined for anything less. Let your glory and splendor overwhelm me until all that is left is a pure and unselfish bride who radiates with the beauty of her Beloved.

Fountain of the Lamb

He is like a bouquet of henna blossoms—
henna plucked near the vines at the fountain of the Lamb.
I will hold him and never let him part.
—Song of Songs 1:14

*H*enna blossoms emit an intense fragrance like the tenderness and beauty of Jesus, which intoxicates the soul. His atoning love carries the most beautiful scent. It drowns our sorrows and frees our souls.

His love is a fountain that never runs dry. He floods our soul and refreshes our spirit as we drink of His living waters. He came alongside of us when we were dead in our sins and brought us back to life through His precious blood. As we meditate upon the revelation of the cross and experience the fragrance of His love, we want nothing more than to live our lives to honor and please Him. Our theology becomes one of love, instead of duty and works, and we lean into His love with total abandon.

Jesus, I come to you, the Fountain of Living Waters. Let me drink of your presence for all eternity. I bask in the beauty of your radiance. The fragrance you carry is so pure and delightful. I've become addicted, drunk with love. Take me by the hand and lead me into the holiest place of your presence. I cannot get enough.

Never Let Go

He is like a bouquet of henna blossoms—
henna plucked near the vines at the fountain of the Lamb.
I will hold him and never let him part.
—Song of Songs 1:14

You were called to live a lifestyle of intimate devotion to the Lord. This invitation to divine romance, given by the Lord Himself, shatters the mentality that we must work for God's approval. He loves you, and there is nothing you can do to earn that love. You will never be good enough, holy enough, or have memorized enough Scriptures to deserve what He offers you.

Once the revelation of His love pierces your soul, you recognize your great need for Him and determine that nothing else will satisfy. You pull Him close and never let Him go. On a practical level, pulling the Lord close starts with your attention. As you turn your attention to Him throughout the day, you will notice that the awareness of His love becomes stronger and stronger. You can live in this awareness, regardless of what you're doing. Your life becomes a habitation for the Lord—even if you're having a bad day.

Lord, I lay every struggle to be perfect at your feet. You love me even when I'm having a bad day, and you feel a million miles away. You enjoy me, even when I mess up. So today, I simply turn my heart to you and rest in your love. I pull you close and hold tight to your presence.

My Reflection

The Shepherd-King

Look at you, my dearest darling,
you are so lovely!
You are beauty itself to me.
Your passionate eyes are like loyal, gentle doves.

—SONG OF SONGS 1:15

Look closely at the person you see in the mirror. Because of God's redeeming love, you look a lot like Him. As you gaze at your own reflection, you'll see Jesus looking through your eyes. You were created in the image of God—day by day, transforming into the person He's always known you to be. As you grow in your identity, you not only see yourself differently but see the world around you differently as well.

Seeing yourself the way He sees you is a vital component to fulfilling your purpose. You must believe you are who He says you are. You are lovely to Him—beautiful inside and out, filled with glory, and completely righteous, whether you feel like it or not. You are beautiful because of Him. You are holy because of Him. You are perfect.

Father, I invite you to wash over my soul with your love and encouragement. Cleanse me from self-doubt and a negative view of myself. You are in me and with me—together we are glorious and can do anything. Put a guard over my mind and my words, so I only think and speak about myself in line with your Word. I am yours. I am worthy of this love. I will see myself the way that you see me.

You Are

The Shepherd-King
Look at you, my dearest darling,
you are so lovely!
You are beauty itself to me.
Your passionate eyes are like loyal, gentle doves.

—Song of Songs 1:15

*Y*ou are not just beautiful; you are the very definition of beauty. Jesus loves to remind us how He sees us. He longs for you to know that He didn't make a mistake when He chose you. There is no fault in you.

When you believe that you are beautiful, admired, and esteemed by God, you carry yourself that way. Beauty is seen in kind gestures, a giving heart, and a humble, compassionate, and patient attitude. It is believing the best about others and extending mercy the same way Jesus does to us. It is joy, hope, and peace. Beauty is all of these things and more, but the amazing part is that even when you have days where you are the opposite of everything listed above, He still sees the beauty in you. He is amazing!

Jesus, your belief in me is more than I can fathom, but I embrace it wholeheartedly. You know everything about me, and despite it all, you still call me your dearest darling. You always find the good in people. While others point out faults, you focus on the heart. When we focus on offense, you extend mercy and compassion. You're the example I want to follow.

Dove's Eyes

The Shepherd-King
Look at you, my dearest darling,
you are so lovely!
You are beauty itself to me.
Your passionate eyes are like loyal, gentle doves.
—Song of Songs 1:15

What an amazing description Jesus gives in this verse! He compares your eyes of tender devotion to that of a dove, which can only focus on one thing at a time. He declares that your loyalty and affection for Him are untainted and sincere. The way you look at Him thrills His heart. He cherishes your love and dedication to Him.

The Holy Spirit is breathing upon you and illuminating your vision, so you can see Him more clearly. He is pulling you so close that you will not be distracted by the cares of this world. Revelation of His love for you is taking over your outlook on this divine relationship. Worldly idols and temptations will no longer divert your attention. Turn your eyes to Him and let Him fill your vision and touch your heart.

Lord, here in your presence I am completely at peace. As I turn all my attention to you, nothing else matters. You are the One I long for. I want to see you more clearly—to know you and live with unveiled vision and deeper revelation. I willingly yield all other pursuits to walk with you. I want to forever be your radiant bride—to shine with the joy and holiness that stirs within me.

Beyond Words

My beloved one,
both handsome and winsome,
you are pleasing beyond words.
—SONG OF SONGS 1:16

The more we see Him, the more we love Him. Our hearts, unguarded and fully open to Jesus, overflow with expressions of our deepest emotion. We've fallen in love with Him, yet regardless of how hard we try, we scarcely find the words to describe what we feel or how lovely He is. His presence stirs such deep emotion, it's impossible to convey. No stroke of the paintbrush, no dance or lyric, not even the strum of an instrument can adequately depict what He means to us, yet we try because He is worthy of every effort.

As we peer into the mystery of His love, revelation continually unfolds. We're struck with awe that becomes addictive. We will forever reach beyond what makes sense to our minds and delve into the reality of His touch. Jesus is the purest, holiest obsession anyone could have. Sometimes, all we can do is sit in the stillness that screams of passion and wait. Hoping the movement of our heart touches His. And it does!

Jesus, I'm undone—totally overwhelmed by your love, yet longing for more. I wish it were possible to express how much you mean to me. Reveal yourself to me, over and over again. I can't get enough of this sacred love.

Find Rest

Our resting place is anointed and flourishing,
like a green forest meadow bathed in light.
—SONG OF SONGS 1:16

There is no safer place to be than in the arms of the Lord. In the sanctuary of His presence, nothing can harm us. Fear, confusion, and anxiety—they all vanish when the abundance of His love surrounds us. Our overworked minds and swirling thoughts find rest when we yield our reasoning and allow Him to fill our soul. Striving becomes a thing of the past as rest and trust work together in harmony.

Through revelation, we understand *our resting place* is a place for two. Jesus enjoys being with you, just as much as you enjoy being with Him. As you lean back into His embrace, remember He cherishes this time. His heart delights in you.

Jesus, I lay every burden and overwhelming concern at your feet. Everything else can wait for just a moment as I rest in your arms. Hold me. Let me feel your peace infusing my mind. You are my hiding place and shelter from every storm. Breathe upon my soul as I whisper my words of love to you. Come let me bless you with my worship.

Illuminate

Our resting place is anointed and flourishing,
like a green forest meadow *bathed in light*.
—Song of Songs 1:16

*C*lose your eyes and feel the warmth of His radiant smile upon your face. He is there, with you now, directing your attention to His glorious light. For every disappointment, He is there to encourage you. In every heartache, His love restores. During every season, He is the answer and the joy that chases away the dark clouds.

The Most Glorious One lives inside of you and illuminates your spirit and soul. You can live from the place of victory every day. The journey of happiness begins with your decision to let God's presence, Word, and power affect you more than the darkness around you. Invite Him into your daily situations, and peace will be your portion, wisdom will guide you, and favor will surround you. You are destined to live a flourishing life that truly makes you happy. Not only are you God's child, you are His chosen one.

Father, illuminate my life. Let every dark place radiate with you. Illuminate my thinking, brighten my path, and lead me with wisdom. Let the light of your love and faithfulness spark hope and faith within me. Throughout the day, I will remember your loving-kindness and choose to be thankful, in good times and in bad, because I know that you are with me.

Safe

Rafters of cedar branches are over our heads
and balconies of pleasant-smelling pines.
A perfect home!
—Song of Songs 1:17

The woods of cedar and fir represent death and life. Jesus' death and resurrection have become your security and covering. The Lord has become a shield of protection around you. The blood of Jesus, recognized by every spiritual force in heaven and earth, covers you and sets you apart. With confident trust, you can follow Him anywhere. Fearlessly, you can go about the Lord's work, knowing He will defend you. Even His angels have been given charge over you.

Reminding yourself of the unlimited, unmatched power of the cross should create confidence. The Lord wants you to know the *rafters of cedar branches* over your head are strong enough to shelter you from every storm. He has built you a home in His presence—stay there. Sing your praise and offer your songs of thanksgiving. Fill your home with the atmosphere of heaven and remain under the covering of His protection and love, regardless of the storms that rage around you. Lean into Him, the strength of your life.

Jesus, with faith and confident trust in your ability to protect me, I yield my fears to you. Victory is mine because victory was yours first. Every plan of the enemy to destroy me will be annihilated by your glorious might. You are my Champion!

My Friend

Rafters of cedar branches are over our heads
and balconies of pleasant-smelling pines.
A perfect home!
—Song of Songs 1:17

*I*magine you're sitting on a balcony, overlooking the beauty of nature. Songbirds are singing, the air is fresh and fragrant, and you and Jesus are sharing a cup of your favorite beverage. He is not only your Lord and King. Jesus is also your Friend.

No one cares more about you, has more patience, or listens as intently as the Lord. He enjoys having fun with you, and He knows how to brighten every day. He doesn't run when things get tough, and He's always there to lighten the load. So, the next time you're enjoying a sunset, running errands, feeling alone, or even happily tucking your kids into bed, remember that your Best Friend is by your side.

Jesus, thank you for being my Best Friend. When I feel alone or misunderstood, all I have to do is turn my attention to you, and you come rushing in. You are the friend I've always wanted. Teach me how to listen more intently, to commune with you more often, and to extend the hand of friendship to others, the same way you have to me.

Dwelling Daily

Rafters of cedar branches are over our heads
and balconies of pleasant-smelling pines.
A perfect home!
—Song of Songs 1:17

There is no place like the place you call home. It's where you're completely yourself. Home is where you laugh, cry, and dream. Daily, as we lavish the Lord with our love and praise, our worship and attention, He wraps His arms around us and welcomes us home.

The home we have in His presence is a real place of holy encounter. It isn't a figment of your imagination or a pleasant-sounding idea. His presence is real, tangible, and available to you right now. Once you've experienced it, you know it is undeniable. Even if you've never encountered the Lord this way, accept the invitation He's extending to you today. Simply believe you can feel God's love and ask Him to surround you with it. Now close your eyes and get ready! God is there.

Father, I want to feel the reality of your touch. I yearn for the peace and joy that only you can give. Come. Surround me. Speak to me. I believe your capacity to speak to me overshadows my inability to hear you. I open my heart to you without reservation. I know you're real. Now, let me experience this perfect home in your presence.

You Are His Rose

I am truly his rose,
the very theme of his song.
I'm overshadowed by his love,
growing in the valley!
—Song of Songs 2:1

As you come to understand your value, it's easy to see why He calls you His rose. Jesus laid down His life for you. You're His inheritance; the rose that the Father handpicked to give to His Son. The entire book of the Song of Songs is a story of His unending love for you. You are intoxicating, beautiful, and full of His glory. You represent the fullness of everything Jesus desires. He cherishes you, enjoys you, and believes in you.

He chose to live within you and now compassion streams from *your* eyes, healing flows from *your* hands, and virtue covers you. Everywhere you go, His glorious fragrance drips from your life. It's time to stop seeing yourself as unworthy of His love but as a rose that intoxicates His heart. You are beautiful. You are His rose.

❧

Father, I'm beginning to understand how beautiful I am to you. I want to live each day as an offering of love I want every thought, word, and deed to reflect the holy One who lives inside of me. I am exquisite, powerful, and made in your image. I am filled with your glory, and I will freely release it to the world, so others may encounter your love and discover their true identity.

Songs of Love

I am truly his rose,
the very theme of his song.
I'm overshadowed by his love,
growing in the valley!
—Song of Songs 2:1

Of all the spectacular things in this world—in the heavens above and the oceans deep—you are the one that Jesus sings about. His heart overflows with love for you, His bride. Let that revelation sink deep into your heart. You are not just some random person that He occasionally remembers. You have the attention of the Father, Son, and Holy Spirit all the time. You are His beloved—the one Jesus came to earth to redeem, by paying the ultimate price.

The Lord knows you—every thought and intent of the heart, and He invites you to get to know Him. Step into one of the most fulfilling relationships you will ever have, and you will stand amazed by your beautiful metamorphosis. Come closer to Him. Lean in and listen as He sings over you.

No one moves my heart the way that you do, Lord. To think you're even more in love with me than I am with you is mind-boggling. I can't help but rejoice when I think about it! You know me, you see me, you care about me, and you're so touched by my love that it causes your heart to sing.

Overshadowed

I am truly his rose,
the very theme of his song.
I'm overshadowed by his love,
growing in the valley!
—Song of Songs 2:1

*H*is presence is with you right now. Regardless of what you're facing today, know that He overshadows you with Himself. He is for you. His love will never stop. He is with you, even during the most horrendous times, and His love and grace will strengthen you and get you through.

He is forever faithful. Don't judge His nearness by what you feel. Take a deep breath and believe He is there. Allow His love to consume you and to absorb every thought, feeling, and emotion that overwhelms you. His peace doesn't make sense—it's beyond understanding. When you live in the awareness of His overshadowing presence, there's a silent conversation continually happening between you and Him. Prayer doesn't always vocalize itself; you simply *become* prayer. You live in a state of constant communion with the Lord that is deep and real, even if neither of you speak.

Father, consume me with this love that melts my thoughts into yours. I want to become so aware of your overshadowing presence that I can sense you everywhere I go. Flood me with your grace, so I can face every situation with peace and confident trust. You are with me and for me, and you will never let me go.

In the Valleys

I am truly his rose,
the very theme of his song.
I'm overshadowed by his love,
growing in the valley!

—Song of Songs 2:1

*E*ven in the darkest times of your life, Jesus is there. It's during these valley seasons—when you feel alone, confused, fearful, and sometimes angry—that His love is solidified in you. Trials become a launching pad for glorious transformation and victory. Even if you don't have the strength to pray one single word, keep your heart toward Him, and He will see you through. His strength is made perfect in your weakness (2 Corinthians 12:9).

How would you know God is faithful if you never needed Him to come through? How would you be sure how devoted you are to Him, if that love were never tested? To discover His power, you must first need it. God is a good God, and He will never inflict suffering or sickness to prove He can overcome. But He will prove His love and unlimited power *despite* these things.

Father, in every season of my life, I will declare that you are good. In painful times, I will cling to you, and in joyous times, I will celebrate your faithfulness. Help me to glean from every situation and to mature, so I become the radiant bride you say I am.

March

Unique

The Shepherd-King
Yes, you are my darling companion.
You stand out from all the rest.

—Song of Songs 2:2

When I think about God, I imagine a brilliantly cut diamond. Hold it under the light, and you will see its many different facets as it sparkles and shines. God is so glorious and brilliant that it would be impossible to display His diversity through a handful of people. Each of us carry a different characteristic of God. We are unique—created to shine a significant aspect of His personality to those around us. To hide that gift is to deprive the world of the part of God you carry.

You don't have to have a title or a large platform, or even be famous or outspoken. You only need to be comfortable in your own skin and believe in the God who lives within you. Don't try to be like someone else. God wants to pour Himself out through the part of you that looks just like Him.

It's amazing to think I've been chosen to shine with some of your most beautiful aspects. Help me to never doubt what I have to offer—all I have to do is be myself and witness a part of you flowing through me. Thank you for unshackling me from the chains that bound me to unrealistic expectations and for teaching me to be comfortable in my own skin.

Effortless

For though the curse of sin surrounds you,
still you remain as pure as a lily,
even more than all others.
—Song of Songs 2:2

Pure, holy, and fragrant. Your life radiates with glory in the midst of a dark world. Simply by staying connected to the Lord, without striving, you remain beautiful. Your righteousness is a gift, purchased with the price of blood. You don't have to work to earn anything from the Lord. If it were possible to buy your way into heaven, then Jesus died in vain. Why would He have needed to sacrifice Himself if we could attain perfection without Him?

How exciting it is to know you're sanctified simply because you're His. When you realize you have holiness roaring inside of you, you want to live in a way that reflects it. Walking in purity when you're surrounded by temptation becomes effortless. Obedience isn't even something you think about—it just happens naturally when you're totally and completely in love with Him.

Father, you have paid the ultimate price to make me holy and righteous. It isn't a sacrifice to turn away from temptation; it's a choice that becomes easier and easier every time I make it. My obedience flows from a heart of love. Now, I want to live in a way that honors this gift of righteousness. I surrender all and love you with effortless devotion.

Who Is He?

The Shulamite
My beloved is to me
the most fragrant apple tree—
he stands above the sons of men.

—Song of Songs 2:3

Who is Jesus to you? When you think about Him, how does it stir your heart? Apart from what your church, friends, family, or leaders think about Him, you must know how *you* feel about Him. This is probably the most important aspect of the Christian life—discovering exactly who Jesus is to you.

Revival isn't revival unless individual hearts encounter the Lord on a personal level. As you grow, He will uncover wrong beliefs that don't reflect who He really is. These aren't times to hide in shame. God wants you to know Him. He wants you to dive in and discover more about Him. He wants to shine on areas of your thinking that have been tainted and clouded over. Be honest about how you feel and ask Him to shine the light of His truth upon your heart.

Lord, I know that you're powerful, beautiful, and magnificent. Shine upon my soul—I want every part of me to experience the truth of who you are. If I hold any beliefs about you that are wrong, show me. I want everything I believe about you to be in line with what is true. I open my heart to you—search me.

Refreshing Love

The Shulamite
My beloved is to me
the most fragrant apple tree—
he stands above the sons of men.

<small>SONG OF SONGS 2:3</small>

A bountiful apple tree is a symbol of Jesus. Trees themselves speak of humanity. Here the Shulamite declares that Jesus is more pleasing to the eyes and more satisfying to the soul than anyone else. He stands above all others—fulfilling our deepest longings. Jesus alone supplies the needs of our hearts. No one can do for us what Jesus can. Like the Shulamite, as we rest beneath the shadow of His love, we discover how refreshing and pleasing His love is. It is unmatched by any other.

Jesus is the Tree of Life. Apples are the Word of God. Come eat your fill—feast upon His promises until they become a part of you. As you eat from Him and rest in Him, you too will bear the fruit of the Spirit in your life. You will become a tree overflowing with copious amounts of fruit to feed others.

Jesus, no man or woman on earth compares to you. You offer me a place of refreshing in your presence that soothes my soul and revives my spirit. I love the way you speak to me. The love you show is exhilarating. Breathe upon my heart and feed me with your promises until they come alive in me.

Rest

Sitting under his grace-shadow,
I blossom in his shade,
enjoying the sweet taste of his pleasant, delicious fruit,
resting with delight where his glory never fades.
—Song of Songs 2:3

Jesus' shade represents His grace, rest, and healing. Let's be honest, this world can drain you of hope and strength if you let it. The good news is that when you're tired and weary, Jesus beckons you to rest under His shadow. He never kicks you when you're down. He is gracious and tenderhearted.

Let His love overshadow you today. There you will find everything you need. The Lord knows exactly when you should forge ahead and when you need to rest. Pay attention when He offers you time to pause and be still. Heed His counsel, and you will be strengthened and come alive. Listen, and He will encourage you and give you wisdom and direction. He will soothe your frazzled soul and heal your body.

Lord, I want your love and our continual connection to be the driving force of my life. I never want to get so busy that I lose sight of you. I'm so thankful that you notice when I'm burnt out. You pull me close and blow away the dusty fragments of stress that tried to suffocate me. In your presence, I can breathe again.

Invigorate

Sitting under his grace-shadow,
I blossom in his shade,
enjoying the sweet taste of his pleasant, delicious fruit,
resting with delight where his glory never fades.
—SONG OF SONGS 2:3

You were created to enjoy your life and your relationship with the Lord. The spark for life is found in Him. He alone holds the hope and joy you crave. The friendships, creativity, and adventures that make you come alive are gifts that He desires you to have.

Life in His Kingdom should be exciting and fulfilling. God wants every area of your life to prosper. Spirit, soul, and body—you were designed to be whole, happy, and healthy. The choice to pursue these things and believe they are yours for the taking is up to you. It may take a mind and heart shift, but the Lord is willing to help you with that too. God wants you to live the best life imaginable. Believe again and start enjoying life the way He intended.

Father, today I make the decision to enjoy my life. I'm not going to sit and wait for everything to be perfect before I can be happy. I release discouragement, anger, and disappointment to you. Fill me with hope, joy, and confident trust. You already know the desires of my heart and the things I've believed you for. You are faithful and will answer my prayers right on time.

Unending Glory

Sitting under his grace-shadow,
I blossom in his shade,
enjoying the sweet taste of his pleasant, delicious fruit,
resting with delight **where his glory never fades**.
—Song of Songs 2:3

His glory is in you and around you. It courses through your being and surrounds you like a cloud. There is no end to it. It heals, speaks, and comforts. His glory releases wisdom and favor. The very Spirit that raised Jesus from the dead lives inside of you. You're a walking container of His goodness and power, waiting to be released.

When you laugh, let it be contagious. When you love, let it be without condition. When you help others, serve with compassion. Be merciful and without hypocrisy. Always look for the good in others, especially those who have wronged you. Speak well of everyone you meet. Lay hands on the sick and release light into every dark chasm.

Never fear what the Lord has already given you the victory over. Stand in His presence, and He will infuse you with faith. Worship Him, fall deeper into the place of love, and you will come alive! His glory never fades, and He's chosen you to contain it.

❧

Lord, flood every part of me with your brilliant splendor. As I go about my day, help me to remember that I not only carry your glory, but I must release it everywhere I go. You are the hope of the world, and you live inside of me!

Suddenly

Suddenly, he transported me into his house of wine—
he looked upon me with his unrelenting love divine.

—SONG OF SONGS 2:4

Just when you least expect it, God manifests His love in ways you never knew possible. The Creator of all that is seen and unseen is not short on ideas of how to extend His hand of blessing to you.

Prayers that have long been prayed, situations that have seen no forward momentum, the waiting that makes you wonder if He's forgotten—He sees it all, and He has the answer. Whether He meets you with a whisper of hope, a momentary idea, or a full-blown miracle that knocks your socks off, He will come. Pay attention to His gentle nudges; they could be your greatest answers to prayer. Expect the huge surprises that astonish you and thrust you into the biggest breakthrough you've ever known. Never give up hope! Nothing is impossible for God, and He loves to surprise you! He is the God of "suddenlies."

Lord, you're not only a miracle-working God, but you're my Father in heaven. You love me. Even when it seems that everything is falling apart, you have a plan. I simply need to stop trying to figure things out and trust you with unlimited faith. I look forward to seeing how you will answer me. You alone are the God of "suddenlies"—and you are coming with the breakthrough that I need!

Intoxicating Love

Suddenly, *he transported me into his house of wine—*
he looked upon me with his unrelenting love divine.
—Song of Songs 2:4

The overflow of life in the Spirit is more intoxicating than the finest wine. Over and over, the Holy Spirit beckons you closer. He yearns for you to experience the bliss of His presence. Nothing can compare to the distinct awareness of His affection.

In every season, in every mundane task, during life's deepest loss or most painful trauma, His love can transport you beyond what you feel and into a glorious healing encounter. His love has no limits. It is heavenly, mystical, and magnificent. It's where everything but God gets swept out of view. It's found by focusing upon the Lord and pouring out your worship without reservation. Here, where heaven and earth collide in an explosion of glory, nothing else competes for your attention. This place of joy and freedom that goes beyond understanding—this is His house of wine.

Father, sweep me up in a hurricane of your love. I look to you and turn away from all distractions that mentally tie me to the cares of this world. You are my joy and my strength. My worship to you rises from the depths of my being. Come; intoxicate me with the bliss of your presence that washes away all other cares.

Relentless

Suddenly, he transported me into his house of wine—
he looked upon me with **his unrelenting love divine**.

—Song of Songs 2:4

The Lord's love is relentless. He will never give up on you. He doesn't look at you one way when you're good and another when you're going through tough times and your faith is challenged. Your weaknesses don't surprise Him. He loves you despite them.

The heart of the Father always seeks to release you into your unfulfilled destiny, even if you're broken and undone—even if you've questioned Him or felt angry with Him. He only needs your yes—even your hesitant, shaky yes that is peppered with discouragement and doubt. God's love is zealous, forgiving, and unrelenting. He knows the way to your heart. He knows how to set you free.

Thank you, Father, for your unrelenting love. You never back down or walk away from me, even when I mess up. You're so gracious, so tender and kind. Your love amazes me. Infuse me with faith as I yield myself to you. Strengthen me with your grace. You paid the highest price, so I can walk in victory!

Revive Me

Revive me with your goblet of wine.
—SONG OF SONGS 2:5

*I*t isn't until we go through difficult times that we truly understand our great need to be revived. We yearn and even ache for God to breathe life back into our dry bones. Nothing can refresh us the way He can. No vacation, spa, or conference is going to make you feel alive unless Jesus meets you in the midst of it.

Jesus, the Son of God who burns with holy, sacred love, is reaching out to you. The fire of His love will move you from passivity to passion. Even while dark shadows linger nearby, the glory of His love will propel you into the light. Grace will strengthen you and set you on your feet again. Where discouragement has stripped you, hope will infuse you. Just a drop of His love will flood your soul like waves crashing upon the seashore. You don't have to wait; you only need to release all the negativity that has bombarded you and ask Him to replace it with His power and grace.

God, revive me! I need a fresh touch of your grace, glory, and love. I shake off everything that's been trying to bring me down. I am not a quitter. I'm a conqueror! I'm a child of the Most High God! Breathe upon me—spirit, soul, and body, and give me back my momentum and zest for life. I lift my voice to sing your praises and declare my victory.

Promises

Revive me with your goblet of wine.
Refresh me again with your sweet promises.
—Song of Songs 2:5

God's promises are sweet and refreshing. His Word sparks hope and life into the darkest situations. His truth fans away the gloomy clouds and fills you with joy. Life, wisdom, revelation, and untold mysteries are waiting to be discovered as you dive into His presence with expectation.

Listen. Still your soul and tune in to the frequency of love. God wants to encourage you and give direction for your life from the words that flow from His throne. Revelation will rest upon your heart as He infuses your spirit with the sound of His voice. His written Word will come alive as you read with faith-filled anticipation. Put His promises on your lips and declare the truth that has touched your heart. Saturate the atmosphere with faith and expectancy. Let the certainty of His love sink deep into every part of your being until you expect nothing less than God's unstoppable power and faithfulness to break through.

Lord, give me an injection of faith as I tune my heart into yours. I will drench doubt and fear with my declarations of hope and truth. Illuminate and refresh my mind and soul with your presence. You are good, and you have the answers and the breakthrough I need. You are faithful, and I expect your promises to come to pass.

Lovesick

Revive me with your goblet of wine.
Refresh me again with your sweet promises.
Help me and hold me, for I am lovesick!
—Song of Songs 2:5

Living in His sacred chamber means living life beneath the continual outpouring of His love. At times, it's overwhelming. It seems we can hardly stand because of the tangible glory that overwhelms our human frailty. Oh, but we were made for this! We were created to live in realms of holy splendor that few have ever known.

This is our God and King! This is the very person of love Himself! To experience the bliss of His nearness shatters every wrong mind-set that tries to explain away the spiritual aspects of Christianity. Theology, rules, and doctrines explode in the fires of His holy passion. Dignity takes a back seat when you've truly been touched by love. One can scarcely stand in the presence of such splendor, majesty, and unconditional devotion. We long for more, yet cry out for His grace to be able to contain it.

Lord, help me and hold me—the glory of your love has overwhelmed my soul! You're here with me now, and everything else is growing dim in the light of your face. Breathe upon my soul. Though it may burst into a thousand flames, I don't care! I want to experience the reality of your embrace. I want to taste both the sweetness and power of your presence.

His Touch

**His left hand cradles my head
while his right hand holds me close.**
I am at rest in this love.
—Song of Songs 2:6

The same hands that hold the universe cradles you. His touch is undeniable. With compassion, He reaches for you and draws you near. You may not always see His hand tucked beneath your head, but you will feel it. This is the reality of the world you live in. You were created for the Kingdom of God that is all around you and dwells within.

Jesus longs to make His touch known to you. He doesn't simply want you to learn about Him. He wants you to experience His reality. When Jesus comes close, everything changes. When He wraps you within the power of His embrace, there's no denying it. His all-encompassing love is your confidence and comfort. Protection, health, and miracles are found in the safety of His arms. How absolutely mysterious and beautiful it is to know that the King of kings loves you unconditionally. Fall wholeheartedly into His embrace today.

Jesus, I want to feel your arms around me. Swaddle me in the mystery of your love. I want to rest in your embrace forever. Whisper secrets that have yet to be revealed and impart wisdom and compassion to my soul. Let me feel the sweet caress of sacred love. Hold me tight and never let me go!

Close

His left hand cradles my head
while his right hand **holds me close.**
I am at rest in this love.
—Song of Songs 2:6

God's love is with you, in you, and surrounding you always. He's as close to you as the air you breathe. There are depths of His love yet to be discovered, but it's up to you to acquaint yourself with them. Lean in and lay your head upon His chest. Our loving Father has reached out and wrapped Himself around you through Jesus. Nothing stands between you and perfect love. You're not hindered by your past, your insecurities, or your humanity.

Feel His breath upon your life. Look into His eyes. Inhale the sweet fragrance of His presence. Gaze upon His majesty and splendor. He is with you. The way you enjoy His love is a gift to Him—the reward of His suffering. Your worship is His delight. He's chosen you to stay close to Him for all eternity, and eternity starts here and now.

Lord, my heart longs for you. My soul yearns for your touch. Thank you for not being angry with me when I lose sight of you. Your loving-kindness fascinates me. Your tender mercy leaves me undone. Your love is unlike anything I've ever known. Pull me close—even closer—and never let go.

The Place of Peace

His left hand cradles my head
while his right hand holds me close.
I am at rest in this love.
—SONG OF SONGS 2:6

Relinquish all control, the right to understand, and the fear that plagues your soul and find peace in His presence. Yield your will and fully surrender yourself to His. Let go of everything you once presumed you knew and lean into His embrace. In this glorious place of trust, nothing can move you. Fully persuaded that God is on your side, you can relax and let go. Discouragement, hopelessness, and frustration won't find a place in your soul when your heart is fixed upon His goodness.

A heart that is set upon Him is confident and at peace. This is the telltale sign of one fully resigned to this faithful, loving God. He is so much greater than you can possibly conceive. As you rest and release your cares to Him, nothing can shake you. Fear cannot be found in the atmosphere of overwhelming love. Jesus is the Prince of Peace.

❧

Jesus, consume me with your love! Drown every mind-set that contradicts your goodness. I place the reins of my life in your hands and trust you to steer me in the right direction. Hold me and protect me. I let go—fully and without reservation. Here in your presence, I'm completely at peace.

Words of Affection

The Shepherd-King

Promise me, brides-to-be,
by the gentle gazelles and delicate deer,
that you'll not disturb my love until she is ready to arise.
—Song of Songs 2:7

Even when Jesus needs to get His point across, He still speaks to you with love. Using words like *gentle* and *delicate*, He continually reminds you who you are and how He sees you. He is not a mean taskmaster. His words always build up and never tear down. His love never changes.

This is how He expects us to treat others. Showing honor, even during quarrels or misunderstandings, is the way of the Kingdom. Truth spoken in love has more power than judgment and criticism. Build others up, just as Jesus does. Remind them of who they are and encourage them. Let your life be an example of tender mercy and unwavering devotion. As you love others and speak as Jesus does, you become even more radiant—a true bride of Christ, shining in purity and righteousness.

Lord, when you speak to my heart, I come alive. Your words, so loving and tender, heal every wound. I love the way you encourage me and speak light and purpose into my life. Teach me to be like you—honoring and supportive—always believing the best and extending mercy to everyone I meet.

Seasons of Rest

The Shepherd-King
Promise me, brides-to-be,
by the gentle gazelles and delicate deer,
that **you'll not disturb my love until she is ready to arise**.

—SONG OF SONGS 2:7

How comforting it is to know that God's timing is perfect. He knows when you need to rest and when you're ready to run. He'll never force you in directions you aren't willing to go, nor will he demand action before you're ready. When *He* knows you're ready but you don't agree, He still doesn't force you. Instead, He blows His awakening breath and simply waits until you're ready to rise.

God knows what lies ahead, and He prepares you by allowing, even encouraging, seasons of rest. Being lost in holy love is the best preparation possible. Cultivating intimacy with the Lord becomes the foundation for everything. In good times and in bad, He is the home you continually return to. Seasons of grace and rest are gifts from God. Enjoy them. Journal the secrets He whispers to your heart. All that you receive during these times will become the food you will use to feed others.

Father, I'd rather stay here, resting in your presence and enveloped by your love, than anywhere else. Transform me as I soak in your living waters, and I will emerge more gloriously in your likeness. When you call me forward, together we will minister love, healing, and forgiveness to the world.

It's Him!

The Shulamite
Listen! I hear my lover's voice.
I know it's him coming to me—
leaping with joy over mountains,
skipping in love over the hills that separate us,
to come to me.

—SONG OF SONGS 2:8

Sometimes the Lord comes on the scene as the lion whose unmistakable and overwhelming power is exhilarating—there's no denying He's there. At other times, He is the gentle lamb who speaks so softly that you must lean in close to hear Him. He comes in a myriad of ways, sensitizing us to His voice and teaching us how to recognize Him. The journey of acquainting ourselves with His presence is one of intrigue and excitement.

The more intentionally you look and listen for Him, the more sensitive you are to even the smallest nudge. Even the tiniest, fleeting image that tumbles across your mind will not be ignored when you pay attention. The Lord desires us to be in tune with what we sense, think, see, and hear because He is often the spark behind it. Pay attention to what goes on inside of you and what you notice in the world around you. It may be the Lord speaking to your heart.

Father, I want to know you and recognize you when you're trying to speak to my heart. With great resolve, I will pay more attention to what is going on inside and outside of me. Speak Lord. Sensitize me to your Holy Spirit. I'm listening.

Joy

The Shulamite
Listen! I hear my lover's voice.
I know it's him coming to me—
leaping with joy over mountains,
skipping in love over the hills that separate us,
to come to me.

—SONG OF SONGS 2:8

When Jesus thinks about you, He jumps for joy. He's thrilled about you! With perfect vision that sees in every direction and wisdom that contemplates the past and future simultaneously, He leads you on an incredible journey. He knows what He's planned for your life and it's always good. The joyful Shepherd asks for your hand, so He can guide you into the best life ever.

When the enemy comes against you, Jesus laughs in his face and hopes you will do the same. Faith and trust in the Lord will liberate you and set you free. Life with Him is meant to be filled with joy and celebration. You are the joy that moves His heart; how much more should He stir yours with holy bliss. The joy of the Lord is contagious and irresistible!

Jesus, your smile sparks faith in the deepest part of me. The sound of your laughter is like a lightning bolt to my soul. It demolishes every lie that bombards my mind and unlocks the chains that restrict me. Permeate me with your joy. I willingly take your hand and will trust you with sheer abandon. In your presence, I am free!

Obstacles

I know it's him coming to me—
leaping with joy *over mountains,*
skipping in love over the hills that separate us,
to come to me.

—Song of Songs 2:8

No mountain can keep the Lord from reaching you. Problems don't restrain Him from running after you. In fact, they're a way for Him to prove His power and faithfulness. His love for you is so strong that nothing will hold Him back. He will effortlessly leap with joy over the mountains of your unbelief and skip over the hills of your struggles, as if they were nothing.

Never fear the mountains you face. The One who has conquered them faces them with you. Now you will know Jesus as your Champion and discover that you are strong and created to live in triumph. As you climb mountains with Him, you'll be strengthened and build character. You'll view things from a different perspective and mature into the bride He's called you to be.

Lord, these mountains I face feel insurmountable. I honestly don't know how to get to the other side of them, so I turn to you. You have told me that nothing is impossible if I believe. Today, I choose the path of faith, even if it takes me to unknown places. I want to conquer these mountains and experience the thrill of victory with you!

Nothing Can Separate You

I know it's him coming to me—
leaping with joy over mountains,
skipping in love over the hills that separate us,
to come to me.

—Song of Songs 2:8

*N*othing can separate you from Jesus' extravagant love. He has no problem dancing and skipping right over the things that hinder your relationship with Him. He knows how to find you. He knows about every area of your soul that is a hindrance to mature love. He will not leave you the same.

Jesus alone can reveal what is true and right. Reach out; invite Him to illuminate every dark chasm of your being with His glory. God put a longing in your heart to live in constant awareness of His love. The Cross sealed the gap that once separated you from Him, but walls of sin and wrong mind-sets offer a place of disconnection. Fortunately, it is His desire and pleasure to jump over them and rapture you once again. Not even the mountain of Calvary could stop Him!

Jesus, come save me from myself. Set me free from anything that would hinder our love. I want nothing to come between us—not fear, self-doubt, impure motives, or selfishness. Sovereign King, I want to run with you in resurrection power. I invite you to permeate every area of my life with your glory.

Discover

Let me describe him:
he is graceful as a gazelle—
swift as a wild stag.
—Song of Songs 2:9

Take some time today to be still. Look into His eyes. What do you see? Notice the color of His eyes and the brilliance of His smile. Never be satisfied with what others tell you about Him. Allow the yearning of your soul to launch you into an encounter of your own. Jesus wants to reveal Himself to you. He's inviting you to uncover the hidden treasures of His Kingdom.

This discovery is meant to free your soul and spirit. He longs for you to soar upon fresh revelation, to saturate you with glory, and then release it to the world around you. Everyone has their own way of expressing the magnificence, grace, power, and love of the Lord. Whether it is with words, art, prayers, or acts of service, give others a glimpse of the One who holds the stars and stirs your soul.

Father, I long to know you. I'm not content with occasional glimpses or intermittent conversations. I desire to walk with you and hear what moves your heart. I want to uncover realities that no one has ever seen. Reveal yourself to me, so I will ascend above the clouds of indifference and passionless Christianity.

Facets

Let me describe him:
he is graceful as a gazelle—
swift as a wild stag.
—SONG OF SONGS 2:9

There are many facets to the Lord's character. He is tender and kind, majestic and powerful. This beautiful Savior, who cradles us in His arms, is also the King who beckons us to rule by His side. As we get to know Him, we realize that His divine nature is complex and limitless—a mystery, worth a lifetime of exploration.

The fear of the Lord brings us to our knees in breathless wonder. The joy of the Lord resounds throughout the earth and sets the captives free. It's easy to understand why the twenty-four elders in heaven continually fall before His throne and declare His worth and power.

These many facets of the Lord are seen in you and me. He's created each of us with diverse personalities and differing gifts. What a glorious example we are of God's inexhaustible complexity. Life with Him is never boring.

Lord, life with you is exhilarating! I love when you uncover facets of your personality that I've never experienced before. Unveil my eyes, so I may peer into the wonders of your beauty and learn all there is to know about you. Teach me to recognize you in the lives of others, so I can celebrate and honor your nature within them.

Hidden

Now he comes closer,
even to the places where I hide.
He gazes into my soul,
peering through the portal
as he blossoms within my heart.

—Song of Songs 2:9

There is no shame in perfect love. You don't have to hide. Jesus longs to fill every area of your life—especially the places where you aren't secure. It isn't until you feel the penetrating gaze of the Lord upon your life that you realize there are still places you've closed off to Him. Jesus has called you to freedom.

When you long to walk with Him in total abandon, He will answer the cry of your heart. No aspect of your life is off-limits. Even the walls you built to protect yourself from pain, have caught His attention. But your well-constructed hiding places will not hinder the Healer. He will patiently wait for you to yield. In this new season of maturing love, you'll discover how safe His love is. Open your heart and invite Him in. Let nothing hinder your sacred intimacy with Jesus.

Jesus, I open my life to you and ask you to be Lord of every area. Change me. Purify me. Let me see myself the way you do, so I may realize my true identity. When I focus on you, I am confident and courageous—truly alive. So, I will keep my focus on you, and together, we will victoriously overcome my shortcomings and weaknesses.

Seen

Now he comes closer,
even to the places where I hide.
He gazes into my soul,
peering through the portal
as he blossoms within my heart.
—Song of Songs 2:9

There is no one, not even your closest friend or family member, who understands you like Jesus does. He knows you—truly knows the very depths and movements of your heart. The things that stir within your being—the hopes and dreams, fears, and torments—are visible to Him. Not only are they visible; they touch His heart. He doesn't peer into the core of who you are just to gain information; He loves you and enjoys you.

When He gazes into your soul, He leaves behind imprints of love. The longer you remain in His presence, the more you begin to look and sound like Him. In turn, when you search your own soul, you will notice Him emerging through your personality and opinions. You are becoming the person He's always believed you are.

Lord, I'm so touched by the way you cherish me. I won't try to hide who I am, or what I think and feel, because you see it all. With you, I can be as vulnerable as I want to be and know you understand. Breathe upon my life. Wash me in your forgiving and powerful love. I want all that you see within me to bring you glory. I yield myself to you without reservation.

Peering through the Lattice

Now he comes closer,
even to the places where I hide.
He gazes into my soul,
peering through the portal
as he blossoms within my heart.

—SONG OF SONGS 2:9

Jesus has already torn the veil that separated you from Him. He paid the ultimate price to prove his love. Neither death nor the grave could keep him away from you, so don't think that any wall that you build will keep Him out. He knows the way in. Even now, He's peering straight into your soul. He knows what makes you tick. He understands your hesitations, but He longs to remove them.

The Lord is excited about you! He can't stop looking at you. He's delighted with the areas of your life that you've opened to Him, and He's eager to fill the places you've yet to invite Him into. He longs to be with you, and He enjoys your company. As He gazes at you, you'll sense His excitement and longing, and it will stir your heart.

Jesus, the way you yearn for me leaves me undone. I feel you tugging at my soul, drawing me away into the chambers of your presence. I have no desire to resist you. I turn to you—spirit, soul, and body—and worship you. I honor you for the price of love you paid. I praise you for the glory that lives inside of me. I am yours—totally and completely.

Blossom

Now he comes closer,
even to the places where I hide.
He gazes into my soul,
peering through the portal
as *he blossoms within my heart*.

—SONG OF SONGS 2:9

The moment you welcomed Jesus into your life, He filled you with Himself. As you devote yourself to Him, you're transforming into a radiant bride. Character, maturity, and wisdom begin to shape your personality. Confidence, courage, and compassion start to define your identity.

Jesus doesn't stare at you and make a list of what He wants to change. He's moved by what He sees and celebrates your grace. The simplicity of saying yes to Him daily is a powerful force. It pulls Him toward you like a magnet. He comes alive within every crevice of your spirit and soul. Soon, seeds of acceptance and passion blossom and release the essence of His beauty and compassion. You carry the fragrance of Jesus Christ, and it exudes from you everywhere you go.

Jesus, I've known you as Savior, but I long to know you as King. Rule my heart and guide my decisions. I want to reflect the glory of your majesty and live with honor and dignity. I water the seeds of holiness and righteousness that you've planted within me, with every decision. Bloom within me until every part of my being is saturated with the fragrance of your beauty.

Arise

The one I love calls to me:
The Bridegroom-King
Arise, my dearest. Hurry, my darling.
Come along with me!
—Song of Songs 2:10

Jesus wants to breathe resurrection life into you and all that you do. This flow of power and glory is a gift that resides within you. He asks you to pour out of your fullness into the lives of others. With excitement shining from His face, He does more than extend the hand of friendship—He beckons you to run with Him. His love imparts courage to leave the places of comfort.

You are the beautiful one He delights in. Listen as He calls you His dearest and His darling. You are glorious and magnificent, simply because you're His. He's so excited to share this journey with you. His fiery love has power to break off every desire for the world and its artificial pleasures. Let His love consume every other ambition and passion. Jesus has come to make you as victorious and powerful as He is!

Jesus, extend your hand to me and strengthen me by your grace. I hear you beckoning me, but I'm hesitant. I want to run with you, and I believe that you live inside of me, but I need courage. I place my confidence in you alone. Fill me with compassion, faith, and boldness, and I will do what you ask.

Because You Asked

I have come as you have asked
to draw you to my heart and lead you out.
For now is the time, my beautiful one.
—Song of Songs 2:10

The Lord never forgets a prayer that you've prayed. Even when you forget, He remembers. When you pray radical prayers of zealous love, it thrills Him, and He will answer. You always have the ear of the King. It's the joy of His heart to fulfill every request that leads you into a deeper relationship with Him.

Often, what you ask for is the culmination, or peak, of what's in your heart. It may take years before some answers fully manifest. One prayer may catapult you on a lifelong journey. Jesus is perfected wisdom, and He knows exactly how to lead you. He nurtures, watches, and meticulously prepares you for what lies ahead. Time serves as a teacher, instructing you through your greatest lessons. Though waiting can be hard to endure, He has not forgotten you. Day by day, through trials and varying seasons, He will guide you down the paths that lead to the answer.

Father, my life is in your hands. You know the prayers I've prayed, and you've heard the cry of my heart. You love me and delight in answering my prayers. I will trust your timing and the way you lead me. Everything you do, you do for my good. Your ways are perfect.

Ready or Not!

I have come as you have asked
to draw you to my heart and lead you out.
For now is the time, my beautiful one.

—Song of Songs 2:10

When the Lord declares that you're ready to run, you are! Unfortunately, you may not _feel_ ready. Perhaps you feel ill equipped, fearful, or maybe you've just become too comfortable. This is why faith and trust must be the anchor of your soul. Faith leads your spirit and makes no sense to your mind. Despite feelings, circumstances, or inconvenience, when Jesus says it's time, it's time!

The days of heaven on earth are ahead, and you were created to carry His glory to the ends of the earth. You are filled with the same Spirit that raised Jesus from the dead. He is the God of strength who abides within you. Take a deep breath, grab His hand, and jump into the deep waters of faith. Acquaint yourself with His perfect love, and it will drive fear far from your heart. Don't worry; He won't let you drown.

Jesus, I hear you calling me to run with you. Some days I think I'm ready, and other days, I don't think I'll ever be. But you know all things and see through the eyes of eternity. I lean into your grace and rely on your power. Apart from you I can do nothing, but with you I can do all things. This is what I was made for!

April

A New Season

The season has changed,
the bondage of your barren winter has ended,
and the season of hiding is over and gone.
The rains have soaked the earth.
—Song of Songs 2:11

Jesus was faithful to you in the gloomiest of winters, and He will be faithful to you in the blossoming of spring. The cold winds of trials have ended. The warmth of love has arrived with new hope. A new season has come!

Light shines against the backdrop of darkness, illuminating the many lessons you've learned during your barren winter. As you step over into this new season, you can see how faithfully He's cared for you. He held you close, strengthening and encouraging you all the way. Invite Him into your most traumatic memories, and He'll remove the painful sting. He's good at taking what the enemy meant for your destruction and turning it around. He fills the darkness with glory.

Father, I feel the warm winds of springtime. The fragrance of your love floods my senses. You've come to escort me out of the darkness and into the light. Thank you for everything you've taught me. I honor you for your patience, even when I kicked and screamed in protest. Now, let my life be as a fruitful vine, so others may eat from the wisdom I've gained.

Unveiled

The season has changed,
the bondage of your barren winter has ended,
and *the season of hiding is over and gone.*
The rains have soaked the earth.

—SONG OF SONGS 2:11

Before she walks down the aisle, every bride must go through a time of preparation. She prepares herself physically, mentally, and spiritually. The same is true with us. Those who have been tucked away with God, learning who they are, have been preparing to be unveiled. When the Lord says He's ready to reveal your beauty to the world, the time for hiding is over. Your season has come.

Even the shiest person has been called to shine. You are a glorious bride who carries the brilliance, compassion, and power of God within you. There are endless ways to release the gifts that the Lord has given you. You have a story to tell, a listening ear, a wise heart, or perhaps a creative edge. The point is you have something worth releasing, and to hide it is to deny the world a glimpse of His presence and love that abides within you.

Father, I'm so honored that you have chosen me to be a carrier of your glory. You've done such a beautiful work inside of me. Your love and mercy have changed me. With confidence in you and in what you've given me to share, I will be faithful to release your love to those you bring across my path.

Drenched

The season has changed,
the bondage of your barren winter has ended,
and the season of hiding is over and gone.
***The rains have soaked the earth
and left it bright with blossoming flowers.***

—Song of Songs 2:11–12

There's nothing like being flooded with the presence of the Holy Spirit. He's answered your cry to be saturated with Him, and nothing dry and dusty will remain. The Word of God has permeated you and filled you with truth powerful enough to move mountains. The rains of His love have soaked you—infused you with His reality, so you are literally one with the Lord.

The power of His redeeming love has washed away the remains of sin, despair, and fear. All that is left is the brilliance of the Lord Himself. You don't just look like your Father in heaven; you are one spirit with Him. New life—the very glory of God Himself—abides within you. The flowers of holy passion and confident faith now bloom within your heart. You are not the same as you once were. Joined in perfect union with God, you are powerful, beautiful, and glorious!

Come, Holy Spirit. Saturate me with your overwhelming glory and drench every part of me with your holy love. I'm yours—totally and completely. Blur the boundaries between heaven and earth and let me live in your glorious presence always. Sensitize me, so I become aware of our continual and holy union.

Find Your Song

... and left it bright with blossoming flowers.
The season for singing *and pruning the vines has arrived.*
I hear the cooing of doves in our land,
filling the air with songs to awaken you
and guide you forth.

—Song of Songs 2:12

As the barren winter ends, nature rejoices, announcing the arrival of springtime. The scent of fragrant flowers fills the air, the birds seem to dance as they flit from tree to tree, and new life is bursting all around. It feels as if the earth has found its song as it ushers in something new.

Now it's time for you to find your song. It's time for you to raise your weary head and lift your voice in anticipation of this glorious end to barrenness. Sing with joy and praise the Lord for what He's doing in your life. Praise Him for the change of season, because it has surely come. Release your songs of hope and faith as new life blossoms within you. God is calling you to begin a journey unlike any other. A journey of passion. A journey of adventure.

God, I am filled with your joy! Hope and faith have found their home in my heart, and I am so excited for what is to come! I feel like a little kid, dancing and singing at the top of my lungs. My songs of praise and declaration shift the atmosphere as they agree with your faithful promises. I release the song of my heart to you. You're a good father.

What Do You Hear?

The season for singing and pruning the vines has arrived.
I hear the cooing of doves in our land,
filling the air with songs to awaken you
and guide you forth.

—Song of Songs 2:12

The sound of love is gentle and soothing. It is inviting, promising, and intriguing. It isn't simply the call to bask in its warmth but also an encouragement to step out and experience life with the One you love. It stirs you and beckons you forward.

There is a message of love being released over you today. The air is charged with anticipation. Listen and you will hear the sound of doves announcing the time of harvest. Yes, the very Spirit of God is singing the Song of all Songs over you. He's awakening you to the melody of mercy, hope, and compassion that flow through His heart. Once you hear it, make it your anthem. Let it stream from your life as you go forth into the harvest with the Lord. This is your season. You're ready to impart to others.

Father, I hear the sound of your voice. Your songs of love have left me undone and without excuse. I am stirred in the depths of my soul to follow you. Lead me by your Spirit and flood me with your truth. I will celebrate your love and release your life to those around me.

See

**Can you not discern this new day of destiny
breaking forth around you?**
The early signs of my purposes and plans
are bursting forth.

<small>SONG OF SONGS 2:13</small>

*J*ust as Elisha of old prayed for his servant's eyes to be opened, Jesus declares it is time for you to see (see 2 Kings 6:17). The days of unbelief, which clouded your eyes, have ended. Promises of destiny and fruitfulness are all around you, waiting to be embraced.

The reality of God's faithfulness is unfolding before your eyes. He wants you to become aware of His devotion to you and commitment to bring His promises to pass in your life. As He illuminates your vision with fresh perspective, you receive the wisdom, creativity, anointing, and direction for your future. Favor smooths the path that once was littered with stones of disregard. Grace and ease become your friends. Your faith is being rewarded, and what once was hidden is being revealed. Once you see clearly, you can go forth in confidence and live in victory. This is your season of destiny!

Father, open the eyes of my heart. I want to see the mysteries that once were hidden. Illuminate the path before me, so I may walk in sync with you. Let favor guide my steps and your anointing pave the way. I cling to you, knowing you will do all that you've promised. You are my hope, my joy, and my great reward. ·

Purpose

Can you not discern this new day of destiny
breaking forth around you?
The early signs of *my purposes and plans
are bursting forth*.

SONG OF SONGS 2:13

The Lord knows exactly where you are on your timeline of spiritual growth. His plans for you aren't ruined when you make a mistake or take a wrong turn. His mercy always finds a way to get you back on track. You may think that you must act a certain way to find the Lord's favor, but His favor has already found you.

You were born with a divine purpose. You are fearfully and wonderfully made. Where one season may leave you feeling stripped and bare, another season will cause you to burst forth in victory. The highs and lows of life don't confuse God. He is wise enough to lead you, despite any diversions you may take. You don't have to fully understand every detail of His plans for you. You simply need to believe they are good. Pay attention to what stirs in your heart. Even the smallest glimmer of an idea or desire may be the Lord shining the light of His purpose upon your life.

Father, guide me with your wisdom into my destiny. I know you have a purpose for my life that's filled with peace and joy. If I get off track or lose sight of you, grab me and pull me back to you. My life is in your hands, and I trust your leadership.

Bloom

The budding vines of new life
are now blooming everywhere.
The fragrance of their flowers whispers:
"There is change in the air."
—Song of Songs 2:13

*Y*ou have been grafted into the budding vine of perfect love. Jesus' life flows through your veins. His holiness has blossomed within you and made you beautiful. As you learn to abide in Him, acknowledging Him throughout your day and listening for His tender voice, your blossoming beauty becomes evident to everyone around you.

Everything about you changes when your life is filled with Him. Your worship adorns you with incomparable radiance. Your smile reflects the joy within. Wisdom, truth, and hope season your speech. Your hands release healing to all they touch. Everywhere you go, the beauty of the One who consumes you splashes on those around you. Enjoy Him, stay close to Him, and share His beauty with the world.

Jesus, I want to live my life from the overflow of your glory within me. You have wrapped me in your love and filled me with your grace. As I learn to see myself the way you do and walk in my true identity, I will release your power with confidence. Thank you for teaching me how truly beautiful I am to you. You are the treasure within me.

Fragrant

The budding vines of new life
are now blooming everywhere.
The fragrance of their flowers whispers:
"There is change in the air."

SONG OF SONGS 2:13

Still your thoughts and inhale deeply. The delicate fragrance of Jesus has filled your life. From the depths of your soul, the scent of love and forgiveness rise to the surface. He is there with you now. The aroma of heaven is all around.

You are one spirit with the Lord. Humanity and deity have merged inside of you. If you could see yourself as He sees you, you would see the mirror image of Jesus. Embrace this truth. Breathe it in and let it flood your senses. As a vessel of His glory, you now carry that same refreshing scent to the world around you. It exudes from you and fills the atmosphere, everywhere you go. You are His, and everything about you has changed.

Jesus, your beauty has flooded my life. I feel you near—like whispers of hope to my soul. Let your presence come as a fragrant cloud of glory and infuse me with its power. I want to look like you, smell like you, and walk like you. I want to know you more than any person ever has. I want to be known as one who carries the scents of joy and faith.

Run with Me!

Arise, my love, my beautiful companion,
and run with me to the higher place.
For now is the time to arise and come away with me.

—Song of Songs 2:13

The Lord has more confidence in you than you have in yourself. He has already extended the hand of holy union and now reaches to draw you into your purpose. No one wants to see you fulfill your calling on this earth more than He does.

Release frustration. Stop striving to discover who you are by looking around you. Who you are and what you are meant to do comes from within. It's already there. The only way to recognize it is to learn to be happy with being you. When you identify as God's very own, your strengths will become evident. Desires and ideas will stir within you. You're a perfect companion for Jesus. He longs to reach through you to share Himself with others. The way you are meant to touch the world is unique. As you step into this way of thinking, faith will launch you forward.

Father, I believe that you have called me for a divine purpose. I may not understand the details, but I know my destiny begins with you. Each day I will acquaint myself with your wisdom, love, and truth, knowing that as I release my life to you, you will lead me.

Higher

Arise, my love, my beautiful companion,
and *run with me to the higher place.*
For now is the time to arise and come away with me.
—Song of Songs 2:13

Skipping over the mountains with Jesus means you must leave yourself behind and follow Him. In order to run in freedom, you must first be willing to release anything that screams of self: sin, impure motives, and pride. These are the things that can drag you down and hold you back from victory.

Resurrection power was designed to fit you perfectly. You are destined for much more than you ever dreamed possible. You've been called to live from a higher vantage point than you currently have. You were created for the high places of faith and power, not the lowly places of fear and selfish love. Let Him lift you from one level of glory to the next. Shake off uncertainty and doubt. All you have to do is believe and let go of all that holds you back. Trust Him. He is reaching for you and wooing you higher. Don't hold back.

❧

Father, give me eyes to see and ears to hear all that you have in store for me. I repent of selfish mind-sets that have limited your love from reaching others. I want nothing to do with self-indulgence that leads me away from you. I choose to live with you in the highest place of your glory.

My Dove

For you are my dove, hidden in the split-open rock.
It was I who took you and hid you up high
in the secret stairway of the sky.

—Song of Songs 2:14

In your moments of weakness, when you're struggling with fear, temptation, or unbelief, Jesus cups His hands around your face and speaks words of tender affection and strength. One of the most powerful statements of Jesus' heart is revealed when He calls you His dove. He reminds you of your identity as a vessel of purity and perfection, because a dove is also a symbol of the Holy Spirit. He looks into your eyes and encourages you, "Don't worry, I still see me inside of you. You're going to be just fine."

God sees your deep devotion. He knows that your heart is toward Him, even when you botch things up or give fear a place. Instead of punishing you for your immature faith, He comes as a loving parent and creates a place of safety in the wounded side of Christ. His mercy is limitless. His grace defines you. His love for you is pure and unselfish.

Lord, my heart is overflowing with love and gratefulness. I want to be single-minded with my heart fixed firmly upon you. Give me clear spiritual vision, so nothing could ever entice or deceive me. Thank you for believing in me, even when I struggle. I choose you over all others.

Secret Stairs

For you are my dove, hidden in the split-open rock.
It was I who took you and hid you up high
in the secret stairway of the sky.
—Song of Songs 2:14

God loves to share His secrets with those He loves. The greatest mystery of all, Jesus' resurrection, is no exception. The ultimate secret place—the chamber of the King—has brought you close to God and set you free. You are already seated with Him in heavenly places. Jesus has paved the way before you. Once you know the way, you can go anytime you desire.

His love is the stairway to heaven. It is also the place of protection. Here in the safety of His arms, no enemy can defeat you. Though he may have stolen from you or hurt you, he cannot defeat you. United to the cross, you can live above the circumstances of life that are filled with pain and testing. Abiding in the wounds of Christ may sound like a mystery, but it is one you have been created to uncover. There you will remain victorious, as you choose the secret life with God over all else.

Lord, you are my shelter and hiding place. I love diving into the mysteries of your Kingdom and learning my part in it. Thank you, most of all, for the secret of the cross and for tucking me away in the safety of its power.

Face-to-Face

Let me see your radiant face and hear your sweet voice.
How beautiful your eyes of worship
and lovely your voice in prayer.
—Song of Songs 2:14

Look into the eyes of the One who loves you unconditionally. You are His delight—the reward of His suffering. No longer does a veil of shame cover your face. You are beautiful, free, and courageous! Believing that you're thoroughly accepted by the Lord gives you the confidence to look Him in the eye—face-to-face. Gratefulness overwhelms you as you stand before Him in humble assurance of His love.

Pour out your heart to Him and lift your voice! It's music to His ears. Lavish Him with your praise—He's worthy of your adoration and wholehearted devotion. He deserves your trust. Your faith pleases Him, regardless of how weak or strong it is. You are His radiant bride. Your life is no longer your own, when you live for the honor of the King.

Jesus, I praise you! I celebrate who you are in my life. I rejoice over the grace you've poured out to me. You've filled me with courage and faith that annihilates every lie I've ever believed. You've redeemed me by your miraculous love and set me free. Let my praise and unyielding devotion honor you and thrust me into a lifestyle of expectancy. You love me, and you'll never let me go.

Catch the Foxes

You must catch the troubling foxes,
those sly little foxes that hinder our relationship.
For they raid our budding vineyard of love
to ruin what I've planted within you.

SONG OF SONGS 2:15

Faithfully, God will reveal areas in your life that need attention. Tenderly, He corrects the attitudes, behaviors, and ways of thinking that hinder your relationship. You can't help but want to become a better person when such a merciful father corrects you. It doesn't feel like a hardship to live above the appetites of the flesh when He has won your heart.

Anything that pricks your awareness (places of compromise, contention, or mistrust) must be surrendered to the Lord. Affections can be easily misplaced when you make accommodations for the gray areas. Even the most minor things can wound your love for Him. It's encouraging to know that the Lord not only highlights these little foxes for you to see, but helps you catch and dismiss them.

What a gracious Savior you are! Your plan for my life includes living above the reproach of anything that would hinder our love. The way you tenderly care for our relationship makes me want to do the same. I want to live in a way that exemplifies this love that knows no bounds. So come! Help me catch the little foxes that seek to hinder our love.

A Budding Vineyard

You must catch the troubling foxes,
those sly little foxes that hinder our relationship.
For they raid **our budding vineyard of love**
to ruin what I've planted within you.

—SONG OF SONGS 2:15

The astonishing seeds of His Kingdom have been planted within you. Springing up from the depths of your soul, a beautiful and fruitful garden has come to life. The dry, dusty remains of who you once were and how you believed no longer exist. Your history hasn't been buried beneath it; it's been washed clean by the power of the cross.

You have so much to offer others. As you tap into the anointing and gifts that Jesus has entrusted you with, remember, they are meant to be shared. This fruit that spills from your vineyard can feed the multitudes. Guard it with all your heart. Continually water it with a lifestyle of unrestricted love and devotion. Quickly tend to the weeds of wrong thinking, bad attitudes, and worldly behaviors, which seek to choke the fruit of your garden. Let nothing hinder the love that has filled your being with unprecedented beauty.

Father, every good and perfect gift comes from you. When I look at the person I'm becoming, I scarcely recognize myself. I look like you! My life is filled with faith, hope, joy, and peace. I see the world through your eyes and have hope and power that will encourage everyone I meet.

Together

Will you catch them and remove them for me?
We will do it together.
—Song of Songs 2:15

Jesus is so kind. His mercy truly does lead to repentance. He isn't shocked by the frailty of your flesh. He doesn't push you away and tell you to come back once you've got your act together. In fact, He offers you His hand and draws you close. He's in this with you. Your sin has already been conquered.

At this very moment, you have His undivided attention. Whatever you're facing, He wants to face it with you. You don't have to do it alone. As a matter of fact, love is the only thing that will change you. You are everything He died for, and He longs to have you fully. Cultivate your love for Him. Tend the fires of holy passion. His exquisite love will ruin you forever. Become His happy captive and His prisoner of hope, and together, you will leap over every obstacle.

Jesus, I belong to you. Not to the world, not to the church, and not even to myself. Everything that I have—every victory, every hope, and every joy—comes from you. Without you, I'd be a mess. Together with you, I can live in purity and holiness with no mixture in my heart. You've conquered my sin; now overtake me with your love.

I Am His and He Is Mine

I know my lover is mine and I have everything in you,
for we delight ourselves in each other.

—Song of Songs 2:16

The King of the universe has given everything to prove His love for you. You are His heritage, His chosen one, His bride. Nothing that God has created compares to you. Your life here on earth is meant to be filled with encounters of this remarkable love. You don't have to wait until you go to heaven to experience His glorious presence and undeniable touch.

Jesus wants you to be so convinced of how He feels about you that you never question it again. Consecrate yourself to Him fully—spirit, soul, and body. He longs to infuse every part of you. This lifestyle of sacred love will strip away selfishness. Unrestrained devotion will burn so fiercely within you that it will blaze a trail for you to run on. Hand in hand with your Beloved, you'll become all He created you to be!

Lord, I am yours, and you are mine. I want to live a life of holy devotion that catapults me into divine encounters of your love that few have ever known. I'm not content with simply receiving this love. I want to lavish you with my worship. Let my thoughts be pure, and my actions be filled with power. I want to be fully yours. I want every part of my life to reflect this holy passion that burns within me.

Unselfish Love

I know my lover is mine and I have everything in you,
for *we delight ourselves* in each other.
—SONG OF SONGS 2:16

True love delights in giving. It is unselfish and sacrificial, just like Jesus. Sometimes, in the comfort of love, it's easy to forget that Jesus has called you to freely give from the overflow of your heart. As much as we would like to simply enjoy Him and rest in His arms, it isn't His perfect plan. It's time to discover the delights of mature love.

God wants to remove a worldly mind-set of love that is selfish, comfortable, and easy. Divine love draws you deeper into the place of unconditional, unselfish, sacrificial love. This means you're no longer content with only receiving; you're determined to find ways to honor and bless the Lord in return. Knowing that He's called you to co-labor with Him, you rise, dedicate yourself to Him fully, and declare, "I am yours, Lord!"

Lord, I so enjoy your love and glorious presence, but I know you've called me for more. You've called me to climb the mountains with you and declare your goodness. I repent for any selfishness that has ruled my heart. I want to honor and bless you in all I do and say.

Fearless Love

But until the day springs to life
and *the shifting shadows of fear disappear,*
turn around, my lover, and ascend
to the holy mountains of separation without me.

—Song of Songs 2:17

*A*dventure awaits you, but fear can hold you back. Veiled under the shadows of concern, apprehension, and anxiety, fear highlights every thought that doesn't agree with God. It silently screams from within and seeks to kill every ounce of faith you have. But fear cannot torment the one who is fully convinced of God's love.

Opposition to your destiny has already been defeated. The darkness of fear is repelled by the brilliant glory that shines within you when His love becomes your confidence. You are no longer afraid of what you cannot see or understand because you're convinced He loves to take care of you. If fear has beaten you down and consumed your thoughts, love can heal you. Saturate yourself with His Word. Change the atmosphere around you and the way you think and feel by agreeing with what He says. Speak it, sing it, declare it, and experience His power in your life.

❧

Father, today I declare my freedom from fear. I will be led by the truth of your Word and your powerful love. I expect goodness and mercy to follow me. I believe you're with me and protecting me. You are who you say you are, and anything that contradicts these truths will have no place in my life!

You Are Significant

But until the day springs to life
and the shifting shadows of fear disappear,
***turn around, my lover, and ascend
to the holy mountains of separation without me.***

—Song of Songs 2:17

The treasures of anointing, creativity, and wisdom that abide within you are meant to be shared, not hidden. Your value is a gift of grace. God created you with meticulous precision. He designed you as a person of significance.

Trust the leading and timing of the Lord when He says you're ready to step into something new. Don't look at others and think they're better prepared, more anointed, talented, or brave. You are significant! Your purpose in life encompasses many areas and often takes many different paths. It's multifaceted, touching different people in varying seasons of your life. Don't keep looking to the future, as if you won't be happy until you arrive at some holy destination. Fulfill each day's purpose and live with intention. Be the best parent, or the most approachable person, and do your best to release the Christ inside of you everywhere you go, then you'll experience lasting joy.

God, I'm excited about where I am now and where you're taking me. I believe I'm significant to you and to the people you've placed in my life. Help me to be the best version of me I can be, fully convinced that you've given me everything I need to walk in my purpose.

Dawn

Until the new day fully dawns,
run on ahead like the graceful gazelle
and skip like the young stag
over the mountains of separation.
—Song of Songs 2:17

In the natural, it's easy to tell when the seasons change. But a shift in a spiritual season must be discerned. New assignments, changes in career, things the Lord wants you to focus on—these and more are revealed to you as you spend time in His presence. Once you've been made aware, it's your responsibility to forge ahead with Him.

Seasons of breakthrough are exciting, but sometimes that breakthrough is a direct result of stepping into unchartered territories as the Lord leads. Fear will attempt to hold you back by reminding you of past failures or disappointments. But I have great news for you—a new day has dawned! You're awakening to His voice, you're gaining confidence in His love for you, and you're experiencing His unlimited power. The dawn of a new season means encountering dimensions of His faithfulness that you've never seen. You'll also discover beauty within yourself that you never knew existed.

❧

Father, I sense the light of a new day shining upon me. I know it's time to release every hindrance and step into something new. Unite my heart and mind, so I can move in full cooperation with your Spirit. Lead me, and I will go with you.

Mountain of Spices

Go on ahead to the mountain of spices—
I'll come away another time.

—Song of Songs 2:17

Have you ever noticed that when you're afraid to do what the Lord asks, in the back of your mind you're also aware of how beautiful the journey might be? To follow the Lord into the mountain of spices is to risk the unknown and trust Him. Be brave. Your fears must be conquered. There is no reason to wait. Let faith propel you with excitement into what lies ahead. Fragrant, exhilarating, and beautiful is the place He's called you to.

Believe in yourself. Believe in who He's created you to be. Don't wait until your imperfections cannot be seen. Now is the time to arise and run with Him, running out of the shadows and into His glorious light. The dawn of a new day is upon you. Trim your lamp and fill it with the oil of holy and zealous devotion. Look into His eyes again and remember that in the light of His brilliance, darkness has already been swept away.

Jesus, I want to be known as one who passionately follows you. I want to live with courage and determination, fearlessly prevailing over the obstacles I face. You are my firm foundation. When I'm weak, you are the strength that carries me. In you, I am truly alive, and wherever we go, I will flourish.

Where Are You?

Night after night I'm tossing and turning on my bed of travail.
Why did I let him go from me?
How my heart now aches for him,
but he is nowhere to be found!
—Song of Songs 3:1

It's a painful season when we cannot seem to find the Lord's presence. Whether we have simply lost focus, become distracted, or turned away in disobedience, God will never leave us. He will never cast us away, even when we push Him away. The issue is one of the heart, and this is always the Lord's main focus. He sees what has stolen our affections and, in His great wisdom, patience, and love for us, He knows how to woo us back.

This is the dark night of the soul—the time where it *feels as if* He's left us. And His seeming absence is more than we can bear. God uses this difficult season for our good. It softens our hearts and helps us understand how much we need Him. Though He seems far during these times, His love is always reaching; His tender whispers, gently entreating.

Lord, I need your presence. Forgive me for allowing busyness to distract me from cultivating my relationship with you. I've allowed weeds—the cares of this world—into the garden of my life, but no longer. I want you more than anything else. I turn my heart, and all my attention, to you.

The Yearning Heart

Night after night I'm tossing and turning on my bed of travail.
Why did I let him go from me?
How my heart now aches for him,
but he is nowhere to be found!

—SONG OF SONGS 3:1

Have you ever experienced such a longing in your heart for the Lord that it consumes you? This yearning, this movement of your soul that reaches out to Him, is one of the most beautiful pictures of love. It is one that God Himself cannot ignore.

The yearning heart prevails over every force of darkness that seeks to hinder it. It is powerful—prompting the Lord to respond with grace and glory. The yearning heart is one that burns with unquenchable desire to know Him more. It causes your soul to sing, even during the darkest of times. It stirs hope, releases joy, and incites the most dynamic praise. It is raw, unpretentious, and undeniable. It is true love—the kind that will never be satisfied by anything else.

Jesus, I am overcome by this longing in my soul. Come closer. Let me experience your presence in every fiber of my being. Flood me with your glory and drown out anything that is contrary to love. Speak to me. Dance with me. Show me things no mortal has ever seen.

Searching

So I must rise in search of him,
looking throughout the city,
seeking until I find him.
—SONG OF SONGS 3:2

One of the biggest hindrances to your relationship with the Lord is distraction and busyness. When your thoughts are inundated with mental *to-do* lists, worries, or fears, you'll have a hard time sensing His nearness. When you live fixated on what's happening around you, instead of directing your attention to the One who lives in you, you'll begin to feel dry, irritable, and moody. These are telltale signs that it's time to change your focus.

God loves spending time with you. He is always available to you. It's up to you to rise from the complacency and search for Him. For your life to truly change, He must become the center of it—the first and foremost motivation of your soul. As you cultivate your relationship with Him, you'll become so saturated with His love that turning to Him often will become effortless.

Father, I want your presence to be my daily inspiration. I've allowed other things to steal my affections, but no more. I shake off laziness and ask that you strengthen me. Fill me with grace to seek you above all else.

Unstoppable

*Even if I have to roam through every street,
nothing will keep me from my search.*
Where is he—my soul's true love?
He is nowhere to be found.

—SONG OF SONGS 3:2

There is no desire more powerful than the longing of a soul to know Jesus. When your heart is filled with passion, nothing will stop you from finding the One you love. Religion, with all its requirements, will never satisfy the lovesick bride. Only the urgency of desire will propel you on this most excellent quest.

Once you've tasted the love of God, you understand you were created for it. Others may not understand, but you do. It doesn't matter what you look like, sound like, or act like when you're driven by this holy obsession. The Lord's tangible touch is a glorious and life-changing experience. Everything else fails in comparison. Temptations are no longer alluring, sin holds no power, and compromise isn't a consideration when Jesus becomes your holy pursuit.

Lord, you have wrecked me with the beauty and power of your love. I'm completely undone—obsessed with the glory that courses through my veins. You are my desire. You are what I long for. I am fascinated by the reality of your Kingdom that abides within human flesh. I worship you and seek you with all my heart.

True Love

Even if I have to roam through every street,
nothing will keep me from my search.
Where is he—*my soul's true love?*
He is nowhere to be found.

—Song of Songs 3:2

When you're consumed with the love of God, you'll see it everywhere you look. When you wake in the middle of the night, you'll feel Him near. As the morning sun awakens the sky, you'll sense His holy kiss. Peace will still your soul. Joy will overtake sadness. Every thought will lead to Him.

No one compares to your true and first love. Anointed sermons, church services, and the like speak to your heart, but His presence alone is your daily bread. Jesus has become everything you live for. He is magnificent, amazing, and approachable. He is the light of the world, radiantly shining upon you and drawing you near. This glorious One has loved you since before you were born. His love is a foundation of grace for you to walk on. Listen and you will feel the call of true love.

Jesus, I love you. I want your glorious smile to illuminate my life. I need the substance of your love to penetrate my spirit, soul, and body. The world with its counterfeits has left me malnourished. I want to feast upon your love. Nothing else will satisfy.

The Shepherds

Then I encountered the overseers as they encircled the city.
So I asked them, "Have you found him—
my heart's true love?"

—Song of Songs 3:3

*I*f you've been hurt or felt disillusioned by leaders in the church, God wants to heal those wounds. Often, He will use other leaders to do just that. Being vulnerable and opening your heart takes humility and forgiveness. But these are key ingredients to true greatness in the Kingdom. When God presents you with an opportunity for people to speak into your life, consider it a gift—one that not only heals but also causes you to grow in grace.

Shepherds who lead according to God's heart are anointed with authentic spiritual authority, wisdom, and compassion. They build you up and encourage you to believe in yourself and in the glory that you carry. Most importantly, they must point you to Jesus and not to themselves. If you are surrounded with amazing leaders, praise God! If not, trust God to show you where to find some.

Father, surround me with leaders who know how to love the way you do. Give me shepherds according to your heart. May they speak with wisdom and compassion into the lives of those you place in their care. I forgive any leader who has ever wronged me. Bless them by drawing them into a deeper relationship with you.

Have You Found Him?

Then I encountered the overseers as they encircled the city.
So I asked them, *"Have you found him—
my heart's true love?"*
—Song of Songs 3:3

Whether you carry the title of a pastor or not, each of us are called to a lifestyle of ministry. We must be able to point others to Him, share His love, and release His Kingdom into every situation. In order to do this, we must know Him ourselves. Our relationship with Jesus must be so vibrant that it flows from us with ease.

Your encounters with Jesus will lead others into encounters of their own. All you need is passion for Jesus and the courage and compassion to touch the world around you. Fan the flames of holy fire that burn within you. Zealously pursue His presence as you regularly set aside time to be alone with Him. Lean into His still small voice inside of you every time you step out of your home, and let His love reach others through you.

Father, I believe I'm a vessel of your Spirit and you want me to release your light everywhere I go. Bless me with the humble confidence and courage I need to deliver that transforming power to others. Let healing, deliverance, hope, and love flow into each person I come across.

May

Beyond

Just as I moved past them, I encountered him.
I found the one I adore!
I caught him and fastened myself to him,
refusing to be feeble in my heart again.

—SONG OF SONGS 3:4

One of the most significant keys to a relationship with Jesus that is tangible, fulfilling, and undeniable is spiritual hunger. Many things can choke the life out of your walk with Him. Aiming to please others more than God, believing that religious action always reflects the heart, and seeking to draw solely from others what you should be drawing from the Lord are just a few examples.

Learning *about* Him should stir desire within you to know Him for yourself. Church attendance should add to your already satisfied soul. First and foremost, you must move beyond the outward grasping for what others can feed you and feast upon His revelation for yourself. The way you cultivate the connection between you and the Lord is more important than anything else. No one can take the place of Jesus in your life.

Lord, forgive me if there is any spiritual apathy in my life. You focus on the depth of our connection and not on how well I convince others of my knowledge or anointing. I want a relationship with you that is real. I want to hear you, feel you, and experience your love. I want to be led by your Spirit and to know what moves your heart. I want to know you.

Encounter

Just as I moved past them, ***I encountered him.***
I found the one I adore!
I caught him and fastened myself to him,
refusing to be feeble in my heart again.

—SONG OF SONGS 3:4

*G*od wants to encounter you with His presence. He longs to saturate your being with the glory that first breathed life into your mortal body. He desires to fill you with the reality of His love. You were created for face-to-face encounters with the Lord. You can have a relationship with Him that is tangible and miraculous.

No one moves His heart the way you do. He loves you more than you can possibly comprehend. What an honor to stand in His presence and experience this inexplicable love. Such a privilege to call Him Father. If you long to encounter Him in deeper, more meaningful ways, there is no special method—no right or wrong way of coming before Him. Simply believe that He loves you. Let words of desire and worship pour from your heart, and soon, you'll be overwhelmed by the reality of His love.

Lord, with desire that drowns out all other desires, I reach for you. Come meet with me. Let me feel the warmth of your embrace. Let me see your glorious face and become acquainted with the ways of holiness. I honor you with my sincere devotion. I long for you with every fiber of my being.

Find Him

Just as I moved past them, I encountered him.
I found the one I adore!
I caught him and fastened myself to him,
refusing to be feeble in my heart again.
—SONG OF SONGS 3:4

God doesn't withhold His presence from you in order to punish you. We go through dry seasons for many reasons, but all of them have the potential for an outrageously good out-come and a renewed desire for the Lord. There really is nothing like sensing His nearness after a period of stale, lifeless prayer.

If you're going through a time of discouragement, desperately in need of His touch, I have good news for you—He is with you right now. It's time for you to find the one that you adore, again. Find time for stillness. Focus on the love that is in you and all around you. Call for Him and trust Him to manifest His love again. God's ability to speak to you is greater than your inability to hear Him. Do this day after day until you become so focused on Him that everything else fades away.

Lord, you are the overwhelming desire of my heart. Help me to move past the distractions swirling through my mind and to tap into your presence. I want every thought I think, every emotion I feel, and every agreement of my soul to be saturated with your truth. I'm running into your arms with fresh desire to know you more.

Fastened

Just as I moved past them, I encountered him.
I found the one I adore!
I caught him and **fastened myself to him,**
refusing to be feeble in my heart again.

—SONG OF SONGS 3:4

There's nothing like that moment when you sense the presence of the Lord flooding the atmosphere. It is undeniably real. It touches your heart unlike anything else. Incomprehensible joy crashes unexpectedly into places that once were heavy with fear. Hope refreshes even the most discouraged soul.

Whether it's been seconds, weeks, or even years since you've felt His closeness, when He comes, you cannot deny it. However, you can choose whether or not to nurture it. The Lord isn't looking to visit you occasionally. He seeks to bless you, speak to you, and enjoy you every moment of every day. He wants continual communication to become a lifestyle—where you tap into His heart in every situation. Let this holy resolve consume your life—to hold Him close and never let Him go!

Lord, break through my darkest seasons with your glorious love. Though these dry times seem unbearable, I'm grateful for them. They've taught me to appreciate your mercy and grace in ways I never have before. I've learned how desperately I need you. Meet with me, and I'll never let you go.

Mercy

Just as I moved past them, I encountered him.
I found the one I adore!
I caught him and fastened myself to him,
refusing to be feeble in my heart again.

—Song of Songs 3:4

*A*ll of us are in need of God's great mercy. Though we wish it weren't true, everyone has moments of weakness. A bad attitude, a time of fear or unbelief, disobeying the Lord's leading—we all go through times when we've yielded to our flesh. No one is exempt.

We serve a tender, compassionate God whose love is inexhaustible. Knowing our human frailty, He never condemns us. Instead of punishing us, He entreats us with mercy and holds us close. Here, in the hands of mercy, we discover our endless need for Him. On our own, we will never be good enough or holy enough to merit a love like this. Without Him, eternity would hold no value. Thank God that nothing can separate us from His unconditional love.

God, I humble myself before you and declare my great need for you. I want to live in the bliss of unyielding devotion and obedience, but without your grace, I can't. Even the love that I love you with is a gift from you. Thank you for being patient with me. Thank you for your mercy.

The Temple Within

Now I'll bring him back to **the temple within**
where I was given new birth—
into my innermost parts, the place of my conceiving.
—SONG OF SONGS 3:4

As you resolve within yourself to open your heart to Him fully, something incredible happens. You rediscover the joys of first love. You can feel it. Right there, in the holy place where He dwells, you're coming alive again. Your focus has returned to its proper place, and there's no joy that can compare.

Oh, the breathtaking moment when you realize you don't have to search for Him in some distant place because He's made His home in you! You're a temple of the Holy Spirit. You're already as close to the Lord as you could ever hope to be—this is the mystery of the One you love. Set your affections upon your glorious Savior. You are His betrothed, and He will never betray His vows to you. Though the path that leads from complacency to zealous devotion isn't always easy, it is always worth it.

Lord, you are glorious and majestic, mysterious and powerful—yet you've made your home in me. Thank you for looking straight into my soul, seeing every movement of my heart, and still choosing me. I consecrate myself to you as a vessel of honor. I devote myself to a lifetime of holy pursuit—that I may fall deeper in love with you.

Hold Me

The Bridegroom-King
Promise me, O Jerusalem maidens,
by the gentle gazelles and delicate deer,
that *you'll not disturb my love until she is ready to arise.*

—SONG OF SONGS 3:5

The journey to maturity begins in the safety of His arms. This is the place where you're infused with holy passion that will wreck your life. Nothing remains the same when He wraps Himself around you. Total and complete immersion in His love is all-consuming—at times it feels as though moving is an impossible task. This is the reality of His presence. This is the place where heaven and earth collide.

He understands that sometimes you need to stay in His secure embrace, and He will never push you away. You were created for this intimacy, and Jesus will allow you to remain in this place of rest, but you are also destined to rule and reign with Him. In His great wisdom, He knows that becoming strong in His love must come first. Allow your heart to come alive, overflowing with His love and compassion, then get ready for the adventure of your life, because this journey will take you from glory to glory.

Jesus, hold me. Breathe your refreshing wind into my every part of me until I can stand again. I want to join you on this quest of releasing your love, healing, and restoration to the world. Thank you for being so patient with me and loving me so well. The wonder of your touch has brought me to life.

Believe Again!

The Voice of the Lord
Who is this one ascending from the wilderness
in the pillar of the glory cloud?
—Song of Songs 3:6

Jesus is not only your intimate Friend but the Almighty King arrayed in splendor. He's the victorious Lord who overcame every form of evil and has called you to share in His conquest. He rose in glory and brought you with Him. His triumph echoes through the ages with lessons of God's magnificent power, love, and faithfulness. Look to Him. Look to this One who could not be defeated, even by the clutches of death.

We are called *believers*, not doubters, for a reason—we believe. Disappointments happen. It's part of life. But how you respond to your trials is what sets you apart from those who live in defeat. You've been called to a glorious life! You can have an amazing future, regardless of how life has been. Never fear the past or current hardships. Happiness starts with choosing to agree with faith and letting go of the past. Change your perspective and believe again!

Jesus, I choose to believe. I lay aside every mind-set that doesn't agree with your goodness. Ignite me with hope and faith. Strengthen me by your Spirit and refresh me. Nothing is too hard for you! Absolutely nothing. I trust you. I believe.

Anointed with Splendor

He is fragrant with the anointing oils
of myrrh and frankincense—
more fragrant than all the spices of the merchant.

—Song of Songs 3:6

The Lord carries an unmistakable fragrance, and you are anointed with the same fragrance. It is the scent not only of suffering but of splendor. As you live and abide in Him, you begin to smell like Him. You diffuse His presence and change the spiritual atmosphere around you. Your outlook on life, your thoughts, and your attitudes are infused with the essence of holy persuasion.

You are the pearl of great price that Jesus has redeemed. He gave everything to have you by His side. You are stunning and highly valued—anointed with the oil of costly love. Embrace this truth and live in a way that both reflects your worth and reminds others of theirs. Let encouragement drip from your lips like honey. Mend broken hearts with healing and compassion. As His vessel, you have the honor of releasing His beauty to the world around you.

Lord, I want to look and smell like you. Saturate me with your fragrance, and let it seep into every part of my being. Let me be so drenched with the essence and purity of who you are that it splashes upon everyone I meet. When I walk into a room, may the substance of your glory flood the atmosphere.

Most Fragrant

He is fragrant with the anointing oils
of myrrh and frankincense—
more fragrant than all the spices of the merchant.
—SONG OF SONGS 3:6

Inhale deeply. Allow the fragrance of His suffering love to flood your senses. Find your worth in who He has declared you to be—His bride—the one He gave His life for. His sacred blood was shed for you. His love is all-inclusive. It never ends. All that you are, or ever hope to be, is found in the center of His love.

He is the most fragrant of all. His presence melts away every care. His love is invigorating. It blazes through every hindrance and sets your soul on fire. Earthly pleasures will never satisfy the yearning in your soul. Nothing will fill the void that His glory is meant to occupy. Saturate yourself in the pleasant aroma of spices that surround Him, and you will come alive.

Lord, as I sit in your presence, I'm aware of the fragrance of your sweet love. The fountain of glory that flows from your throne has flooded my soul. I'm grateful for the power that has set me free, confident in the strength of the arms that hold me. I open my life to you and know that nothing will separate me from your love.

The Chariot of Love

Look! It is the king's marriage carriage.
The love seat surrounded by sixty champions,
the mightiest of Israel's host,
are like pillars of protection.
—Song of Songs 3:7

Jesus wants to lavish you with radiance and elegance. No one will ever treat you as well as He does. He is gracious and full of mercy. His ways are higher and beyond comparison. His love is strong enough to conquer the grave. As you commit yourself to Him without reservation, He will surprise you with glory encounters you never knew were possible.

You are His bride—the one who has decided to follow Him anywhere, even to the mountains that once made you afraid. You are maturing—ready to go forth in full assurance of His love and faithfulness. In response, He sets before you a magnificent carriage that will transport the two of you to places you've never been. When He invited you to the mountains, this was the secret He didn't divulge. He will carry you there on the seat of mercy—the King's glorious marriage carriage.

Jesus, whisk me away to the place where my cares fade away. Consume my every thought. When I'm overwhelmed, hold me tightly to your side. I repent for being afraid of what awaits me. The mountains loom in the distance, but together we will not only conquer them, we will ascend even higher—to the heights of heaven.

Safe

Look! It is the king's marriage carriage.
The love seat surrounded by sixty champions,
the mightiest of Israel's host,
are like pillars of protection.
—Song of Songs 3:7

There is no safer place than to be with Jesus in His majestic carriage. This is the place of intimacy, where you become confident in your position as His bride and in His faithfulness as your Protector. The finished work of the cross, where Jesus triumphed over all His foes, has become your safeguard. Your life is hidden in Him, concealed from the enemy.

You are extravagantly protected—surrounded by the power of love. Lean back, relinquish the right to be afraid, and trust the Lord as He carries you through life in His covenant of grace. Over every mountain of difficulty, His presence is a place of rest and refreshing. Let His love cast out every fear and fill you with confidence, so you can live your life to the fullest.

Jesus, I believe you're with me upon every mountain path. Though the road ahead seems bumpy, I will lean back in your strong embrace and trust you. It doesn't matter how difficult the journey or how dangerous it is because you will never fail to protect me. I will stay close to you, and you will be the momentum that leads me forward.

Angelic Warriors

They are angelic warriors standing ready with swords
to defend the king and his fiancée
from every terror of the night.

—SONG OF SONGS 3:8

*G*od has assigned his most noble angels to watch over you. Trained for war and seasoned in His glory, they are ready to defend you and minister to you. How comforting it is to know that wherever you go, you have a team of holy bodyguards. They lift you upon their shoulders, like the palanquins of old, and are ready to fight on your behalf.

As you recline with the King behind the veil of His royal chariot, you are hidden from the clutches of the enemy. Stay close to Jesus as He imparts His promises to you. Declare them over your life and the lives of those you love. Angels act on His holy words, including those that come out of your mouth in agreement. This is not the time to retreat. Go forward with confidence. Trust in the safety of His presence and the multitudes of angels protecting you.

❧

Father, thank you for your angels. Thank you for the many ways you protect and defend my life. When fear tries to rear its ugly head, I will remember your perfect love and receive your peace. I will trust you and believe that your angels are fighting on my behalf. There is no place safer than being with you.

Even While You Sleep

They are angelic warriors standing ready with swords
to defend the king and his fiancée
from every terror of the night.
—Song of Songs 3:8

Great confidence comes when we believe all that God declares to be true. Sweet and protected sleep is one of God's promises to you. Your sleep is meant to be peaceful and refreshing, filled with sweet dreams and holy encounters. Angels have been assigned to you, to guard you day and night. Your bedroom is the very doorway to God's presence.

Fill your thoughts with the faithfulness and love of God as you rest your head upon your pillow each night. Before you fall asleep, take a few moments to thank Him for His blessings and faithfulness. Even if you've had a rough day, there are always things to be thankful for. Picture your angels standing guard as you carelessly drift off to sleep. Let Him give you a good-night kiss as He whispers words of hope into your soul.

Father, there's a song in my heart as I drift off to sleep tonight. My mind is filled with thoughts of you, and my spirit meditates upon your love. I will lie down tonight in total peace and sleep soundly—secure in your arms. I expect to dream beautiful dreams, to have sweet and refreshing sleep, and to wake with wisdom for tomorrow. Thank you for hiding me beneath your secret shadow where I'm hidden in your strength.

Mercy Seat

The king made this mercy seat for himself
out of the finest wood that will not decay.

—Song of Songs 3:9

The seat of mercy, which gives you access to our King, wasn't only designed as a gift to you; it was designed for Jesus. It was a way for Him to bring you close to God again. Where sin once separated you, His mercy has brought you near.

The Father's heart ached with longing for *you*. The omnipotent Creator of the universe filled the world with glory yet desired your heart. Nothing besides you could satisfy the yearning of your heavenly Father, who granted you access into the holiest place of all—His presence. He has seated you beside your beloved King Jesus. Let the revelation of this unmerited, unpredictable love penetrate your heart, and overturn every doubt. You're exactly what He wanted and gave His life for. You are amazing!

Father, thank you for carrying me upon the seat of mercy over the barrier of sin. Thank you for loving me in ways I didn't know I could be loved. It seems unfathomable that I am worth the price of perfect love, but I willingly accept your holy gift. You've asked for my heart, and I give it to you—unreservedly.

The Beauty of the Mercy Seat

The king made this mercy seat for himself
out of the finest wood that will not decay.

—Song of Songs 3:9

The Creator of the universe spoke into existence the very tree that would become the cross of Christ. The same wood that once held our suffering Savior also formed the mercy seat. It was sprinkled with blood and overshadowed by angels. We are now seated upon this seat of mercy, carried along in the safety of the cross, and granted forgiveness by His loving-kindness and outrageous compassion.

In Scripture, wood also symbolizes humanity. *You* have become the seat of His mercy—the resting place for His mercy and glory. The mercy seat was made of wood and gold, inside and out. This illustrates how God infused Himself into humanity, and the two became one. You are in Him, and He is in you. You are a chosen vessel of His glory. Your true beauty will never fade away with age. It is eternally filled with the glory of love.

There is nothing as outrageously beautiful as your mercy. Your sacrifice of love has saved me, healed me, and given me a foundation to dance on. Mercy has set me free and filled me with hope. The glory of the cross has extinguished every sin and infused me with your likeness. You are the radiant splendor that fills my life.

The Glory of Love

Pillars of smoke, like silver mist—
a canopy of golden glory dwells above it.
The place where they sit together
is sprinkled with crimson.

—Song of Songs 3:10

Pillars of justice, power, love, and faithfulness provide the covering for your life. The very air you breathe is filled with the substance of redemption. It saturates every fiber of your being and invigorates your soul. Not even the freshest mountain breeze can compare.

When you spend time in the presence of Jesus, you will sense His glory as it fills the room. Stand in the midst of the glory cloud and you will feel it whirling around you, inviting you into its dance of bliss. The mystery of His nearness cannot be understood with your mind. Profound and miraculous, it must be experienced. His love is timeless; it carries the scent of hope and makes you feel at home. You will feel its substance as you reach by faith into a world not fully seen, but undeniably real.

Father, I'm undone by your whispers in the air around me. I hear you calling to me, reaching for me with incomprehensible love. I feel you, and though I cannot see you clearly, I know you're here. I can scarcely stand in your glorious presence. Consume every part of me that has yet to be infused with the glory of your love.

Crimson

Pillars of smoke, like silver mist—
a canopy of golden glory dwells above it.
The place where they sit together
is sprinkled with crimson.
SONG OF SONGS 3:10

*Y*ou don't often hear people say that blood is beautiful. Yet these are the words that overflow from thankful lips when we discover the power of the blood of Jesus. Songs have been written, poems have been scribed, and paintings have been created to portray the glory of something that would normally seem offensive or gruesome. To the Christian, it is a symbol of sacrificial love and redemption.

Crimson is a deep purplish-red color, signifying the royalty of Jesus and the blood that paid for our salvation. It gives us boldness to enter His presence. Our King's holy blood stands as a covenant of unmerited love and unity. His life now flows through our veins. It is more powerful than the hosts of hell and gives us the strength to overcome.

Jesus, thank you for the blood that you shed to set me free from the bondage of sin and death. The riches of your mercy and grace are beyond comprehension. Your covenant of love is unbreakable. You will never change your mind about me. From the cross to the throne, you are love personified. I bow before you, grateful for all you've done.

Priceless

Love and mercy cover this carriage,
blanketing his tabernacle throne.
The king himself has made it
for those who will become his bride.

—SONG OF SONGS 3:10

The priceless love and mercy of Jesus covers you everywhere you go. You are royalty. You are the beautiful bride of Christ. You move His heart—not just humanity as a whole, but *you* specifically. Though you weren't yet born on this earth when Jesus died on the cross, I believe your face flashed before His eyes. He knew exactly who He would give His life for.

Love brought Jesus to earth. Love led Him to the garden of suffering. Love nailed Him to the cross. And it's love that brings Him to our hearts. You need not live one day without enjoying His manifest love. This is a relationship that should never get boring. The mystery and wonder of perfect love will stir your heart and enrapture your soul. Spend some time basking in this love today.

Kiss me with your holy love and cover me with your endless mercy. I've fallen in love with love Himself—left awestruck by the wonder of it all. You've lifted the cloak of heaviness and clothed me with hope, life, and joy. I'm soaring upon the breath of my Beloved.

A Beautiful Life

Love and mercy cover this carriage,
blanketing his tabernacle throne.
The king himself has made it
for those who will become his bride.
—Song of Songs 3:10

*H*ow astounding it is that the King of Glory has taken it upon Himself to make sure we are well taken care of. Not only has He blessed us with salvation, but also everything we need to live a victorious, godly, and successful life.

God is not a harsh ruler sitting on a heavenly throne, dictating our service to Him. Instead, *He* serves *us*. He took it upon Himself to carve out an infallible way to eternal bliss that starts now.

To access an amazing life, you must allow His promises to sink down inside of you until they become a part of the way you think. His Word is powerful enough to change even the most doubt-filled and discouraged mind. As you meditate on His promises, let words of faith spill forth from an expectant heart. There is no magic pill for a happy life, but start by believing that with God anything is possible, and He wants the best for *you*!

Father, thank you for the way you love me. I choose to believe you have the best in store for me. I repent of fear, discouragement, and negativity and release them to you. From now on, I will live with hope, faith, and expectancy, as an encouragement to others.

Brides-to-Be

Rise up, Zion maidens, brides-to-be!

—Song of Songs 3:11

You are the beautiful bride of Christ, filled with grace and compassion. As you become secure in your relationship with Him, you'll begin to see others through His eyes. You'll sense His love for them, you'll believe He designed them for a glorious purpose, and this heavenly perspective will change the way you treat people.

We serve a God whose mercy is unlimited. When He looks at someone whose life isn't following a healthy, safe, or holy path, He doesn't turn away. Instead, He encourages, loves, and builds up. We should follow His example. People who are miserable don't need judgment; they need a God who loves them enough to set them free.

Point the brides-to-be in the right direction. True lovers of God make the best ministers. Don't wait for a title; you already carry His name.

Father, I want to see others through your eyes—as your brides-to-be. I want to feel your love for them even when I see their mess. Give me words to say and actions that display your heart. Your mercy and love have set me free; now help me to love others as graciously as you love me. Unlock their hearts, as you have unlocked mine.

Feast Your Eyes

Come and feast your eyes on this king
as he passes in procession on his way to his wedding.
—Song of Songs 3:11

So many things vie for our attention. From the moment we wake, responsibilities, hopes, dreams, and concerns bombard our minds. Distractions can consume us, especially in this day of social media. At times, our lives are dictated by what happens around us.

Yet Jesus must be the foundation of all we believe. All that we do, say, and think must flow from the core of who we are in Him. Though our thoughts may wander and we don't consciously think about Him every second, we can live with the awareness of Him, continually. He becomes the very essence of each thought, both consciously and subconsciously. Every action and word becomes seasoned with Jesus, when He's the substance of our lives.

Take time each day to feast on His love and His promises. Fill yourself with Him continually, and you'll be amazed at how your thought life transforms!

Lord, nothing matters more to me in this life than you. Help me to live in a way that reflects this. I want you to be the thought I always turn to, the peace that chases away stress. Throughout the day, nudge me and draw me close to you. You have built a home inside of me—a constant reminder of your ever-present love.

Joy

This is the day filled with overwhelming joy—
the day of his great gladness.

—Song of Songs 3:11

Never underestimate the joy you bring to Jesus. The countless times you've made mistakes and the faith that sometimes feels too small to move a leaf, let alone a mountain, are no surprise to Him. When He hung on the cross, you were the joy that was set before Him. You're His inheritance—the perfect gift God will give His Son. Oh, how He longs to receive you as His bride on your wedding day!

If Jesus is filled with joy over us, how much more should we be filled with joy because of Him! One moment in His glorious presence strips away depression and sadness, and floods you with gladness. Unrestrained joy has a voice—it's the sound of laughter. When your heart is saturated with faith, you can't help but laugh at the enemy. When you believe God has the answer, opposition and bad news can't overwhelm your soul.

Today, take a moment to rejoice, dance, and laugh at your problems. Refuse heaviness and let His joy be your strength.

Jesus, your joy blazes into the depths of my bones. Even when the enemy rises against me, I will not let him steal my joy. No matter what happens, my trust in you becomes a substance of joy that defies logic. You make my heart happy.

Remind Me

The Bridegroom-King
*Listen, my dearest darling,
you are so beautiful—you are beauty itself to me!*
—Song of Songs 4:1

Jesus is more tuned into our needs than a spouse, parent, or even ourselves. No matter how many times He affirms us as His darling and tells us how beautiful we are to Him, He never tires of reminding us. He knows we need it.

How you see yourself is reflected in the way you speak and in what you do or don't do. When you sense His loving reassurance, don't shrug it off. Jesus is speaking to your identity as you allow His words to penetrate your heart. You are brave, worthy, loved, smart, and strong. You are these things and more because the One, who created you in His image, says that you are. No one can make you believe otherwise. No one can take that away from you, unless you let them.

Jesus, I love the way you speak to my identity and remind me who I am. I am yours, and I was made in your image. I am powerful and anointed. I am beautiful and strong. I am not afraid to try new things, and I'm not ashamed of who I am or how I look. I will carry myself in humble confidence, lean upon you, and live unafraid.

Eyes of Devotion

Your eyes glisten with love,
like gentle doves behind your veil.
What devotion I see each time I gaze upon you.
You are like a sacrifice ready to be offered.

—SONG OF SONGS 4:1

When Jesus gazes into your eyes, what does He see? Despite how you feel or what you're going through, He sees your tender heart of devotion. He sees the yes in your heart that started you on this holy journey and gave Him permission to lead you and fill you.

Jesus isn't looking for a perfect track record of religious duty. Your love mesmerizes Him, regardless of the trivial things that momentarily steal your attention. Every moment you spend with Him matures you—from glory to glory you continually grow. With eyes of wisdom and grace, you're beginning to understand how faithful He is. Your heart is open and glistening with love for Him. Let His love sweep you off your feet.

Jesus, I stand before you unashamed. Though my thoughts are not always pleasing to you and my actions are far from perfect, I know you see my heart. Have your way in me. I say yes to you all over again.

Behind the Veil

Your eyes glisten with love,
like gentle doves behind your veil.
What devotion I see each time I gaze upon you.
You are like a sacrifice ready to be offered.

—SONG OF SONGS 4:1

The Lord loves to be near those who have a humble and contrite heart. There is no pressure to impress Him. Religious actions or words that sound holy but carry no power mean nothing to Him. Mercy takes us where our revelation and works cannot.

It is in our moments of humility, where we conceal what we know, that we are like the Shulamite behind the veil. True spiritual maturity understands its worth but doesn't flaunt its revelation or experiences with the Lord. Too often we live for the approval of others and don't safeguard our most precious revelations and encounters. A humble heart is beautiful in His sight. Everyone has a need for acceptance and approval, but until you are fully assured of your worth in Him, the applause of mortals will always seem insufficient.

Father, I repent of any pride or desire to please people more than you. I want to live with a gentle and meek spirit. Thank you for teaching me who I am in you and feeding my spirit, so I'm not starving for applause. I pray that every motive of my heart would honor you and reflect my love for you. You satisfy me.

Living Sacrifice

Your eyes glisten with love,
like gentle doves behind your veil.
What devotion I see each time I gaze upon you.
You are like a sacrifice ready to be offered.

—Song of Songs 4:1

*Y*our devotion moves God's heart. The strength of your love is uniquely yours. He doesn't compare you to anyone else. It isn't your weaknesses that He pays the most attention to; it's the commitment of your life. This yes that streams from the depths of your soul and the many times you've followed Him, even when it was hard, are symbols of living sacrificially.

This lifestyle of devotion extends beyond ourselves and reaches to help others, at times with great personal cost. Sometimes it can feel like a thankless job. There is so much we do in private, so many times we've sacrificed for family and even strangers, and it appears no one sees. But God does. He sees it all—every time you've poured out your life for Him in service to others. Nothing goes unnoticed. When you honor Him in secret, it's true devotion, and it's beautiful in the sight of God.

Father, you've done so much for me. It's my delight to live in a way that honors you. I want my lifestyle to reflect the gratefulness I feel and the love that streams from my heart. May my sacrificial yes and all that I do in secret be pleasing in your sight.

Open

When I look at you,
I see how you have taken my fruit and tasted my word.
Your life has become clean and pure,
like a lamb washed and newly shorn.
You now show grace and balance with truth on display.

—Song of Songs 4:2

Right now, the Lord is looking at you. He's drawing near, not as a reprimanding father, but as One who knows you, loves you, and believes in you. You can be as real with Him as you need to be. No wall can keep Him out, and He sees past every disguise. He loves you through every season of the soul.

All of us are dependent upon His grace and in need of His mercy. When He looks at us, He knows everything there is to know. As you stand before Him, allow His penetrating gaze to not only examine you but to strengthen and refresh you. When you're hurting, He's the Healer; when you're sad, He's the Comforter; and when you're discouraged, He's the Hope you need. One look, one momentary glance from Him is enough to turn everything around.

Lord, I open my life to you. When you examine me, I pray that you will find a heart filled with sincere devotion, integrity, and love. If there is darkness hiding within the crevices of my soul, reveal it, and give me the grace to overcome. I want all that I think, say, and do to reflect your radiant beauty.

The Word

When I look at you,
I see how you have taken my fruit and **tasted my word.**
Your life has become clean and pure,
like a lamb washed and newly shorn.
You now show grace and balance with truth on display.

—Song of Songs 4:2

There is nothing quite like the Word of God. It brings healing and wisdom, imparts faith and hope, and teaches us the will of our Father in heaven. The power of His Word sets us free and teaches us what it means to be Christlike. The Word of God reveals His character and His love.

His truth is infinitely greater than the facts we face. It is the anchor that holds us steady in the midst of a storm. It guides our decisions, feeds our spirits, and is the power that overcomes evil. As we study it and meditate upon its wisdom, it comes alive within us. When we process His truth and ponder the Scriptures that move our heart, our spirits grow stronger, and our souls surrender fear. His Words on our lips color us with beauty that cannot be defined.

Father, I love to discover the treasures in your Word. Pour out fresh revelation upon my heart and unlock the secrets I've yet to know. As I declare your Word, may it become a path for me to walk upon and a sword that slices through every opposition. Your Words are spirit and life, and I feast upon them for they are the joy and delight of my heart.

Pure

When I look at you,
I see how you have taken my fruit and tasted my word.
Your life has become clean and pure,
like a lamb washed and newly shorn.
You now show grace and balance with truth on display.
—Song of Songs 4:2

*Y*ou are clean and pure. As a blood-washed child of God, you have been made as righteous as Jesus. Never again do you need to believe that you are anything less than God's holy child. The enemy cannot throw lies at you and confuse your identity when you know who you are in Christ.

The sheared sheep in this passage illustrates the need to remove the excess wool of fleshly zeal. We must leave behind the energy of the flesh so we can move into the Holy Place with God. We enter His presence by grace alone. The flesh doesn't need to work harder to please God; rather, it needs to be shorn.

When you come into His presence, you must leave striving behind. Come with the essence of love, humility, and gratefulness streaming from your heart. Jesus paid a beautiful price to call you His own and make you pure. He's all you need.

Jesus, thank you for the unfathomable price of love that has set me free. Nothing but the blood could ever qualify me to come into your Holy presence. You are my beautiful King whose passion has awakened me to life. Your extravagant love has cleansed me and made me pure.

Grace

When I look at you,
I see how you have taken my fruit and tasted my word.
Your life has become clean and pure,
like a lamb washed and newly shorn.
You now show grace and balance with truth on display.
—Song of Songs 4:2

Maturity and grace go hand in hand. When you embrace your identity in God, you can stand confidently, but only because you know that He alone has made you whole. An air of grace and poise surrounds you. You have no need to impress anyone when you are secure in Him.

When you fully rely on Him and understand how much He loves you, it feels as if your heart has been uncaged. You carry yourself differently, speak differently, and treat people with more respect because your great need for Jesus has been met. Truth is spoken in kindness—always honoring and encouraging—because you've learned to love without judgment. When you're secure in His love, you walk with compassion and mercy as your guide, knowing how much you have needed it. You become truly beautiful—inside and out.

Lord, my heart is soaring because of your mercy and grace. All that I am, I see in you. Though sometimes it doesn't feel that it could possibly be true, you say it is. Be my equilibrium and steady me as I live to honor you.

June

Speak

Your lips are as lovely as Rahab's scarlet ribbon,
speaking mercy, speaking grace,
the words of your mouth are as refreshing as an oasis.
What pleasure you bring to me!
—Song of Songs 4:3

*Y*our lips have been anointed with redeeming grace. Lifting others with words of hope and imparting value sets you apart and causes you to shine. Others will be drawn to Jesus by the grace-filled words that you speak.

Guard your lips. Remember that what flows from them reveals what is in your heart. Use your words wisely and generously. Learn to listen with God's heart of compassion, remembering that we all need someone who believes in us and can see us from God's point of view. You have been called to love and forgive—not judge or criticize. You were created to speak words of life, hope, and wisdom, words that heal, encourage, and bring unity. Love always wins over judgment. Love and mercy are what set you apart.

Father, set a guard over my lips, so I only convey encouragement to others and honor to you. May I be known as a person of hope, joy, wisdom, and faith. Touch my heart with compassion that knows no bounds, so the words I speak bring life and freedom. Teach me to listen to you and communicate with a voice of wisdom and hope.

Words of Worship

Your lips are as lovely as Rahab's scarlet ribbon,
speaking mercy, speaking grace,
the words of your mouth are as refreshing as an oasis.
What pleasure you bring to me!
—Song of Songs 4:3

Not only are your words refreshing to others; they bring pleasure to the Lord. Each time you speak life and truth in the face of hopelessness and opposition, you delight His heart. When you declare His praise, although you'd rather give up, His strength becomes yours. Words of faith illuminate the darkness when they agree with His Word.

Your worship is like kisses upon His heart. He cherishes every word of love that pours from your lips. Your devotion is beautiful because it isn't forced or phony. What you say reflects the intimacy that burns within you and draws His attention. Your words not only reveal your heart, but they provide a framework for your life. They carry power, attracting either light or darkness, so choose your words wisely. Fill your heart with His love, and it will stream from your lips.

Father, I want every thought and intent of my heart to be pure and pleasing in your sight. I want my words and heart to flow in unison with your Holy Spirit and your Word. Surround me with your presence and unite me to your heart, so our words will be one.

Embracing Vulnerability

I see your blushing cheeks
opened like the halves of a pomegranate,
showing through your veil of tender meekness.

—SONG OF SONGS 4:3

Cheeks speak of emotions. Raw, messy, beautiful, and unguarded, they erase every blurry line of demarcation and reveal the real you. Allowing yourself to be vulnerable and completely genuine means risking rejection. You may not want to be totally open with everyone, but God will bless you with people who make you feel safe.

Embracing vulnerability is one of the most liberating and healing things you can do for yourself. Though it may be hard at first, it will get easier with time. Start by accepting yourself and believing that the One who created your emotions isn't offended by them. To Him, your emotions are beautiful, even in instances where they reveal wrong mind-sets or wounds. He knows how to get to the root and bring healing. God created you to be your authentic self, comfortable in your own skin and unafraid of being you.

Father, thank you for creating me. I am unique and wonderful, even with my quirks and imperfections. Today I strip off the mask that shields my emotions, and I invite you into every area of my soul that needs your healing. I will embrace vulnerability and discover the joys of being me.

Strength

When I look at you,
I see your inner strength so stately and strong.
You are as secure as David's fortress.
Your virtues and grace cause a thousand famous soldiers
to surrender to your beauty.

—Song of Songs 4:4

Your humility and submission to God make you strong. Knowing who you are in Him gives you security. The power of love, the fruit of your relationship with Him, makes you resolute and secure in all that He is. Just as He is, so you are in this world—brave, powerful, wise, merciful, and creative.

It isn't prideful to know your identity when it's established in Him. God wants you to be confident in His unconditional love, knowing it's by grace alone that you stand. He carried the weight of the world so you don't have to. A fully surrendered will contradicts the wisdom of the world, yet it's the epitome of godly wisdom and strength. Doing the right thing no matter the cost is beautiful in His sight. It signifies a life that is poured out to Him and stronger than every opposition.

Father, your strength is my confidence. No matter what I'm going through, I can reach out my hand and know that you're here. You're eternal and powerful. You're the substance of my life and the reason I will never quit. You alone are my strength.

Secure

I see your inner strength so stately and strong.
You are as secure as David's fortress.
Your virtues and grace cause a thousand famous soldiers
to surrender to your beauty.

—Song of Songs 4:4

*G*od is for you—always. His love knows no bounds. He is good and kind. Though you may face temporary setbacks or disappointments, He will turn things around and work in unexpected ways that prove His faithfulness and strengthens your faith.

After time, you learn that trusting and praising Him in the midst of pain is your greatest weapon against fear. No matter what happens, you know He will never fail you. This type of boldness reveals not only a strong person but also a humble one, submitted to the will of God. You become resolute, determined to do the right thing with no double-mindedness. Like David, you have a heart after God.

David's tower was a place where the weapons of warfare were stored. Your decision to follow the King—your inward life and confidence in Him—is like a storehouse of mighty weapons that you wield against the enemy.

Father, I release all my cares to you today. I allow my spirit, soul, and body to rest confidently in your love. I say no to fear and plant my feet firmly upon your Word. I choose to trust you despite every swirling thought. In you, I am safe.

Grace

I see your inner strength so stately and strong.
You are as secure as David's fortress.
***Your virtues and grace cause a thousand famous soldiers
to surrender to your beauty.***

—Song of Songs 4:4

You are beautiful, filled with His grace. Whether you have a strong or timid personality, when it's seasoned with grace, there's little anyone can say to discredit you. You see situations and people with God's perspective, and words of affirmation, honor, and hope stream from your lips. You look and sound just like Jesus.

Grace runs deep within you. It isn't only seen by the way you speak or act; it's evident in the way you depend on God. This humility, founded in your reliance upon the Lord, is a beauty that's apparent. It defines you. People know there's something different, even if they don't fully understand what that is, and they're drawn to your nature. What a refreshing person you become when you accept God's unconditional love and know how to share it with others.

Lord, I want to be known as a person of grace, confidence, and compassion. I want others to feel your presence when they're around me, to be encouraged by the way I treat them, and to know it's only by your grace that I stand. I want to live free from offense and without offending others. Help me to live in a way that glorifies you and reveals your heart.

Infused with Faith

Your pure faith and love rest over your heart
as you nurture those who are yet infants.
—Song of Songs 4:5

Two of your most attractive qualities are faith and love. You become more and more like Jesus as you yield your life to Him. Never despise the seasons you go through. The good times wouldn't be as savory if you didn't taste the bad. You'd never know the power of His Word if you didn't need to wield its power. Victory wouldn't be appreciated if you couldn't fail. His arms wouldn't feel so rejuvenating if you didn't need to be refreshed.

God is with you every step of the way. In every battle, you're discovering His unlimited power. In times of celebration, you're reminded of His faithfulness. At all times, faith is taking root deep within your heart. As you walk with Him and learn His ways, faith and love infuse your life. Each victory becomes a golden truth imprinted upon your soul, which can never be erased.

God, you are with me, instructing, leading, and helping me through every season. Love and faithfulness now rest upon my heart because I believe you're a faithful, wise, powerful, and loving God. You will never forsake me. I yield myself to you, so every situation will bear fruit in my life and become substance that I can share with others.

Impart

Your pure faith and love rest over your heart
as you **nurture those who are yet infants.**

—Song of Songs 4:5

The journey with Jesus will always lead you beyond yourself. This life of faith and these gifts of grace, strength, and love not only mature *you*; they enable you to nourish and impart life to others. As you delight yourself in Him, you become a fountain of living waters—a refreshing drink for thirsty souls.

God's diversity spans humanity. No one else carries the facet of Him that you do. You are different and unique—imparting wisdom and compassion that is a distinct reflection of God's character in you. The lost are filled with questions that only He can answer, but He desires to speak through you. To love through you. Impart what you have.

All you need is a heart of compassion.

Father, fill my heart with compassion for others. May I be humble, yet filled with faith that boldly and generously touches the world. You have restored me to yourself; now I want to be known as a loyal lover who runs alongside you in ministry. I want to discover just how glorious your power can be through me.

Brave

The Shulamite
I've made up my mind.
Until the darkness disappears and the dawn has fully come,
in spite of shadows and fears,
I will go to the mountaintop with you—
—Song of Songs 4:6

So often we resist the challenges of spiritual growth, afraid of what lies ahead. Fear of the unknown looms like a dark shadow, obscuring our view of the Lord. With tender affection, He patiently waits, whispering words of love that dispel uncertainty. He knows that with time, we will say yes and reach for His hand.

Trusting Him is one of your greatest weapons against darkness and fear. Faith replaces fear, not because you grit your teeth and try harder; it comes as you relinquish everything that is contrary to His nature and allow yourself to fall in love with Him—over and over again, every day. Suddenly, you're as bold as a lion, roaring with faith and laughing in the face of storms that normally would take you out. You feel courage rising within as the Lord melts your fears with His love.

Lord, at times my faith is nothing more than a smoldering wick, yet you run to me with fire in your eyes, ready to kindle a greater flame. I want to be so consumed with your love that fear's voice can no longer be heard. Strengthen me and give me courage. I reach for you and will not resist love's invitation to freedom. I trust you.

With You

I will go to the mountaintop with you—
the mountain of suffering love
and the hill of burning incense.
Yes, I will be your bride.

—Song of Songs 4:6

Though the road that leads to the mountaintops is long and winding, you don't have to travel it alone. The journey of life is both joyous and arduous. It's filled with many heartwarming and festive moments, yet littered with obstacles of pain and suffering. It's unpredictable, glorious, passionate, and at times, difficult. Yet through it all, God is by your side and He will never leave you.

There are always options about which roads you can take—the comfortable and predictable or the surprising and adventurous. God is calling you higher to a life that challenges you in the most beautiful ways. He wants you to dream with Him, to hope in the face of countless disappointments, to believe in miracles, to laugh even when you stumble, and to discover just how faithful He really is.

Lord, take my hand and don't let go. Life is unpredictable and, at times, scary, but the longer I walk with you, the more I realize how faithful you are. You steady and encourage me, when no one else does. You're my hope, my strength, and the peace that anchors me. You breathe fresh resolve into my soul.

The Mountain of Myrrh

I will go to the mountaintop with you—
the mountain of suffering love
and the hill of burning incense.
Yes, I will be your bride.

—Song of Songs 4:6

To say yes to the mountain of myrrh is a lifetime commitment of embracing the cross. It is the place where selfishness dies and holy love takes root. The reality of the cross is transformational. It stirs holy passion within your heart and empowers you to live for Him, regardless of the cost.

Every seeking heart will eventually arrive at this place—discovering Him in ways only the mountain of suffering can teach. This is where you're taught the ways of God and learn what true love looks like. To embrace suffering love is to acknowledge not only what Jesus did for you, but to learn how to love without limits. When you become His holy bride, you no longer live for your own pleasure. You're consumed with love that longs to give to Him and to those He's given His life for.

Jesus, your love is more beautiful than any other. You have paid love's ultimate price, as a testimony of passion's power. I say yes to a life of holy pursuit where I embrace the message of the cross and its place in my life. I will seek to follow you, even to the mountain of suffering love.

Fragrant Offering

I will go to the mountaintop with you—
the mountain of suffering love
and *the hill of burning incense.*
Yes, I will be your bride.
—Song of Songs 4:6

*Y*our life is a fragrant offering unto the Lord. The scent of your unrestrained commitment rises to Him as a gift of true love. Your prayers of dedication and intercession touch His heart. Your worship ascends to His throne like the costliest perfume. As your soul passionately pours itself out to bless Him, He takes notice.

When you live in agreement with who He is and who He says you are, you release His essence into every situation. Not only have you embraced the cross; you carry the Lord's very nature within you. You're a holy vessel. Redeeming love drips from your being everywhere you go. His love has enflamed your heart.

Lord, your beauty blossoms in my soul, stirring praise that cannot be restrained. You are my joy and my example of true love. Let my life be an offering of total and complete devotion. I want every part of me—spirit, soul, and body—to be so in tune with your Spirit that everywhere I go I release the fragrance of heaven.

Yes!

I will go to the mountaintop with you—
the mountain of suffering love
and the hill of burning incense.
Yes, I will be your bride.

—SONG OF SONGS 4:6

There is nothing more beautiful and life changing than the moment you say yes to God! From this point forward, everything changes. Nothing else will ever make as much sense as He does. Living for Him propels you into a new and exciting way of life. Culture, career, business, and environment no longer define you when you are a child of the King.

This is more than your initial yes. Day after day, you accept His invitation to run with Him. His love has conquered your heart, matured you, and made you brave. His eyes of passion melt away the fears. Though you may still deal with insecurities, or have unanswered questions, nothing compares to your desire to be near Him.

Lord, the way you lavish me with your love sets my heart on fire. Every part of me is yours, and I never feel the need to resist. I want to be so confident in your faithfulness that nothing hinders my commitment. Help me to stay right in the center of your love, so I will always say yes to you.

Beautiful Bride

I will go to the mountaintop with you—
the mountain of suffering love
and the hill of burning incense.
Yes, I will be *your bride*.

—SONG OF SONGS 4:6

When the Lord looks upon the earth at the many spectacular things He's made, His eyes settle on you. In all of creation, nothing compares to your beauty. He created you and awakened your spirit with the kiss of life. Then He gave you a choice. Free to say yes or no to this holy invitation of love, you said yes!

His love has washed you, cleansed you from all sin. For all eternity you are clothed in radiant splendor—wrapped in the finest linens of extravagant love. You're the pure and spotless bride. His perfect partner that has embraced truth and become one with Him. As you lean into His love each day, you discover the treasures He's placed inside of you. You truly are beautiful, powerful, confident, and compassionate. Even when you're shaken, you will rise victorious!

Lord, I'm undone. This revelation of the way you see me is changing the way I think. You have made me in your image. Fear cannot defeat me. Suffering is not my portion. I am powerful and strong because I'm filled with your Holy Spirit. Let the beauty of holiness, confidence, and compassion define my life and glorify you. I am your bride.

Believe

The Bridegroom-King
Every part of you is so beautiful, my darling.
Perfect your beauty without flaw within.
—Song of Songs 4:7

Too often we define ourselves not by what we are, but by what we are not. We focus on our weaknesses instead of our strengths. We allow past failures to dictate our future. We can easily think of a million reasons why we can't have what we want; yet the Lord is shouting from the sideline, "Only believe!"

Your world is framed by what you believe. It's time to see your life from His perspective and allow His truth to drown every lie. Don't look at others and wish you were like them. God created you with all you need to succeed and be happy. It's time to believe in yourself. It's time for freedom to flood your soul. Take hold of His truth and hold it tight. It has the power to unravel self-doubt and make you the happiest, most courageous, and successful version of yourself that you can be.

Father, I choose to believe that anything is possible. I'm seeing life through new lenses. I am beautiful, powerful, and courageous. The past is in the past, and nothing defines me except you. I choose freedom. I choose faith. Not only am I going to dream about what the future may hold; I'm going to stop procrastinating and make a change.

You Are

The Bridegroom-King
Every part of you is so beautiful, my darling.
Perfect your beauty *without flaw within*.
—SONG OF SONGS 4:7

*Y*our beauty stems from a transformed heart. It is not defined by your height, how much you weigh, how toned your body, or how perfect your smile. You are a glorious masterpiece, designed by God. Your identity is inscribed upon your spirit. It is not based on your career, where you live, how much money you have, or what you wear. It's who you are, not what you do. You are a royalty—a child of the Most High King.

God describes you in ways that may seem like fiction, but they're true. God cannot lie. Today, allow what God says about you to sink in: You are flawless, beautiful, and sublime. You're the apple of His eye, His treasure, and His bride. You're His temple, His garden, and His voice on this earth. You are wise, favored, and successful. You are the fragrance of Christ, complete in Him, prosperous, and healthy. You are an overcomer.

Father, from now on, my life will be defined by what you say about me. Hope and confidence are rising within me. The power of your truth is like a breath of fresh air. I am all that you say I am, and though I may not understand it, I choose to believe it.

Now

> **Now you are ready,** bride of the mountains,
> to come with me as we climb the highest peaks together.
> Come with me through the archway of trust.
>
> —Song of Songs 4:8

Picture this: Jesus is standing before you, holding your hands, and looking you in the eyes. "Wow! You are beautiful," He says. He exhales purposefully, and a smile unlike any you've ever seen alights His face. A look of satisfaction and love glimmers in His eyes. "It's time. You're ready."

The Lord's ways are higher than ours. His wisdom and understanding is perfect and untainted. When we think we're ready to take on the world, He tucks us away with Him, matures us, and strengthens our faith. Then, just as we become comfortable in the secret place of His love, He lifts us up and tells us that we're ready to run. Jesus wants a bride who will co-labor with Him because of love. He isn't looking for workers to serve Him. He's looking for lovers who will run with Him because they've discovered His heart.

Jesus, I want to be by your side forever. It doesn't matter if you tuck me away or ask me to travel the world. All that matters is that I'm where you want me. Take me by the hand and lead me to your holy chambers or to the edge of adventure. You have given me the courage to trust you, and I wouldn't have it any other way.

Bride of the Mountains

Now you are ready, **bride of the mountains,**
to come with me as we climb the highest peaks together.
Come with me through the archway of trust.

—SONG OF SONGS 4:8

The mountains that once hindered you from running with Him have become the floors you dance upon. God's love has become the foundation of your life. From this perspective, things become clear. His ways, His wisdom, and His faithfulness have been settled in your heart and nothing can obstruct your view of the truth.

If you're stuck staring at the same valley wall, it's time to change your perspective. Focus on what is eternal, holy, and true, and you will rise to your rightful position in His Kingdom. Never let the valleys steal your passion for the Lord. You were made for the mountains, but it's in the valleys that your devotion is proven.

Lord, your holy mountains were created to bless me, not hinder me, from following you. Thank you for the way they've strengthened me and revealed your faithfulness. Through the eyes of faith, I can see things from your point of view. I am convinced that your love will always be enough.

Things Revealed

We will look down
from the crest of the glistening mounts
and from the summit of our sublime sanctuary.

—Song of Songs 4:8

You were created to walk with God in glory, every day. Your life doesn't have to be mundane and ordinary when you're a child of the King. From the sanctuary of His presence, He will unveil startling revelations that have been hidden until now. You can intercede from the place of victory when His will has been revealed.

God wants you to live in the place where spiritual realities are a regular part of your life, where you've learned to recognize His voice and the many different ways He speaks. To live from the realm of heaven means that you seek Him with all your heart, listening and looking with the eyes of faith.

Lord, I want to live from a higher realm of awareness, where I expect to encounter your holy presence every day. Infiltrate my thoughts and give me a transfusion of faith, so every imagination is illuminated by your truth. Anoint my eyes, so I can see with your perspective. Touch my ears, so I will hear the secrets you long to share.

Conqueror

Together we will wage war
in the lion's den and the leopard's lair
as they watch nightly for their prey.
—SONG OF SONGS 4:8

*I*ntimacy with Jesus equips you to stand in victory against the enemy. Though you aren't called to be in a constant state of warfare, you do need to know how and when to fight. Jesus never said that you would fight the enemy alone. He is your Champion, and His Spirit within you has made you a conqueror.

To face demonic forces with holy power, you must daily embrace the cross and live life from the place of divine intimacy. His kisses prepare you for battle. Worship and praise become your greatest forms of warfare because they flow from a life that fully trusts God. His presence gives you confidence to use your authority and conquer every form of evil. You defeat the enemy, not because you scream louder, but because peace and faith have filled your heart. From the position of bold love, you are victorious.

Jesus, your love makes me brave. There is no power greater than yours. Through the power of the cross, you have already defeated the enemy, and all I have to do is step into your victory. Because of you, I am already a conqueror. Together we stand triumphant!

Ravished

For you reach into my heart.
With one flash of your eyes I am undone by your love,
my beloved, my equal, my bride.
—Song of Songs 4:9

*Y*our love enthralls the heart of God. Imagine that! Even with all your imperfections, doubts, fears, and problems, you capture the attention of the Creator of all that is seen and unseen. This all-powerful, all-knowing, mysterious, and eternal God is moved by your love.

When Jesus reveals the depths of His passion, it's overwhelming. This revelation is much too high for us to grasp with our minds; it must be embraced with our hearts. It's overwhelming and glorious. Often, it brings us to our knees in reverent awe and wonder, while other times it fills us with joyous laughter. This is the passion that drove Love to the cross. This extravagant, furious love can never be quenched.

Lord, your love crashes upon me in waves of never-ending wonder. How can it be that my love does the same to you? Yet knowing it does, I will worship you and love you with every fiber of my being. You are worthy of this and so much more.

His Equal

For you reach into my heart.
With one flash of your eyes I am undone by your love,
my beloved, my equal, my bride.
—SONG OF SONGS 4:9

Four times in Song of Solomon, Jesus calls us His sister and His bride. The word *sister* can actually be translated as equal. God has said in His Word that we must not be unequally yoked. With that in mind, He would never go against His word and yoke His Son with someone who wasn't His equal.

How incredible and humbling that Jesus would take our nature upon Himself, and by the resurrection, give us His. Because of this, God could choose the perfect bride for His Son—one who is able to rule and reign with Him. Now you have an equal role with Jesus upon the earth. You present His glory, His merciful and joyous personality, His hope, His wisdom, and His redemption to the world. You're a perfect partner for Jesus—loved by the Father the same way He loves Jesus.

Lord, thank you for loving me with such perfect love. Because of it, I have become your bride—your perfect partner. You've anointed me with grace, power, and wisdom. You've equipped me to carry your presence to the world in a way that truly represents all that you are. May I truly reflect the glory of the One who lives inside of me and calls His own—His very equal.

One Glance

You leave me breathless—
I am overcome
by merely a glance from your worshipping eyes,
for you have stolen my heart.
—Song of Songs 4:9

*I*t only takes one moment of affection to touch the Lord's heart. Whether in times of intentional worship, or choosing to focus on Him instead of the chaos around you, when you make Jesus your focal point, He takes notice.

Your devotion captures the heart of the King! By a simple turning of your attention to Jesus, He cannot resist you. When you know how much He loves you, it demolishes rejection and fills you with faith. Why would you fear the obstacles of life, when this majestic King, who has everything you need, loves you? Let His love dispel every anxious thought. Release your cares as you worship Him. Lift your eyes today and focus on His faithfulness. Remind yourself that this beautiful God loves you, and He holds the solution to everything you face.

Lord, I want my love and my faith to move your heart. In the face of opposition, I will give you praise. You are glorious, faithful, and powerful. You hear my prayers, and each one matters to you. I want every word that I speak and each stirring of my thoughts to bring you honor and reflect a heart of total devotion.

Righteous One

I am held hostage by your love
and by *the graces of righteousness shining upon you.*
—SONG OF SONGS 4:9

No matter how hard you work, you will never be good enough or smart enough, or know enough Scriptures, to earn His love and the blessings that come with it. Your righteousness is perfect and complete—given to you as a gift of grace, purchased with His blood.

The moment you made Jesus the Lord of your life and submitted yourself to Him, you were graced with righteousness. With outstretched arms, He stood before you and welcomed you into His family. He placed a crown upon your head, which you will spend the rest of your earthly life growing into it. You are radiant and beautiful. You carry the family resemblance—you're God's holy child, brought into the most royal family of all. Simply believing you are who He says you are will cause you to want to live in a way that honors Him and portrays who you really are.

Jesus, thank you for the cross. Thank you for loving me so perfectly. It is by grace alone that I stand in righteousness. You tore down the walls of separation and brought me into your family. You have beautified me with your presence. Let everything within me echo your holiness.

The Finest Wine

How satisfying to me, my equal, my bride.
Your love is my finest wine—intoxicating and thrilling.
And your sweet, perfumed praises—so exotic, so pleasing.
—Song of Songs 4:10

Your life of devotion pleases Him more than any other beautiful thing He's created. It intoxicates Him! Jesus is essentially saying that your love for Him is more valuable than anything else in the universe. Your love thrills His heart. He values your love more than any other pleasure there is. He measures it, not by its strength, but by its sincerity. He knows you love Him although you may fail and sin at times.

You are desired just the way you are. Never let these words go in one ear and out the other. Take a moment and meditate on this truth. It will make your heart soar and cause you to live differently. Knowing how much He loves you will ignite passion that becomes an unquenchable fire.

Jesus, the way you love me has set my soul ablaze. Holy zeal—to honor you with a pure heart—consumes me. You have filled me with joy and blessed me with the riches of your glorious kingdom. I offer you my life—my heart, soul, and devotion. May it truly be an intoxicating delight to you.

Praise

How satisfying to me, my equal, my bride.
Your love is my finest wine—intoxicating and thrilling.
And your sweet, perfumed praises—so exotic, so pleasing.

—Song of Songs 4:10

The Song of Songs is an incredible declaration of Jesus' extravagant love for you. Repeatedly, He reminds you how beautiful you are, how strong your seemingly weak love is, and how excited He is for you to dive into all that He has for you.

When you hear these words that flow so freely from His heart, you can't help but praise Him. Shout, dance, sing, and laugh—He loves it all! Every time you genuinely get excited about Him, it captures His attention. The angels of God join in as you praise Him. When you discover the power of praise, you can't help but praise Him even more. Your praise and poured out life is a love feast for the Lord! More than all your sacrificial works of ministry, He longs to hear the joy and affections of your heart. Today, let your song rise before Him like sweet perfume.

Jesus, sometimes I don't have the words to express the love that grips my soul, so I'll dance and shout. I may sound a bit fanatic, but I don't care! Hope and faith just keep rising as I drench myself in your presence. I'm filled with expectation—I can sense you here with me, right now. I lift my hands in praise—you are amazing!

Words of Love

Your loving words are like the honeycomb to me;
your tongue releases milk and honey,
for I find the Promised Land flowing within you.
The fragrance of your worshipping love
surrounds you with scented robes of white.
—SONG OF SONGS 4:11

Your words of love to the Lord and to others are like sweet honey when they are seasoned with love, gratitude, hope, and compassion. Your speech has the ability to release life and healing to your soul. Faith and love stir the atmosphere around you and within you. Never underestimate the power of your words.

There are only two forms of speech: words that agree with God and words that don't. Words that sound like Him, even if they are desperate cries for intervention or answers, carry the essence of heaven. He will never turn away from a lovesick heart. When you pour out your words of love to the Lord, not even the love of all the angels combined can compare. All the joys of paradise are nothing in comparison to the joys He experiences when He spends time with you.

Father, I long to know you more and to release words of life everywhere I go. You are holy, powerful, and kind. Being with you makes me courageous, hopeful, and gracious. May every word I speak and every movement of my heart agree with you and be filled with passion that blesses you, transforms me, and touches all who hear.

Milk and Honey

Your loving words are like the honeycomb to me;
your tongue releases milk and honey,
for I find the Promised Land flowing within you.
The fragrance of your worshipping love
surrounds you with scented robes of white.

—Song of Songs 4:11

Fill yourself with the sweet promises of God. Let them saturate the way you think, and they will drip from every word you say. Others will be fed by the nourishing truths that flow from your lips. The promised land was a land flowing with milk and honey—abundant and rich. This is who you are—abundant and richly filled with living truths. The very Spirit of God, the promised land, so to speak, is within you.

Jesus hears every word you say. Each sigh of your heart, every declaration of love, and every cry for help—nothing goes unnoticed. Every word matters to Him, and they should matter to you as well. If you notice negative, complaining, doubt-filled words, it's time to flood yourself with His truth. Be intentional about what you think about; it will be evident in your demeanor and speech.

Jesus, pour out your presence upon the dry, cracked, and thirsty ground of my soul. Drench me; flood every thought with the goodness of who you are. Consume my thoughts, so they are filled with nothing but your truth. Touch my lips, so my words glorify you and spark hope and life to all who hear.

The Atmosphere of Glory

The fragrance of your worshipping love
surrounds you with scented robes of white.
—Song of Songs 4:11

There is nothing like you in the entire universe. When you adore the Lord and worship Him with unrestrained passion, He is there, infusing you with Himself. There, in the inner sanctuary of your heart, you become one with Him. Flowing out from your being are brilliant streams of glory.

Though you cannot see it with your natural eyes (unless the Lord allows you to), the atmosphere around you, as a believer, is permeated with the presence and splendor of the Lord, especially when you worship. Your songs of love and heart of adoration are an invitation for divine encounters and angelic intervention.

The next time you're worshipping the Lord, pay attention to what you're sensing within and around you. When the atmosphere becomes saturated with His holy presence, press in and ask Him if there is anything specific He wants to say or show you. You just may be surprised!

Lord, you have clothed me with robes of righteousness and purity. I believe I carry the fragrance of heaven, and everywhere I go, I release your perfume into the atmosphere. Even now I feel your presence. You are here with me, wrapping me in your love. Whisper the secrets you long to reveal.

A Garden Enclosed

My darling bride, *my private paradise,*
fastened to my heart.
A secret spring are you that no one else can have—
my bubbling fountain hidden from public view.
What a perfect partner to me now that I have you.
—Song of Songs 4:12

*Y*ou are God's private paradise. Like the garden of Eden, you are sealed with His holy angels, who guard you with flaming swords. You are exquisite—a secluded sanctuary of His eternal love. There in the garden of your heart, He dwells, enjoying the beauty that is found no place else.

No one has access to you the way the Lord does. Your yielded life of devotion and commitment to Him locks out intruders who would seek to vandalize your soul. Guard your heart at all times, so it flows in unison with His Spirit. Pay attention to imaginations and beliefs, which could dirty the beautiful garden within. No longer are you like a wilderness filled with weeds. Your heart has become a place of excitement and pleasure to the Lord. Beauty has blossomed within you.

Lord, I open my heart to you and ask you to make your home within me. No area is off-limits to you. I want every part of me to be a place that you enjoy—a delightful garden you call your own. May every thought, word, and deed beautify my being and bring you joy.

July

A Fountain

My darling bride, my private paradise,
fastened to my heart.
A secret spring are you that no one else can have—
my bubbling fountain hidden from public view.
What a perfect partner to me now that I have you.
—Song of Songs 4:12

You have become Jesus' holy and sacred fountain, sealed with the Holy Spirit. Clean, pure, sparkling waters flow within you, and Jesus loves to drink from your depths. Your secret thoughts and meditations are like cool streams of water to your King. Your inner life is a secret spring, open only to Jesus, who alone holds the key.

The King's garden is covered and watered by a private spring that is not polluted by any outside source. When you refuse to be polluted by the darkness of this world, you are this pure spring, who refreshes the heart of God. You are sealed and covered by His presence—reserved for only Him. Out of your inner being flow rivers of living water. It is the outpouring of your worship, devotion, and dedicated life.

Lord, as I dive into the reality of your presence, I have one thought: May you be as blessed by my love as I am by yours. You have seeped into every crevice of my soul, flooding me with awe and wonder. Help me to keep myself pure and untainted from the world, so together we can pour out the clean, refreshing waters of your perfect love.

Partnering with Jesus

My darling bride, my private paradise,
fastened to my heart.
A secret spring are you that no one else can have—
my bubbling fountain hidden from public view.
What a perfect partner to me now that I have you.

—SONG OF SONGS 4:12

You are not just someone the Lord has been forced to work with. You have been chosen as His perfect partner. Yes, you. With all your fears, failures, moments of doubt, and bouts of pride, you are called to walk with Him and work alongside Him.

God could have given His Son anything—literally anything in heaven or on earth—as a perfect gift, yet He chose you! He isn't waiting until your battle against flesh and temptation ceases and you feel holy enough to touch the world. He's only waiting for you to say yes to His invitation. You don't even have to fully understand exactly what you're supposed to do! One opportunity at a time, you simply must pour out what you have and draw from the power, wisdom, and creativity He's given you.

Jesus, believing I am who you say I am isn't always easy. Sometimes you put me in situations where I don't think I have enough to offer. I feel as if I might let you and others down. But today I make a decision to not shrink back from the opportunities you present me with, whether big or small. I will trust you and the power of your Spirit within me. Yes, I want to run with you!

All of You

My darling bride, my private paradise,
fastened to my heart.
A secret spring are you that no one else can have—
my bubbling fountain hidden from public view.
What a perfect partner to me ***now that I have you.***

—Song of Songs 4:12

When Jesus reigns as King of your life, your heart becomes the chamber room of His glory. Anything is possible, once you yield your life to Him. He doesn't expect you to do everything correctly, pretend life is perfect, or to never battle temptation or doubt. He's simply looking for your yielded heart—one that longs to be fully His.

Is there any part of that you're withholding from the Lord? If fear, disillusionment, temptation, or laziness have risen as seemingly insurmountable walls before you, He has the power to demolish them. He doesn't punish you or withhold His love when your faith is weak. The beautiful work He's begun in you can only be completed by Him. In the meantime, Jesus wants you to enjoy Him and enjoy life! It's time to be free from the weighty burdens you've carried. A fully surrendered life is liberating!

Jesus, take the reins of my life. I give you full control and hold nothing back. All that I am and hope to be, I surrender to you. I let go of everything that is contrary to your will for my life and reach for your hand. Lead me and guide me each day. Fill me with the pleasures that can only be experienced as I live for you.

Fruitful

Your inward life is now sprouting, bringing forth fruit.
What a beautiful paradise unfolds within you.
—Song of Songs 4:13–14

Do you know what Jesus sees when He looks at you? He sees a beautiful garden filled with fruit. He sees life blossoming inside of you that you may not see yourself. Your spirit has awakened to the One who calls you beautiful. Saturated with His love and glory, your heart is the perfect ground for fruit to grow.

God has planted seeds of love and treasures of grace within you. Never underestimate the importance of what you carry. Some of the gifts and talents that you have may still be hidden, saved for a specific time in your life when God knows they'll best serve you and those you're called to share them with. Or perhaps the power and anointing that resides within you has gone untapped and you find yourself doubting if you have anything to offer. Whether you're in a season of barrenness or fruitfulness, God's perfect timing must be trusted. Maintain your posture of worship and stay tuned into the Holy Spirit. The unveiling of your inward beauty is about to be revealed.

Father, unlock your destiny within me. I want my life to be a garden of beauty and fruitfulness that blesses others. Impregnate me with purpose and vision. Give me clarity, so I can walk with confidence and bring light into every dark and hopeless situation.

When I'm near You

Your inward life is now sprouting, bringing forth fruit.
What a beautiful paradise unfolds within you.
When I'm near you, I smell aromas of the finest spice,
for many clusters of my exquisite fruit
now grow within your inner garden.
—Song of Songs 4:13–14

Your love is like costly spices—fragrant and delightful to the Lord. He loves to be around you. The scents of redemption, holiness, and perfect love rise from your being. Your worship is like sweet perfume, poured upon the feet of Jesus. Every time you turn your heart toward Him, it rises before Him and captures His attention.

Like Esther of old, as you spend time with the Lord, you beautify yourself with the costliest fragrances of all—His perfect love, holy presence, and glorious grace. The beauty of your devotion flows from you like the scents of rare and exquisite spices. The forgiveness you release to others and your Christlike character are pleasing offerings to the Lord. When Jesus comes close to you, He's overwhelmed by the pleasing bouquet of faithfulness and passion, which exude from your being.

❧

Father, the deep wells of your Spirit are calling to the depths of my soul. I cannot resist you, nor do I want to. Let my life be a fragrant offering of love, adoration, and complete devotion. Fill every part of me with the perfume of your holy presence.

Abundant

When I'm near you, I smell aromas of the finest spice,
for many clusters of my exquisite fruit
now grow within your inner garden.
—SONG OF SONGS 4:13–14

Have you ever seen a tree chock-full of fruit ready for picking? That is how you are. Your life, the very garden of your heart, is inundated with exquisite fruit. Not just any fruit and not just a little, this is the fruit of the Spirit growing abundantly in your life. It brings you joy in place of sadness; it gives you peace during adversity and strengthens you when you're weak.

This delightful fruit isn't meant for you alone. There is so much of it in your life; it must be shared. Your kindness, patience, and gentleness are rare treasures that bless others. Live in a way that makes others feel valued and supported. Give when you have the opportunity to do so, even if it's with a smile or an encouraging word. Lift others up, be a friend, and look for ways to be an example of Jesus on this earth.

Father, you have filled my life so abundantly. I am rich because I know and serve a good God, whom I call Father. I repent for any selfishness, for any time I have hidden your love by ignoring those around me. I want to release your light everywhere I go and into every situation. Anoint me with compassion. Remind me to slow down and pay attention to those you place in my path.

Fragrant Worship

> Here are the nine ...
> **branches of scented woods.**
> —Song of Songs 4:13–14

The phrase "branches of scented woods" speaks of the fragrant cedars or trees of frankincense. In order for a frankincense tree to release its fragrance, it must be cut or tapped. This is such a beautiful comparison to the life of a Christian during pain and suffering. Your worship to Him is fragrant and costly—a gift of incomparable value. There is nothing more precious to the Lord than the fragrance of your worship in the midst of brokenness. In its purest form, frankincense is sought for its healing properties. Your purest worship will release the scent of healing, the very fragrance of Jesus, to those around you.

Though times of suffering and trials are difficult, they draw you close to God and reveal His faithfulness, which you would never know otherwise. If you were never in need of His intervention, you'd never have the opportunity to experience His miracles, might, and deliverance.

Father, when I'm broken and feel alone, I'll reach for you. I'll lift my heart and declare your goodness, even when things around me are falling apart. You love me and will never forsake me. Come, wrap me in your arms until your strength becomes mine. My hope, my faith, and my deliverance are found in you.

Tears from the Tree

Here are the nine …
myrrh, like tears from a tree.
SONG OF SONGS 4:13–14

Inhale deeply and allow the fragrance of perfect love to flood your senses. The spice of myrrh comes from the pierced bark of a thorny tree. What a clear picture of the cross and sufferings of our Lord Jesus, who was pierced and hung on a tree. The costly sacrifice of Jesus on the cross reminds us of a love that has no limits. Never doubt this love.

If Jesus was willing to come to earth as a man, then die in your place, He certainly won't stop taking care of you now. You are the treasure and delight of His heart. He holds nothing back from you. Embrace the faith you have within. Stir it up and stand upon His Word that will not return void. Shake off doubt, fear, and discouragement. Remind yourself of His goodness and how much He loves you. Let hope arise. He is for you and stands victorious against the enemy of your soul.

Lord, help me to remember that you are in control. With you, I can walk upon the waters of adversity. You are faithful and true. You've given everything to prove your love for me. Today I choose to embrace this love that dispels every fear. You are good. You are for me, and you will come to my rescue.

Light

Your life flows into mine, pure as a garden spring.
A well of living water springs up from within you,
like a mountain brook flowing into my heart!
—SONG OF SONGS 4:15

How magnificent it is to imagine the Spirit of God, living and abiding in us. Yet in this verse, the Lord gives us *His* perspective. Our life, pure as a garden spring, flows into Him and thrills His heart. Jesus doesn't erect walls to separate our nature from His. He isn't concerned that we will contaminate His glory with our humanity. He never shrinks away from us or makes us feel unworthy.

What an example for us to follow! Jesus wants us to be so secure in who we are that we aren't afraid of being around sin. We are called to love the unlovely—those living in iniquity and wickedness. Your purity doesn't become tainted by the filth of sin around you. Be more convinced of the love and glory within, your ability to help others, than you are of evil's ability to affect you. You're one spirit with the Lord; He fills you with power. You're the light that shines in the darkness, drawing sinners to Him.

Jesus, I want to live in a way that allows the radiance of your love to shine through. Lead me into the darkest places, where sin abounds, and we will love the unlovely, together.

Waters of Refreshing

Your life flows into mine, pure as a garden spring.
A well of living water springs up from within you,
like a mountain brook flowing into my heart!
—Song of Songs 4:15

Never again do you need to succumb to the feeling that you are dry and weary when the River of God cascades through your soul. You have a never-ending source of grace inside of you. As a sanctuary for the Living God, your life overflows with abundance. You're washed in love and soaked in grace.

Everyone goes through difficult and dry times, when it seems we cannot find God's presence or hear His voice. It's up to you to drink from the deep well that resides within you. As His garden spring, you never need to stay in the place of weariness. Rise with fresh zeal and affection for Him. Draw strength, hope, and refreshing from the Spirit of God inside of you. You're never empty or alone. He is with you, filling every part of you. Let all restraints, every anxiety and care, fall like broken pieces of a cumbersome shell.

God, you are the waters of refreshing that never run dry. When darkness screams and hope begins to fade, I will draw from your strength within me. I refuse to be imprisoned by anything that contradicts your greatness and love. Instead, I will fasten my thoughts and words to the truth of your power and faithfulness. Flood me with the substance of your love.

Mountain Brook

Your life flows into mine, pure as a garden spring.
A well of living water springs up from within you,
like a mountain brook flowing into my heart!
—Song of Songs 4:15

If you've ever sat beside a mountain brook, you know it's one of the most tranquil, relaxing, and refreshing places on earth. Surrounded by lush green landscape, the waters pour over rocks and boulders, creating a soothing symphony unlike anything you've ever heard. This is what Jesus compares you to.

The sound of your voice is like a symphony of love. He sees the movement of your heart in worship. Your life of devotion exhilarates Him. He's elated when you set time aside to be with Him. You know how it feels when He draws near, but maybe you forget that you bring joy to Him as well. You're like a refreshing brook of water flowing into His heart. He loves to spend time with you.

Father, may my love for you never run dry. As I worship and live my life before you, may it rise to your throne forever. Melodies of love flow from the depths of my being. I want to remain in this place of continual reverence and zeal, bringing joy to your heart for all eternity.

Fully Yours

Then may your awakening breath
blow upon my life until I am fully yours.
Breathe upon me with your Spirit wind.
Stir up the sweet spice of your life within me.
Spare nothing as you make me your fruitful garden.
Hold nothing back until I release your fragrance.
—Song of Songs 4:16

Hold nothing back from Him, for He has held nothing back from you. He loves you with both power and tenderness. His touch has awakened your soul and brought you to life. All that He's done or will ever do is to prove His love and reveal your identity.

Often, God's ways seem to be opposite your own until you see the wisdom behind all He does. The cold north winds of adversity drive you to your knees and remind you of your utter dependence upon Him—embrace them. The warm south winds are meant to refresh and comfort—enjoy them. Each breath, every wind of His Spirit, molds you into the mature bride He's called you to be. When you reply with cries of love to be fully His, He will use every storm to demonstrate both His sovereignty and His passion.

Lord, at times I feel as if my circumstances contradict your majesty, but I know you well enough to realize you will turn things around. Even in the winds of adversity, the whisper of your voice resonates within me, drawing me close. Your love is eternal and just. Your arms of love keep me safe.

Stirring

Then may your awakening breath
blow upon my life until I am fully yours.
Breathe upon me with your Spirit wind.
Stir up the sweet spice of your life within me.
—Song of Songs 4:16

God never asks us to wear a mask and pretend we're okay when we're not. He gave us emotions, and He isn't offended when you allow yourself to feel them. He simply reminds us that He is the answer to everything we go through. When you're having one of those days, lift your voice and ask Him to stir the sweet spice of His life within you.

His love is strong enough to carry you through each devastation. His wisdom will navigate you across the most tumultuous waters. His peace will rise within you and contradict the bellowing chaos. In His presence, your eyes are opened to the wonder of His magnificent and unstoppable sovereignty. Your posture changes and the heaviness melts away when you allow Him to become the center of your attention. He is the sweet scent of victory stirring within you.

Lord, when my heart and mind clash, stir your splendor within me. You are the only truth that matters, and you know how to settle my soul. Before I rush into the busyness of the day or lay my head to rest at night, I will bask in the reality of your love and experience your peace that surpasses all understanding. Your beauty inspires me.

Daily

Come walk with me as you walked
with Adam in your paradise garden.
Come taste the fruits of your life in me.
—Song of Songs 4:16

The mystery of God's beautiful garden began with Adam. Just as the Lord walked with him in the garden, He longs to walk with you each day. You were created for fellowship and deep communion with the Lord. It isn't just the desire of *your* heart. From the very beginning, it has been the longing of *His*.

Expect to hear His voice, to feel His touch, to laugh and rejoice, as you spend time with Him. Let your worship ascend to Him and outshine every dark and cumbersome thought. Expect to experience His extravagant love as it warms your heart. When His presence greets you, open your arms wide and welcome Him. Share this day with Him. Make every moment count as you delight in Him and He delights in you.

Lord, I want to know you more than any person has ever known you. I long to see your face and hear your voice. I want to be acquainted with your holy ways and make them my own. Throughout the day, regardless of what I'm doing, I want my thoughts to land on you. Take my hand and walk with me in the garden of my life.

Enjoy

Come walk with me as you walked
with Adam in your paradise garden.
Come taste the fruits of your life in me.

—SONG OF SONGS 4:16

There is a beautiful shift that happens within you when you recognize Jesus' great desire for your love and company. This is what He died for. This is the love that couldn't keep Him in the grave. You are the joy that ignites His heart and causes heaven to rejoice. You are His glorious inheritance. You delight His heart.

Whether you've been a Christian for hours or years, His glorious work inside of you is amazing and eternal. Invite Him to draw close, to gaze into your soul, and enjoy the fruit of His life within you. Vulnerability and surrender are beautiful to the Lord. Never be afraid to open your heart to Him fully, even if you're aware of areas that need attention. It is by grace alone that you stand.

Jesus, your love is all-consuming and magnificent. It has overcome my darkness and transformed my life. Your glory radiates from within me. I hardly recognize the person I have become. I'm so grateful you have kissed me with redemption. Come taste the fruit of your undeniable work within me.

Confident

The Bridegroom-King
I have come to you, my darling bride,
for ***you are my paradise garden!***
—Song of Songs 4:16

Recognizing that life is about much more than just yourself is a true sign that you are stepping into your bridal role. Confidence in your identity provides the framework for a courageous life—one that takes risks to follow Jesus. Motivation to share His love propels you forward with no concern for what may or may not happen. You simply live from the inside out.

You have become a beautiful, fragrant, glorious home for His presence. When you're rooted and grounded in the soil of God's love, your life becomes a flourishing garden. Everywhere you go, the fragrance of His life exudes from your being. His glory has literally become a paradise within you.

Jesus, let my life be a paradise of your presence, for all to enjoy. As you saturate me with your love, I become confident in what I carry. It is my honor to be a home for your glory. I am undone—overwhelmed by how much you believe in me. The atmosphere of faith has dispelled all fear, and I will step into my role as your bride.

You Are

The Bridegroom-King
I have gathered from your heart,
my equal, my bride,
I have gathered from my garden
all my sacred spices—even my myrrh.
—Song of Songs 5:1

You are not inferior to Jesus. The same Spirit that raised Him from the dead lives inside of you. You are filled with power and saturated with glory. Jesus isn't peering down His nose at you, wondering when you'll ever get it right. Today, at this very moment, He's looking at you with love-filled eyes and calling you His equal.

God is the confidence of the entire world. There is no escaping His might. As you stand in awe and wonder of this One who breathed substance into all that you see, remember that He who holds this power shares it with you. You are told to heal the sick and cast out demons. At your command, the storms will cease. His wisdom is offered to you. You're the salt of the earth and the light of the world, all because He lives inside of you.

God, you astound me. You ignite the day with your splendor and still the night with your peace. You paint the seasons with diversity and color. You hold my heart. With the might of your word, all that I see, and even what I don't see, came into being. Yet in ways much too high for me, you call me your equal and trust me with your power.

For His Pleasure

I have tasted and enjoyed my wine within you.
I have tasted with pleasure my pure milk, my honeycomb,
which you yield to me.

—Song of Songs 5:1

God has reached into your heart and found the perfect work of grace within you. Your sweet offerings of love thrill Him. He gathers them like fruit from a garden, like honey from the honeycomb. You are so drenched with His love, life, and perfection that it fills Him with pleasure. He runs to you to drink the wine of your devotion. Your love and praises satisfy Him.

Heaven and earth have united within you. Everything about you is becoming more and more like Him. You are a creation of *His* making, a story of *His* redeeming power. Every ounce of goodness inside of you came from Him, yet He looks at the work He's done inside of you and tells *you*, "Well done." What a delight it is to Him to look at you and see that all of you belongs to Him.

Lord, you feed me with spiritual bread that satisfies my deepest hunger. As I delight in you, come delight in me. When you look at me, I hope you see yourself reflected in my life. I want to live for you above all others and to bring you joy as I seek to walk in purity, integrity, and love.

You Have Become a Feast

I delight in gathering my sacred spice,
all the fruits of my life I have
gathered from within you, my paradise garden.
Come, all my friends—
feast upon my bride, all you revelers of my palace.

—Song of Songs 5:1

The world needs His touch, His love, His compassion, and His power—all of which reside within you. You don't need to have every Bible verse memorized or be authorized by an organization to share His love and truth. You *are* His truth. As a vessel of the Holy Spirit, you have become a banqueting table for others to feast from.

When Jesus brings people across your path, He's doing it because He knows you have something they need. You have Him. You are the answer to someone's prayer because He is in you. Step out and take a risk today. When you leave the house, expect to encounter people God wants you to talk with, pray for, or simply give a kind word to. You look like Him because you are one with Him. Let His kindness be seen in your life.

Lord, help me to pay more attention to you as you stand in the midst of others and beckon me to share your kindness. Show me the value each person has, even if I don't agree with everything they do or say. Let me be a vessel of dignity, respect, and honor. One who reveals your heart to others.

An Ever-Flowing Fountain

Feast on her, my lovers!
Drink and drink, and drink again,
until you can take no more.
Drink the wine of her love.

—SONG OF SONGS 5:1

The rivers of living water that flow within you never cease. His presence inside of you is an ever-flowing fountain, available at all times. You can experience God's extravagant love, right now. Turn your attention to Him, be still, and feel His nearness. Throughout the day, drink of His presence and continually make yourself aware of His glory. Expect Him to speak. Expect to feel the warmth of His love.

The rains of light and life have saturated the once-dry ground of your heart. You have more than enough to give to others. You have become a refreshing drink that quenches the thirst of weary souls. The presence of God inside of you doesn't run out. Stay in the stream of His love, and you will never run dry. Give this love to others and introduce them to the One who satisfies their every need.

Father, thank you for the Holy Spirit—the river of Living Water flowing within me. I turn my attention to you. Overflow every thought and imagination, each worry and anxiety, and every distraction with your tangible presence. Throughout the day, when my thoughts drift, bring me back to this place of peace and holy encounter. Flood my soul with hope and love, and let it leak from me everywhere I go.

Dream

I dreamed of my beloved—
he was coming to me in the darkness of night.
—Song of Songs 5:2

Your spirit never sleeps. When you lay your head down each night, expect the Lord to bless you with divine encounters. Your Beloved longs to share His heart and unveil His mysteries to you, even while you sleep. Your pillow becomes a pillar of glory and your bedroom, a chamber of angelic activity. There is so much happening around you, and often, the Lord will give you glimpses of unveiled secrets and answers to prayer while you sleep.

Your heart has been awakened to love. Each movement of your spirit reaches for Him, even when you're asleep. Expect Him to come. Invite Him to infiltrate your thoughts and imaginations, day and night. Before you fall asleep, ask Him for dreams that reveal His heart, give you wisdom and strategy, and instruct you how to pray for others.

Father, I believe my bedroom is the very doorway to your presence. As I lie down tonight, I will sleep in total peace because I know you're protecting me. There's a song in my heart as I drift off to sleep. My mind is filled with thoughts of you; my spirit meditates on your love. Speak to me.

He Sings over You

The melody of the man I love awakened me.
I heard his knock at my heart's door
as he pleaded with me.

—Song of Songs 5:2

Oh, how the Lord loves you! In perfect pitch, with a voice more beautiful than a thousand angels, He sings over you. His sacrifice has become the lyrics to an eternal chorus. He celebrates you with joy-filled inflection. Nothing can compare to the Song of all Songs.

The sound of His voice resides within you. It echoes through every cell, infusing you with health and life. It lifts you above the chaos, fills you with hope, and strengthens your faith. It stirs uncontainable passion to know Him more and undeniable anticipation for what He will do. Ask the Lord to let you hear this song of love today. Let it inflame your heart and awaken you to a new season. Listen for the melody that will cause your spirit to blossom.

Jesus, just to think about you singing over me fills me with awe and wonder. Your song impregnates me with joy. I can hardly contain myself! Suddenly, I feel lighter—hopeful. I expect your goodness to manifest in my life. I'm full of life. Serenade me with your songs of love. Take me by the hand, and we will dance.

Knock

The melody of the man I love awakened me.
I heard his knock at my heart's door
as he pleaded with me.
—SONG OF SONGS 5:2

The Lord is standing at the door of your heart, knocking. He's beckoning you and inviting you to something you've never experienced before. Jesus constantly calls us from glory to glory. There is always more of His character to become acquainted with, more of His love to encounter, and more wisdom and grace to lead you.

Your life's calling will propel you straight into His hands, when you respond to His proposal. Though the timing doesn't always feel right, you can trust Him when He draws you away from what is comfortable and predictable. If you will open to Him, He will take you through a door that leads to new revelations of Jesus in your life. He will never knock before it is time.

Lord, I hear you knocking on the door of my heart, and I open to you with joyful anticipation. I'm not sure what the future looks like, but when you take me by the hand, I have no fear. I will run with you wherever you lead. When you call, I will not resist.

Deeper Still

The Bridegroom-King
Arise, my love.
Open your heart, my darling, deeper still to me.
Will you receive me this dark night?
There is no one else but you, my friend, my equal.
—Song of Songs 5:2

The cry of a longing heart desires more—more of His kisses, more of His glory, and more words of loving affirmation. But, if we want to be fully His, we must also invite His searching gaze into the deepest places we've yet to face. We must trust Him so completely that we don't back away from the areas He invites us to overcome. He takes us from glory to glory, but encounters with His holiness will always lead to personal growth and transformation.

While we're on this earth, there will always be things that hinder our relationship with the Lord—habits and mind-sets that He addresses when He knows we're ready. Never shy away from His fine-tuning. Though He wants to walk you into freedom and victory, it isn't necessary to focus on everything that's wrong. Instead, continue to gaze at Him without resisting His cleansing fire. Transformation becomes simple as we yield our all to Him.

Lord, examine my heart and reveal anything that would distance me from you. I will not resist your searching gaze—it's like fire in my bones. Purify me and cleanse me from secret sin. Transform me from the inside out as I yield my soul to you.

He Needs You

I need you this night to arise and come be with me.
You are my pure, loyal dove, a perfect partner for me.
My flawless one, will you arise?
—Song of Songs 5:2

When the Lord invites you to places you've never gone before, He already knows ahead of time what your reservations will be. Whether you are afraid, lack motivation, or only see the obstacles, Jesus notices even your tiniest willingness to follow Him. When your heart cries out for Him to have you fully, He takes you seriously.

He will never push you to do something you aren't willing to do, but He does know how to remove your fears and show you things from His perspective. In His tender compassion, He will speak grace and strength to every reservation and remind you who you are. He calls you pure and flawless, a loyal dove, and a perfect partner. Let His description of you infuse you with faith and break down any barriers that hinder you from following Him.

Lord, unlock your purposes for my life. Impregnate me with desires that will launch me forward and bring you glory. Help me to see the potential I have for greater things. I lay my fears at your feet. I will go where you ask. Let every step I take be filled with more of you.

Gethsemane

For my heaviness and tears are more than I can bear.
I have spent myself for you throughout the dark night.
—SONG OF SONGS 5:2

Our relationship with Jesus, this first love, always comes back to the cross. The mountain of myrrh that unfolds before every believer must be traveled with great confidence in His outrageous love. We must believe in the power of the cross. The commitment to follow Him anywhere and pay any price is not just something that thoughtlessly falls from our lips. It will be tested.

Our Beloved, this righteous King, is also the Man of Sorrows who calls us alongside Him even in His suffering. He was shamed, rejected, and pained. To know Him and embrace His ways means becoming acquainted with both the blessings and burdens of His heart. Partner with Him and be a light in the darkness. Stand up for righteousness. Rise and join with Him in intercession. Whatever our cross, we must embrace it just as He did, knowing it leads to victory.

Lord, you are love's perfect example. You bore the cross of sin and shame and suffered in my place. Though the path to resurrected life leads me through the way of sacrifice, I will not withhold my love from you. I've dedicated my life to following you. The beauty of your victory now flows through my veins.

There's Always More

The Sleeping Bride

I have already laid aside my own garments for you.
How could I take them up again
since I've yielded my righteousness to yours?

—Song of Songs 5:3

Never be satisfied with your current experience with the Lord. Eagerly seek to grow in wisdom and understanding, never settling for the level of maturity that you have. Maintain an open heart that seeks deeper revelation. Continually lean into His presence, believing that there is a greater depth of encounter to be experienced. The Lord's ways are a treasure that will take eternity to fully understand.

When you're willing to lay aside your ways for His, freedom fills your life in unexpected ways. You become satisfied and content in the deepest part of your soul, regardless of your circumstances. Peace surpasses understanding. Confidence in His love trumps every fear. Wisdom and faith settle every question.

Lord, you paid an extravagant price to give me a life filled with glorious revelation and power. I want to live with an attitude of expectancy and humility before you. I never want to hold anything back. I want to continually seek to be more like you, never believing I've reached a level of maturity that gives me the right to be less zealous or committed. Have your way in me.

Reasoning

You have cleansed my life and taken me so far.
Isn't that enough?
—Song of Songs 5:3

No one knows our hearts as Jesus does. He knows that sometimes we take too long to do what He asks. We stall because not only do we count the cost of following Him, but we create graphs and spreadsheets filled with *what ifs*. We focus so much on the price of love and obedience that we lose sight of Love Himself.

Our hearts and heads often battle the will of God. We reason away challenging impositions and try to grasp with our minds what can only be experienced through acts of faith. We won't always understand why He asks us to do the things He does, but eventually the fruit of relentless pursuit will be evident.

Take a risk. Yes, sometimes we make mistakes in hearing God, but the more we purpose to follow Him, the clearer His voice becomes.

Lord, forgive me for reasoning away the things you've asked me to do that are difficult. I don't want thoughts that contradict your sovereignty. I yield myself to you and ask that zeal to follow you would consume my soul. I want to be so captivated by love that any price I pay doesn't feel like a price at all.

Unlock My Heart

My beloved reached into me to unlock my heart.
The core of my very being trembled at his touch.
How my soul melted when he spoke to me!
—Song of Songs 5:4

Every believer goes through times when they feel stuck. Prayer becomes a one-way street, songs of worship trickle from your lips, instead of rising from your heart, and busyness becomes a taskmaster, ruling your days. It becomes obvious that your mind is overpowering your soul and spirit. You know God must be somewhere in the vicinity, because He said He'd never leave you, but you certainly don't feel Him.

The good news is that you never need to stay that way. The fact that you recognize the seasons of dryness means He created you for the rains of His love. With a simple turning of your focus to the Lord in faith, He will make His presence known again. The key is to expect your breakthrough and refuse to be denied. Stop for a moment and be still. Can you see Him reaching in and unlocking your heart? The grace of God has the power to get you unstuck.

Lord, fan away the gloomy clouds of heaviness and draw me close. Unclutter my mind and let your presence rise within me. I've felt stuck, but now you will release me from this cocoon of melancholy and frustration. I will stay in this place of worship and expectation until your glorious love has drenched every dry place.

Burning Heart

My beloved reached into me to unlock my heart.
The core of my very being trembled at his touch.
How my soul melted when he spoke to me!

—SONG OF SONGS 5:4

Deep within us is a desire for more of Jesus. Our hearts burn with longing to be close to Him. Just one touch from Him and our hearts melt with desire to know Him as He really is. We have come to a place of insatiable hunger for His presence.

This is one of the most desirable places for every believer—to know the nearness of His love and yet recognize our need for more. To believe He longs for our company, our affection, and our partnership leaves us utterly undone. We are those with burning hearts. For us there's no turning back to trivial pursuits of the flesh. Nothing else will satisfy. We've fallen in love with the Lover of our soul!

Lord, I long to know you more. The veil has been torn, and you've brought me near. But I yearn for unclouded vision. I want to see you. I earnestly desire to touch you, to reach out and hold the hand that so often holds mine. Whisper words that inflame my being. Draw me closer than anyone has ever been before.

Arise

My spirit arose to open for more of his touch.
As I surrendered to him, I began to sense his fragrance—
the fragrance of his suffering love!
It was the sense of myrrh flowing all through me!
—Song of Songs 5:5

Even when you cannot sense God's nearness, reach for Him. When you're having a season of glorious encounters and it feels as if you cannot handle more of His touch, rise and cry out for increase. Live in a way that continually brings your attention to Him.

Let your desire for Him propel you to action. Never be complacent. Refuse to remain the same. Arise and shake off everything that hinders your relationship with Him. Surrender it all. He is worth any price you must pay.

Ponder His promises. Meditate on His Word. Allow yourself to feel His Spirit enveloping you as you work or run errands. When the dust of darkness tries to obscure your vision, adamantly pursue Him, and let nothing stop you. Get lost in the wonder of His love. Let your heart move closer, even while you sleep.

❧

Lord, I long for the reality of your touch. As I reach for you, come rushing to my side, so I feel the brush of your presence. Flow through my veins, infuse every cell, and illuminate every thought with the glory of your love. Take me over completely and let nothing about my life remain the same.

August

Surrender

My spirit arose to open for more of his touch.
As I surrendered to him, I began to sense his fragrance—
the fragrance of his suffering love!
It was the sense of myrrh flowing all through me!
—Song of Songs 5:5

*L*et go. Release every care, every fear, every agreement you've made with doubt and unbelief, and lift your soul to Him. He is worthy of your total and complete trust. You weren't created for anxiety; you were created for peace. When your thoughts swirl like a hurricane and you feel as if you're barely holding on, it's a good indication that you need to run into His presence and surrender.

Invite Jesus into every aspect of your life. Hold nothing back. Total surrender means leaving behind every thought and belief system that dulls your spiritual senses and delays your destiny. It means giving the Lord total control, even if at first it leaves you feeling out of control. Cast aside the comfort of the known and predictable. Jump into a place of total abandon. Soon, you will sense His fragrance and know He's taking care of everything.

Jesus, revive me. I need your peace that passes understanding. Forgive me for trying to control the things I cannot understand, for not being patient and waiting for you to answer, and for doubting you. I surrender. Have your way. I lay my cares at your feet. Come with the soothing fragrance of your presence and lift me up. I trust you.

Dripping with Myrrh

My spirit arose to open for more of his touch.
As I surrendered to him, I began to sense his fragrance—
the fragrance of his suffering love!
It was the sense of myrrh flowing all through me!

—SONG OF SONGS 5:5

*W*hen the Shulamite leaps from bed and rushes toward the door to open for Jesus, she becomes aware of the most pleasing fragrance—liquid myrrh. As she reaches for the door handle, she discovers a sweet surprise—the beautiful scent that reminds her of her Beloved is actually dripping from *her* hands.

You, just like the Shulamite, smell like Jesus. Your being, as you embrace the suffering love of Jesus and are willing to pay any price to follow Him, drips with myrrh. The fragrance of unquenchable love now flows through you. It is an offering of unselfish devotion that captures the attention of heaven. With an abundance of grace to follow Him, you lack nothing. Even the enemy can smell you coming.

Father, drench me with a desire to walk the way of the cross. Give me grace and fortitude to follow Jesus anywhere. May the depths of my union with you be reflected in all I do and say. Wrap me in the garments of your glory and saturate me with yourself, so the fragrance of your presence drips from my being.

Where Are You?

I opened my soul to my beloved, but *suddenly he was gone*!
And my heart was torn out in longing for him.
I sought his presence, his fragrance,
but could not find him anywhere.

—Song of Songs 5:6

There's a time in every believer's journey when God seems to hide Himself. He never pulls away in order to injure or reject us. He doesn't withhold His presence for any other reason than to draw us out. Discipline is not punishment.

When we go through seasons where we've become dry and God feels distant, we must remember that trials do not define God's nature. God is good, even in the silence. Often, we've allowed spiritual laziness to place a wedge around our hearts. Once we admit it and repent, it's time to demolish every barrier and run to Him. Our need for Him becomes more apparent; we will do anything, go anywhere, and pay any price to experience His nearness again. It isn't until our hearts are filled with longing that we can understand how powerful that longing truly is. Out of this wilderness season, we emerge more powerful than ever!

Lord, come calm the storms of life, especially the ones that are raging within me. When I get distracted and lose sight of you, forgive me. I'm desperate for something only you can supply. I need you. Quench my ravaged soul with your living waters. I know everything I need comes from you.

By Faith

I opened my soul to my beloved, but suddenly he was gone!
And my heart was torn out in longing for him.
I sought his presence, his fragrance,
but could not find him anywhere.

—SONG OF SONGS 5:6

What do you do when tragedy strikes, life is a mess, and worship is a struggle? How do you cope when you cannot feel His presence or hear His voice? The answer is that you worship and declare your love for Him regardless of what's happening. Faith doesn't rely on feelings. Despite what's happening, God is worthy to be lavished with your love.

Turn your attention to Him and lift your songs of passionate surrender. You are called a *believer*, not a *doubter*. You walk by faith, not feelings. It takes faith to worship when you can't sense His presence, but as you choose Him even when you don't feel Him, He will come. In the midst of pain, you meet Him as the Comforter. His sweet voice falls upon your heart like a healing balm. Never give up. He is worthy. He is faithful.

Lord, I lay every care at your feet and wait for you with expectancy. Though chaos may be screaming for my attention, I choose to focus on you. You are worthy. I love you for who you are—my Creator, my Savior, and my Friend. With unselfish abandon I worship you, and here I will wait, knowing you will come.

Search

> I called out for him, yet he did not answer me.
> **I will arise and search for him until I find him.**
>
> —SONG OF SONGS 5:6

*I*n all that God does or doesn't do, His aim is to make you wholly His. Regardless of what you're facing, continually respond by stirring the internal waters of first love, and the sovereign purposes of God will be worked out in your life.

God wants to be found by you! When He feels distant, shake off all that restrains you and determine in your heart that you will find Him again. To search for Him doesn't mean working yourself up and binding every force of darkness. It is a simple and peaceful process. Still your soul and reach within to the place where He dwells. In faith, quiet your mind and turn your heart toward Him until you sense His presence again. It may take several attempts to still your racing mind and tap into His peace, but you will. Like the Shulamite, search for the One you love until you find Him.

Lord, I feel you drawing me closer. I'm coming after you with all I've got and I won't stop until I'm ravished by love, once again. Reach out and tear the veil so I can see you clearly. Hold me close and let your breath infuse my being with hope and strength.

Unquenchable

As I walked throughout the city in search of him,
the overseers stopped me as they made their rounds.
They beat me and bruised me until I could take no more.
They wounded me deeply
and removed their covering from me.
—Song of Songs 5:7

*N*ever let anyone quench your zeal for God. Religious rules and regulations don't foster passion. Instead, they turn your focus away from seeking the Lord to pleasing people. When your love for Him is like a blazing fire, others may not understand. Lukewarm leaders may feel uncomfortable, even jealous around you.

It is a sad reality that while God has given them a mandate to protect and disciple, many use their authority in a heavy-handed way, which quenches the zealous heart. However, when you live to please the Lord, He will correct those who stifle or hurt you. Your main calling is to love the Lord with all of your heart and to love others—even those who are walking in error.

Lord, thank you for the leaders you've placed around me. Bless them with wisdom and passion for you that is undeniable. Give them grace to lead by example. May they become true fathers and mothers to the body—parents who cheer their family on and encourage them to seek you for themselves. Let their love for you be contagious and may they see those around them through your eyes.

When You Are Wounded

They beat me and bruised me until I could take no more.
They wounded me deeply
and removed their covering from me.
—SONG OF SONGS 5:7

What do you do when spiritual leaders fail you? One of the hardest tests is when those who should be leading and guiding you wound you. It's a painful reality that sometimes those placed over us unjustly persecute us. It brings a wounding that's hard to describe. Mistreatment from friends and leaders is a test that few escape. Even Jesus was wounded by those closest to Him.

If you could see those who hurt you the way Jesus does, you would see their wounds, their own need for growth, and possibly spiritual darkness. Mercy and forgiveness would propel you to your next level of glory, freeing you as you began to pray for them with the Father's heart. How you respond determines a lot, not only about your future, but about how fast you will heal from their abuse. If there is anyone you need to release today, let's do that now.

Father, I forgive those who have hurt me. It doesn't matter whether or not they understood how cruel they were. All that matters is that you help them. Let me see them from your point of view. May mercy, peace, joy, and hope fill any place that has been darkened by offense. I release them to you.

Authentic

Nevertheless, make me this promise, you brides-to-be:
If you find my beloved one,
please tell him I endured all travails for him.
I've been pierced through by love,
and I will not be turned aside!
—Song of Songs 5:8

Rest assured, when you're going through the dark night of the soul and everything seems to be crumbling around you, others will be watching. This, too, is part of God's plan.

What a glorious example He's called you to be. Ministering to others in the midst of your own pain and sorrow is the mark of a mature, compassionate bride. Don't bury your head in the sand when you notice other hurting people around you. Let your faith and passion become contagious. Give others a chance to witness God's glory during life's darkest hour. You don't have to pretend you have it all together. Allow them to see you being real, experiencing pain, having questions, and yet finding the One who fills you with hope and leads you to victory. Never underestimate what your life, lived for others to see, can do.

Father, I want to live an authentic life before others. Lead me by your Spirit, so I know what to share and what not to share with those you place in my path. Be the light that illuminates my path, the hope that fills me in dark times, and the answer to someone's prayer. Help me to be aware of the people around me that need an encounter with you.

Endurance

Nevertheless, make me this promise, you brides-to-be:
If you find my beloved one,
please tell him *I endured all travails for him*.
I've been pierced through by love,
and I will not be turned aside!

—Song of Songs 5:8

There is nothing like feeling that the Lord is distant when you're going through a dark and terrible time in your life. The pain makes it easy to fall into self-pity. The Lord's seeming absence strikes a chord of fear and stirs the dust of doubt. Instead, you grasp Him by faith and worship. You may not even be able to lift your head, and your voice may barely be heard. But Jesus hears even your weakest whispers of love.

He may feel distant today, and you may not see how He could ever fix the mess you're in or do the miracle you've been hoping for. But He is faithful. While you don't close your eyes to your problems, you don't focus on them either. Refuse to give the problem a seat on the throne of your heart, where Jesus is supposed to be. Remind yourself of God's miracle-working power and believe.

Lord, I know you hear the travailing of my soul. Come meet me in my need. I'm weary and worn, and it feels as if everything's falling apart. I don't have much to offer, so I simply give you my heart. You are faithful, and you will never fail me.

Pierced Through by Love

Nevertheless, make me this promise, you brides-to-be:
If you find my beloved one,
please tell him I endured all travails for him.
I've been pierced through by love,
and I will not be turned aside!

—SONG OF SONGS 5:8

*L*ove can reach the deepest pain. It can pierce your heart more powerfully than the sting of misunderstanding and rejection. It heals every trauma. The love of Jesus has the power to overshadow the wounding inflicted upon you by others. Your life will never be the same when you live in the reality of what Jesus has done for you. Your days are radically different when you pay attention to what He continues to do for you every day.

The beauty of the cross and the overwhelming passion Jesus shows us has ruined us for anything less than His will in our lives. Nothing will hold us back, especially not the afflictions we've suffered in zealous pursuit. Scars of rejection and misunderstanding become symbols of honor, marking us as lovesick brides, longing for our Beloved. We must have this love forever!

Jesus, pierce my soul with the power and beauty of your love. Heal the places that have been wounded by misunderstanding. Though few may understand my radical pursuit of your purposes, righteousness, and love, I will continue to pour myself out to you. My life is nothing without you, and I will follow you forever.

What Love!

Jerusalem Maidens, Brides-to-be
What love is this?
How could you continue to care so deeply for him?
Isn't there another who could steal away your heart?
—Song of Songs 5:9

Oh, how our hearts swell with love for Jesus! No matter what, He is our rock, our answer, our help in time of need, and the One we live for. Encounters with His glory will leave us refreshed and encouraged, yet utterly undone and longing for more. His love catapults us into a lifestyle of zealous devotion, the fires of which must be tended.

Passionate hearts that are willing to pay any price to follow Jesus are not easily understood, yet people are drawn to those whose lives are marked by God—those who exude encouragement and compassion and who live by example. The testimony of an authentic lover of God, one who doesn't hide behind a mask and pretend life is perfect, will reach more unbelievers than a judgmental "holier than thou" attitude. This is the kind of lifestyle that will cause others to ask, "What love is this?"

Lord, I want my heart to be true—filled with unquenchable passion for you that guides my life. Let there be no mixture in my soul. Shine the light of your glory upon the areas that hide in darkness, and we'll face them together. May my life be a beautiful example of your presence, power, and love.

Idols

> Jerusalem Maidens, Brides-to-be
> What love is this?
> How could you continue to care so deeply for him?
> **Isn't there another who could steal away your heart?**
>
> —Song of Songs 5:9

*N*o one rivals what we have with Jesus. We've fallen in love with the Lover of our soul, and nothing else can compare. People have a hard time understanding this devotion because so many other things compete for our affection and give immediate gratification. The answer to their question, "Isn't there any other?" is a resounding no!

While nothing can steal our hearts away from Him, there are plenty of subtle distractions that dull our relationship. Pay attention to those things that waste your time, steal your connection with the Lord, and leave you dry. Jesus wants us to enjoy life, and He isn't against fun and entertainment. But when outward things consume our inward focus and steal our heart, they've become idols. We must guard ourselves against spiritual laziness and cultivate the most beautiful relationship of all.

Jesus, you mean more to me than anything else, but sometimes, I get so caught up in the busyness and distractions of life that I neglect my time with you. Breathe upon my desire to know you more. Give me grace and strengthen my resolve, so nothing will steal our time together. From the moment I wake and throughout the night, may my heart stay in tune with yours.

You're Beautiful

We see now your beauty, more beautiful than all the others.
What makes your beloved better than any other?
What is it about him
that makes you ask us to promise you this?
—Song of Songs 5:9

You are radiant and filled with the glory and joy of the Lord. Without saying a word, you release God's essence into the atmosphere around you, simply because He lives inside of you. Eventually, others will recognize that you're different. At first, they may not understand, but your willingness to love the unlovely and be an example of the Father's heart will make you shine.

There's no denying the beauty that radiates from you. Live in tune with God's heart and be sensitive to His intentions for those you meet each day. Your integrity and hope, mixed with approachability and encouragement, will point them to Him. When you go through trials, let faith lead you, so your break-through becomes a testimony for others to see. Don't hide the beauty of your devoted life.

Lord, let my life radiate with your beauty. May my actions, words, and beliefs be filled with kindness, hope, and integrity. I want every person I spend time with to know I'm different, even if I'm not talking about you. I want them to feel comfortable with me and walk away feeling encouraged, hopeful, and valued, because they have felt your presence within me.

He Alone

The Shulamite Bride
He alone is my beloved.
He shines in dazzling splendor, yet is still so approachable—
without equal as he stands above all others,
waving his banner to myriads.
—Song of Songs 5:10

Once you've encountered the Lord, you're left with an insatiable desire for more. Though there are times when He seems to have pulled away from you and feels distant, set your heart on Him with renewed passion and refuse to be offended. The revelation of Jesus must fill your heart continually. No matter what happens, keep the fires burning even during the dark night of the soul.

There are times it's quite difficult to call Him your Lover, but the cry of the lovesick heart cannot be snuffed out. Don't let your guard down when you go through times of darkness. When you cannot see His face, you can still trust His heart. Let Him alone hold your affection and refuse to give in to disillusionment and discouragement. Though you may not understand what He's doing in your circumstances, keep your faith alive and don't stop worshipping the One who will turn the shadows into daybreak.

Lord, I know you haven't forgotten about me, but sometimes you feel distant. Even in the darkest valleys of my life, you have given me miraculous signs of your love. Come now and do the same. Put your love on display and reveal your hand in my life. I wait for you alone.

Dazzling

The Shulamite Bride
He alone is my beloved.
He shines in dazzling splendor, yet is still so approachable—
without equal as he stands above all others,
waving his banner to myriads.
—Song of Songs 5:10

Oh, how we long to behold this One who is the very definition of perfected glory. Though our natural eyes may not see Him, our spirits perceive something unmistakable. This is our Lord, Savior, and King. Dazzling brilliance overwhelms our hearts with love and awe. We behold Him with love divine. Drawn to His beauty and grace, we're unable to adequately put to words what our hearts discover—and yet we try.

We long for the ability to express what we sense profoundly—a reality that is just beyond us, hidden for us to discover. Though we write about it, paint it, dance it, and find other ways to convey what stirs within us, we will always fall short in describing this glorious King.

Jesus, I'm leaning into your presence, searching for aspects of you I've never known before. I want to discover dimensions of your glory that cannot be understood with my mind. Surprise me. Dazzle me with your majesty and brilliance, so I'm left utterly astounded and absolutely inspired.

Incomparable

The Shulamite Bride
He alone is my beloved.
He shines in dazzling splendor, yet is still so approachable—
without equal as he stands above all others,
waving his banner to myriads.
—SONG OF SONGS 5:10

*J*esus is incomparably more beautiful and regal than ten thousand great men combined. He stands above them all. Effortlessly, we declare our love for Him when all is going right and we find ourselves in seasons of joy, rest, and encounter. However, in times of pain, when we're alone and discouraged, a true reflection of what we believe will be heard in our words.

It's important to be true to yourself and recognize when you're feeling out of sync—spirit, soul, and body. Allow yourself to feel your emotions, but bring those feelings to the Lord and ask Him to purify them, so they don't consume you. Focus on the One who can take a painful situation and use it to thrust you into your glorious future. Let your thoughts be directed by the power of your declaration, reminding yourself of God's power and faithfulness that knows no comparison.

Jesus, let the words of my mouth and the meditation of my heart, honor you at all times. You are Lord over all things, and your power knows no bounds. I bow before your majesty and remind myself of your love that never fails me. Let a torrent of praise explode from my soul as I declare your goodness in every situation.

Beauty of Holiness

The way he leads me is divine.
His leadership—so pure and dignified
as he wears his crown of gold.
Upon this crown are letters of black written
on a background of glory.
—SONG OF SONGS 5:11

When you focus on God's love and faithfulness, trusting Him to lead you in every situation, you'll experience the awe and wonder of His holiness. There is no leader like Him. No mixture in His crown and no impurity to obscure His view of any situation. Though you'll go through difficult seasons, He is with you in every one.

The highest degree of excellence is found in the leadership traits of the Lord Jesus. He rules with grace and perfection. He leads with compassion, wisdom, strength, and mercy. You can trust Him with full abandon, leaving all your cares in His hands. His infinite knowledge and understanding make Him the choicest Counselor. When Jesus is your King, His sovereignty will rule your life, directing you in all your ways.

Father, you are sovereign in all your ways. You measure my portion and keep every promise. You reign with perfect wisdom and justice. Nothing is too hard for you. You shield me from evil and share your divinity with those who call you Father. Draw me into the glory of your holy presence and drench me with this love that knows no bounds.

Majesty

The way he leads me is divine.
His leadership—so pure and dignified
as **he wears his crown of gold.**
Upon this crown are letters of black written
on a background of glory.

—SONG OF SONGS 5:11

Jesus is the Love that stepped out of eternity. The Son of God, the King of all, whose awe-inspiring majesty deserves the greatest honor. He fills the earth with glory while oceans thunder and fields echo His ecstatic praise. Creation anticipates and yields to His presence; let us do the same.

Jesus took the weight of the world upon Him. His love for us has been proven in the grandest way. He releases incomprehensible mercy, and His eyes are full of understanding. The King of Creation has become the King of our hearts. This is the One we call Lord, Savior, and Friend. Reach out to Him today, and let the revelation of His majesty, divinity, and surprising availability to you pierce your heart.

Jesus, I bow before you with a grateful heart and a spirit filled with joy. You've already done so much for me, yet you continue to pour out your love in the most surprising ways. You are sovereign, holy, and powerful, yet you hold me with tenderness and understanding. Your kiss upon my life has changed me forever.

He Sees You

He sees everything with pure understanding.
How beautiful his insights—without distortion.
His eyes rest upon the fullness of the river of revelation,
flowing so clean and pure.

—Song of Songs 5:12

The Lord sees everything that happens with perfected vision. He is not biased, filled with wrong motives, nor is He cruel in His judgments. Because His heart is clean, He can properly interpret our every intention. How refreshing it is to know that we can trust Him to weigh our thoughts, words, and actions. He is the Lord of all, who truly understands us. He deciphers our deepest meditations yet corrects with mercy and grace.

Jesus doesn't have a glass-half-empty theology. He doesn't sit with a gavel in hand, ready to pronounce judgment. He encourages you, believes in you, always cheers you on, and draws you close. He sees the good in everyone and invites you to do the same. Jesus believes you'll rise in victory, even during your greatest struggle. Now He urges you to see others through this same lens of mercy.

Jesus, you know me—every thought and movement of my heart. You're great in mercy, and your corrections always leave me feeling hopeful and full of holy resolve. Cleanse my heart, so I will see others through your eyes. When people spend time with me, I want them to feel refreshed, motivated towards righteousness, and encouraged. I want to be like you and love perfectly.

Insight

He sees everything with pure understanding.
How beautiful his insights—without distortion.
His eyes rest upon the fullness of the river of revelation,
flowing so clean and pure.

—Song of Songs 5:12

When the Lord shares His revelation, a part of us that was dead comes to life. When we're enlightened by His wisdom, every fiber of our being becomes rejuvenated. It surpasses earthly knowledge. The veil over our soul suddenly lifts, yet somewhere in the caverns of our heart, we've known it all along.

His understanding is perfect and cannot be learned—His Spirit must impart it. His discernment, wisdom, and insight into every situation leave us in awe. No one interprets situations with such clarity. Only He can look at a problem and know the answer. How wonderful that He loves to share His wisdom with us.

Call out to Him! Sit with Him in expectation. Lean into His embrace. Ask for His insight. There is beauty in everything about Jesus.

Jesus, there's nothing like the moment you infuse me with holy revelation. The way you enlighten my heart to understand something is one of the most amazing moments. Today, I ask you for more of these moments. I want to experience the wonders of wisdom and understanding that can only come from you. Fall fresh upon me.

Those Eyes

He sees everything with pure understanding.
How beautiful his insights—without distortion.
His eyes rest upon the fullness of the river of revelation,
flowing so clean and pure.
—Song of Songs 5:12

Gaze into His eyes, and you will see the Father, Son, and Holy Spirit looking back. These are the eyes that are filled with wonder and treasures yet to be discovered. These are the eyes that hold the answers to every mystery. They pierce our souls and interpret every movement of our heart. Nothing is hidden from His sight.

When you know that God sees you and still loves you, you find the courage to live an authentic life. The longer you stand in His presence, being vulnerable and honest with Him, shackles of people pleasing begin to melt away. His opinion of you becomes the only one that matters. He understands you, even when no one else does. This life of freedom releases you to be yourself, to realize how fully you depend upon the Lord, and to live humbly before Him and others. Open your life to His penetrating gaze and find confidence in His never-ending love.

Thank you for seeing me—the real me—and still loving me. You're gracious and kind, yet your eyes blaze with purity. I want to live without any hindrances to your holy love. I want the courage to be genuine and to believe in myself the way you do. Help me to become the best version of me I can be.

The Highest Path

He sees everything with pure understanding.
How beautiful his insights—without distortion.
His eyes rest upon the fullness of the river of revelation,
flowing so clean and pure.

—SONG OF SONGS 5:12

Everything about Jesus is pure, righteous, and untainted. He loves you with perfect love. He judges the world with matchless wisdom. Everything He asks you to do is motivated by His love for you and His passion for the world. Every good gift comes from Him. The desires of His heart are pure and holy. Jesus died for you with the purest of intentions. Now He calls you to live in this same reality—one that is higher than human thoughts.

You can live in a way that sets you apart from the norm. When people fall prey to hopelessness, you become a vessel of hope. When division drives a wedge, His wisdom and compassion show you how to pray. When others succumb to fear, you release God's love, which sets them free. It's time to live on the highest path—one paved with pure intentions and faith that is illuminated by God's truth.

Father, I want to live with a pure heart before you. I want my faith to stand strong through tests and trials. I want to be so confident in your love for me that I have courage to believe for great things. When everyone around me suffers in darkness, may I be the one shining the light that sets them free.

Beautiful Emotions

Looking at his gentle face I see such fullness of emotion.
Like a lovely garden where fragrant spices grow—
what a man!
—Song of Songs 5:13

The longer you walk with the Lord, the more you experience His beautiful emotions. Everything about Jesus is extraordinary. His emotions are diverse and refreshing. We move His heart, and He knows how to move ours as well.

His tender love encourages us to become everything He's purposed, igniting us with faith. When we're bowed down with sorrow, He lifts our head and breathes hope into our hearts. His joy is stirred with every accomplishment we make, even the seemingly insignificant ones. He freely laughs in the face of the enemy and invites us to do the same. Though He does experience righteous anger, He doesn't direct it to those whose hearts are toward Him, even in our imperfect, weak love. Jesus knows how to be all things to all men, and He engages us in ways that leave a lasting impression.

Jesus, the way that you connect with me is so gracious. You created me to feel deeply and you show me how to do it in holiness. I release my inhibitions and will allow my emotions to shine through. I want to experience the diversity of your emotions and be moved along with you. Together we will laugh, cry, love deeply, and enjoy life.

Lovely

Looking at his gentle face I see such fullness of emotion.
Like a lovely garden where fragrant spices grow—
what a man!

—Song of Songs 5:13

Jesus is like a garden filled with delightful fragrances. His life and personality stir a desire within you to know Him more. As the scent of His mercy and compassion wash over you, it awakens your heart to love. When He releases the spices of His unlimited power, it causes your soul to soar.

As you remain in His presence, living each day in awareness of His love, you'll discover His fragrance seeping into every situation. Nothing will feel overwhelming or be too difficult to handle when you recognize that He walks with you through life. He loves you. He enjoys you, and He wants you to come alive in the garden of His love. Let hope arise in areas that once held you back. It's time to live with expectancy.

Jesus, I can feel you tugging at my heart, wooing me into the discovery of unexplored faith. Reveal yourself to me in ways I've never known before. Let the garden of your love spill into my life, diffusing your holy fragrance into every stale and lifeless thought.

Speak to Me

No one speaks words so anointed as this one—
words that both pierce and heal,
words like lilies dripping with myrrh.

—Song of Songs 5:13

You were created to hear God's voice. Most of us don't hear Him audibly with our natural ears but as a still small voice within us. Too often people think they cannot hear Him because they expect a booming voice to come from heaven. The Holy Spirit lives inside of you. He knows how to speak to you and get your attention.

Still your mind and rest in His presence, each day. Thoughts, ideas, and images, which agree with His Word and stir hope and faith within you, are more than likely Him. Listen for Him in every conversation. Often, His love and counsel come through loud and clear. Watch for Him to speak through emails, prophetic words, books, articles, and even in the beauty of creation. God is not confusing. Though it takes time to separate His voice from your emotions, He is patient. If you desire to know His voice, He will make it clear.

Father, speak to me. I want to know your voice more intimately than any other. Teach me to recognize your faintest whisper as it brushes my subconscious. Help me to discern your intentions as they spark my mind like a brilliant idea. I tune myself into you and will listen for you in every situation.

Words

No one speaks words so anointed as this one—
words that both pierce and heal,
words like lilies dripping with myrrh.
—Song of Songs 5:13

*G*od's Word is sharper than any two-edged sword, piercing excuses and revealing the motives of your heart. One word from Jesus has the power to transform your life. His words always impart life. However, resurrection life always begins at the cross.

It's in death to selfishness that you discover the delight of life with Him. The joy and peace of knowing you are walking in total surrender to His will far outweighs anything you'll forsake.

Jesus' words impart life and encouragement—symbolized by the pure and sweet scent of a lily. Yet the secret of their anointing is found in the power of myrrh—the offering of suffering love, which He paid for you. Never underestimate the strength of love that is willing to pay any price.

Jesus, I want to live in the power of your love. I'm not afraid to lay aside my will for yours because I know that your ways are higher than mine. There is nothing I have that didn't come from you, except for the yes, which streams from my heart. I am fully committed to you. I surrender every thought, desire, and action, laying them before your throne.

Holy Hands

See how his hands hold unlimited power!
But he never uses it in anger,
for he is always holy, displaying his glory.
—Song of Songs 5:14

The same arms that hold the universe cradle your heart. Our glorious God, whose hands are full of power, welcome you with love and mercy. An inferno of holy passion, released through Jesus' nail-pierced hands, has cleansed you and made you whole.

God's omnipotence is displayed through all that He accomplishes, and all that He accomplishes is pure and magnificent. Nothing is too hard for Him. With His hands, He crushes the enemy, yet reaches for you in tenderness. He's handed you the keys to His kingdom, and His blessing is upon your life through the power of covenant. His unlimited power is always used for your good. His hands are mighty and effective in accomplishing exactly what is in His heart. Jesus' love for you is so extravagant that He's tattooed your name in the palm of His hand.

Lord, every time I think about you, I discover new and glorious treasures. It will take all of eternity to experience the many facets of your magnificent power, beauty, and love. You never cease to amaze me. Thank you for pulling me close with such tenderness and encouragement. I love you. Let me feel the warmth of your embrace today.

Mercy

See how his hands hold unlimited power!
But *he never uses it in anger,*
for he is always holy, displaying his glory.
—Song of Songs 5:14

What a merciful God He is! His love and patience go beyond human reasoning. Though He could wipe out the entire planet and punish us for our sin, He doesn't. Instead, He forgives us and empowers us for victory.

Our sovereign King rules the earth with deep compassion. In exchange for our frailty, He hands us His strength. His wise skill and awesome power shine throughout eternity. His deeds display His unparalleled might, yet with kindness and goodness. If you look for His blessing upon your life, you'll find it. There is always something to be thankful for—always a gift of provision to be recognized. His activity and faithfulness can be seen in the rising moon and setting sun, given to you with each breath you take. No one else can do what He does. No one else will love you so perfectly.

Jesus, you are holy and faithful. Everything you do is above reproach. Your unparalleled power, coupled with outrageous mercy, is an example all should follow. Give me your heart towards others, so I will never withhold compassion and forgiveness to those you so freely gave your life for.

The Depths

His innermost place is a work of art—
so beautiful and bright.
How magnificent and noble is this one—
covered in majesty!
—Song of Songs 5:14

His innermost place can also be translated, "His belly" or "His yearning heart." In this passage of Scripture, this particular Hebrew word conveys tender compassion and a yearning heart. In our weakness, the Lord approaches us with compassion. In our sin, He bends down and lifts us up with mercy. Out of the His innermost being flow rivers of love able to quench the thirsty soul.

We are called to search the depths of God—to know Him intimately and in ways few have known Him. His presence is limitless. His love is captivating. His beauty creates greater heights of inspiration. His smile chases away the darkness. The mystery of the cross floods your life with glory. The realms of holy revelation are open for exploration. May His secrets be unveiled to you today.

Father, your love is a mystery that I love to uncover. Your tender care is astonishing. The longer I live, the more I want to know you—especially the inexplicable and veiled things of your kingdom. Touch the eyes of my heart and illuminate my understanding, so I can see truths that have long been hidden.

Magnificent

His innermost place is a work of art—
so beautiful and bright.
***How magnificent and noble is this one—
covered in majesty!***

—Song of Songs 5:14

How majestic is this One who sits upon the throne of glory! God's holiness is so pure that instead of it driving a wedge between Him and us, it makes Him approachable. As we lift our voices and declare His majesty and omnipotence, He smiles and replies with love. We bow before the Creator of heaven and earth, and He swoops us up in His arms and kisses us on the cheek.

The character of God has been passed down to His children. Jesus is wrapped in splendor and extends His garment to cover you as well. He has engraved His nature upon your heart. As He is, so are you—holy, merciful, powerful, and righteous. All that you do and say should reflect your royal inheritance. The holy scepter has been extended to you, and you've been given the authority to bring His kingdom to earth—the kingdom that lives inside of you.

Father, I stand in awe before your holy throne. You are magnificent and glorious—a sight that leaves me undone, although I've barely caught a glimpse. Help me live a life that pleases you and reflects the glorious kingdom I've been adopted into.

Steadfast

He's steadfast in all he does.
His ways are the ways of righteousness,
based on truth and holiness.
None can rival him,
but all will be amazed by him.
—Song of Songs 5:15

*J*esus does not waiver under pressure. He is steady and constant, stable and reliable. Everything He does is based on purity, holiness, and truth. His ways are always executed with strength and dignity. He does not fail.

The dependable ways of our King are like marble pillars established upon a foundation of righteousness. There is no other, in heaven or on earth, who compares. He relentlessly pursues you because He loves you and knows you need Him. Nothing you can do will ever make Him change His mind about you. He is constant. His wholehearted dedication to you is unreserved. His judgment upon your life is without fault and led by mercy. He is the Rock of Ages. The strength of your life forever.

Lord, I want to be like you—constant in compassion, relentless in my pursuit of you, and unshakable in my faith. Thank you for your commitment to me, for the way you tirelessly encourage me when I'm weary, and for celebrating even my smallest victories. Your strength has become my foundation and source of joy.

September

Unrivaled

He's steadfast in all he does.
His ways are the ways of righteousness,
based on truth and holiness.
None can rival him,
but all will be amazed by him.
—Song of Songs 5:15

*J*esus is awe inspiring! He has no equal. His love is unparalleled in every way. Tender and merciful, He's also the One who fights for you with unrivaled power.

Nothing can withstand this One in whom all of heaven and earth will one day bow. He is stronger than the power of the enemy. The intensity of His love will conquer every fear you face. Say His name and the storms are silenced. The glory of His presence is a shield around you. His kiss strengthens you for battle, while His breath lifts you to the heights of victory. The roar of His voice breaks the chains of bondage. Not even death could hold Him. In Him you are free!

Jesus, you are my strength, my motivation, and my reason for living. In you, I lack nothing. Anchor me with your love. Let your presence surround me like a shield. When I'm weak, your glory is like a pep talk, reminding me of who I am. You restore my roar and give me confidence.

Stand Amazed

He's steadfast in all he does.
His ways are the ways of righteousness,
based on truth and holiness.
None can rival him,
but **all will be amazed by him**.

—SONG OF SONGS 5:15

Stand in awe of this One who breathes light into darkness, created the world from nothing, and taught your heart to beat. His voice thunders, breaking the chains of injustice. He sings His songs of love over the earth and sets the captives free.

The Lord over all creation calls you His child, friend, and partner. He came to give you an abundant life. Your existence is the very manifestation of His love. His glory is like fire in your bones, and your fiery zeal is a threat to the kingdom of darkness. Jesus rescues you from bondage and causes your heart to sing. His Kingdom knows no end. His power is unmatched. His mercy is never ending.

Lord, you amaze me. You deserve my highest praise! No matter what I face, I want to honor you with absolute trust and complete surrender. You are my Tower of Strength. Righteous King, your dominion and authority shine throughout eternity. I am totally and completely secure in your unfathomable love.

His Kisses Are Sweet

Most sweet are his kisses, even his whispers of love.
He is delightful in every way
and perfect from every viewpoint.
—Song of Songs 5:16

Jesus' kiss of sacred intimacy awakens you to life and catapults you on an eternal path of discovery. Nothing competes with His love. It is pure, empowering, and unique. Nothing is more pleasing or transformational than knowing Him. Every pleasure and temporary joy fades in comparison to the touch of the Holy Spirit upon your life. Just pondering His love can overwhelm your heart with bliss.

You experience His faithful kisses each day in many different ways. When He whispers your name, it sparks hope and faith. His kisses of peace soothe the most anxious mind. When darkness overshadows you, He orchestrates the dawn. Every gloomy thought is infused with truth when He pulls you close. Pay attention to His many blessings upon your life—they are the sweet kisses of a loving King.

Lord, I'm coming close with expectancy enflaming my soul. Your kiss upon my life has both satisfied me and left me longing for more. Your love floods my veins and infuses every cell. I want all of you in every way. I must experience every aspect of your glorious love.

Altogether Lovely

Most sweet are his kisses, even his whispers of love.
He is delightful in every way
and perfect from every viewpoint.

—SONG OF SONGS 5:16

The goodness and beauty of the Lord is found all around you. Seek the light of His face in every sunrise, hear His decrees of breakthrough crashing upon the waves, and reflect upon His wisdom as the stars shine firmly in place. You will find His comfort, joy, and love surrounding you everywhere you look.

Life with the Lord is meant to be captivating and delightful. It stirs our hearts with mystery yet settles every rattling confusion. His love is beyond comprehension. His mercy is above the heavens. Everything about Him is fascinating, beautiful, and gracious. The majestic Lord of all creation loves us perfectly because He knows exactly what we need. He is altogether lovely.

Jesus, you've created a life for me that reflects your goodness and compassion. Help me to remain focused on the beauty of life and not become distracted by the darkness that tries to intimidate me. You are my delight, and today I will count my many blessings, for you are the center of them all.

Let Me Count the Ways

*If you ask me why I love him so, **O brides-to-be,***
it's because there is none like him to me.
Everything about him fills me with holy desire!
And now he is my beloved—my friend forever.

—Song of Songs 5:16

*E*very day is a fresh opportunity to remind yourself of the goodness of God. Focus on His faithfulness. Aim to be more optimistic, and chances are you'll have less anxiety, more peace, and more joy. Light always illuminates the darkness. This is true even in the way you think—truth, faith, and hope will chase away oppression and pessimism.

Find things to be thankful for, whether you're in a season of joy or a time of sorrow. Let your thoughts be filled with His love for you and revive memories of how He's come through in the past. Reminisce with the Lord, allowing your heart to overflow with gratitude. Praise Him for all He has done and declare His truth over every situation you're facing.

Father, thank you for the many ways you love me. You have proven your faithfulness to me, time and time again. Help me to become more aware of the blessings in my life than I am of the difficulties and disappointments. Today I choose to shake off a negative mentality and to embrace an attitude of gratefulness and optimism. I choose to believe you are good, and with you, anything is possible!

Holy Desire

If you ask me why I love him so, O brides-to-be,
it's because there is none like him to me.
Everything about him fills me with holy desire!
And now he is my beloved—my friend forever.

—Song of Songs 5:16

The more time you spend with the Lord, the greater your desire for Him. He satisfies the deepest hunger of your soul yet inflames your being with longing too profound for words. It is almost impossible to voice what you sense when He is near. Holy desire will propel you into a life of encounters with His love.

His ways are trustworthy, and His plans for your life are good. As you become fully convinced of this, it will change your prayer life. No longer will you cry out with prayers that are diluted by doubt. Instead, peace will settle you, and you'll be more in tune with His Spirit. Faith will explode inside of you as matters that once stole your affection become insignificant compared to His glory. Let holy desire for Him, and nothing more, overcome everything else, and you will discover a life of peace and joy unlike anything you've ever known.

Lord, I lay every burden and distracting thought at your feet. Fill me with holy desire to know you more. Fan away the shadows of commotion inside my head, which disrupt our connection. When you are near, nothing else matters. Let me become so aware of your nearness that I become tethered to your heart at all times.

Friend

If you ask me why I love him so, O brides-to-be,
it's because there is none like him to me.
Everything about him fills me with holy desire!
And now he is my beloved—my friend forever.

—Song of Songs 5:16

*H*e is Father, Son, and Holy Spirit. He is Creator, Savior, and Counselor. But He is also your Friend who enjoys your company and loves to be around you. You never have to try to impress Him because He already knows everything about you. You can tell Him anything, without feeling judged or misunderstood. He knows when to speak and when to hold you in silent wonder.

Friendship with the Lord brushes away the pollution of the world, which causes you to see things through a distorted lens. When you include Him in every conversation, seek His wisdom, and open yourself to His point of view, life becomes enjoyable. Knowing He's with you and cares about the things you care about makes your burden lighter.

Jesus, you are my dearest and closest Friend. It's amazing that you, the King of the universe, could enjoy my company. Even when I get distracted and neglect to spend time with you, you reach out to me. You're so kind. I want to know you more and become acquainted with what moves your heart. I want to know the sound of your laugh and to see you in the eyes of a stranger. Come walk with me today.

In You

Brides-to-be
O rarest of beauty
where then has your lover gone?
—Song of Songs 6:1

Everyone was created with a specific facet of God's character and beauty. No one on earth carries exactly what you do in the way that you do. You were created to be a unique example of your heavenly Father. What you have been entrusted with must be shared, or you will deny the world of God's gift to them through you.

Whether what you carry is meant to touch a small circle of people around you or to bring worldwide revival isn't important. What's important is that you believe that you have something to give, even if it's something as simple as an encouraging word. It's time to shine! It's time to let the glory of God within you find an outlet.

Father, some days I feel I have so much to offer, and other days I wonder if I have anything at all. I know you've anointed me for a special purpose. Highlight the attributes and beauty within me that you've called me to share, and I will pay attention. I won't hold back, nor will I overthink and try to work out every detail. I will simply allow the best parts of me to shine, so the world will catch a glimpse of you.

Point the Way

Brides-to-be
O rarest of beauty
where then has your lover gone?
We long to see him too.

—Song of Songs 6:1

*N*ever be hesitant to let your love for Him spill out and splash on those around you. The world is looking for perfect love. Every person on earth was created to know Him. They carry questions that can only be answered by encounters with Him. Tired of dry and lifeless religion, they long to know the One who has moved your heart so profoundly.

Many people live in a state of turmoil. They have closed their ears to condemning Christians for good reason. They long for truth but need to encounter it through you. When you show unconditional love, when you have a different approach to life, and convey hope in times of hopelessness, people notice. Weary hearts need a touch from God, and He wants to touch them through you. Once they encounter Him, they will be gripped with holy passion and begin the Shulamite's journey for themselves.

Father, let your light shine through me. I want to be so confident in your truth and power that I don't hold back when someone's in need. Give me the words to say when someone opens up to me. May my life be a testimony of your faithfulness, introducing others to the greatness of knowing you.

Lead by Example

Where may we find him?
We will follow you as you seek after him.
—Song of Songs 6:1

*W*hat an honor it is to spark hope and awakening in people's lives. Every word you speak, even your posts on social media, have the potential to kindle a slumbering spirit. Your attitudes and actions have the power to revive or destroy those around you. You have more power than you could possibly imagine.

You carry a spiritual torch within you that can light the way for others. Don't hide it or allow selfishness to snuff it out. Give people glimpses of truth by being someone they can look up to. They don't want you to wear a mask of false perfection. They want to know that God is relatable, approachable, and real. They want to understand how you can remain calm in the midst of chaos. They crave peace when war is raging in their souls. You don't have to have all the answers. You only need to point them to the One who does.

Jesus, help me to be a true reflection of who you are. As my life conveys your goodness, may the faith of others come to life. As I live in authenticity, allowing others to catch glimpses of my struggles and breakthroughs, let their desire for you be stirred. Make yourself real to others as I live before them in truth.

Community

My lover has gone down
into his garden of delight,
the place where his spices grow,
to feast with those pure in heart.

—Song of Songs 6:2

One of the most beautiful revelations of all is that the Holy Spirit has chosen to live within believers. We are His garden of delight. Jesus came from heaven to fill the earth with His glory. He came to fill you.

Together we are His body—the expression of His love. He tenderly cares for each of us, often revealing His love through the words and deeds of others. We were created for community. We need each other's support, inspiration, comfort, and friendship. Don't limit yourself by withdrawing and waiting for the perfect opportunity to extend the hand of friendship. In some seasons, you will be the recipient; in others, you will give what you have to offer. But in all seasons, it's important to surround yourself with people who challenge you to be the best version of yourself possible. There is strength in finding where you belong.

Father, surround me with people who share my values and seek you with a humble heart. Bless me with a group of people where I will feel celebrated, known, and accepted. Thank you for trusting me with gifts that you want me to share. As I seek to grow in you, I know you will show me where I belong.

Spice of Life

My lover has gone down
into his garden of delight,
the place where his spices grow,
to feast with those pure in heart.

—Song of Songs 6:2

Never try to fit in by being just like everyone around you. You are one of a kind—created to be exactly the way you are. The gifts you have inside of you are as diverse as the spices that make up His garden. Together the fragrance is refreshing and clean. Individually, they are designed for a specific purpose.

Spices give flavor and awaken our taste buds, just as your personality adds zest to the lives you touch. Embrace who God created you to be and enjoy those around you. Accept yourself and allow yourself to have fun. Find the things in life that bring you joy. Give every situation the chance to mold you into a confident, caring, and unselfish human being. Let others be blessed by knowing you. You are amazing, just the way you are!

Father, today I choose to be happy being me. With all my quirks and unique viewpoints, not everyone is going to like me, but you do and that's what matters. I'm comfortable being who I am. My individuality adds spice to the lives of those around me. I don't have to impress everyone, but I do need to live in a way that honors you. Let my personality mingle with the beauty of yours.

Pure of Heart

My lover has gone down
into his garden of delight,
the place where his spices grow,
to feast with those pure in heart.
I know we shall find him there.

—SONG OF SONGS 6:2

Jesus delights in your worship and dances within the streams of praise that flow from your heart. When He draws near, your adoration fills Him with pleasure. His heart feasts on the purity of your devotion. Even now, as your thoughts turn toward Him, you've captured His attention.

The Lord seeks those whose hearts are loyal to Him and your consecrated life has become His delight. Guard your walk, and fill your life with joy and righteous pleasures. Be quick to forgive and even quicker to say you're sorry to those you've hurt. Never let offenses take root within your heart, and if they have, allow His love to pluck them up. You were created to love and be loved in the most fulfilling way.

Jesus, all that I am is yours. I've devoted my life to becoming one with you, thinking like you, loving as you do, and discerning what moves your heart. I submit this day to you. All that awaits me, we will face together. Be blessed by the longing of my heart to honor you. May it become a continuous flow of pure devotion.

I Know

My lover has gone down
into his garden of delight,
the place where his spices grow,
to feast with those pure in heart.
I know we shall find him there.

—SONG OF SONGS 6:2

As you grow in the Lord, you don't always realize how much you're changing and maturing, until a situation arises that evokes an unexpected response. Courage replaces fear, hope overrides discouragement, and your once-impatient frustrations turn into patient replies. You're becoming more like Jesus every day.

Confidence rises within you as you recognize the power of His transformation within you. Even on your worst days, you know His power is alive within. The revelations that have been unveiled to you become a foundation for you to stand upon. Regardless of what you go through, you will always know the way into His presence. Never doubt the power of your history with Him. It has paved a path straight into His arms, and you can follow it forever.

Lord, you are the way, the truth, and the life that has transformed me. Thank you for the way you have woven yourself into my spirit. All that I am, I am because of you. Continue to unveil to me the revelation of who I am in you. I know that no matter what, you are here, alive inside of me.

Within

He is within me—I am his garden of delight.
I have him fully and now he fully has me!
—Song of Songs 6:3

Stop for a moment and think about this: the Spirit of God lives inside of you. He's not far away. He doesn't come for occasional visits. He's saturating every part of you right now, infusing you with the very essence of His glory.

You are the vessel He chose to pour Himself into. This same Spirit that raised Christ from the dead has come to make you a powerful overcomer. His anointing and power do not diminish based on how you feel. He is the one constant in your life—the one thing that anchors you when storms rise. Fear is not your nature. Failure is not your destiny. Confusion cannot dwell with the perfected wisdom that has made its home inside you. The glory of the Lord, His healing power, the pure and unshakable nature of God—each has become your portion. You have everything you need to live a victorious life and impart this blessing to others.

Spirit of God, rise within me. Let me feel the splendor of your presence and the blaze of glory that is a part of me. Consume every dreary and lifeless mind-set. Wash away all that has been muddied by my past. You are my joy forever—the truth I need to live in victory.

Fully Yours

He is within me—I am his garden of delight.
I have him fully and now he fully has me!

—SONG OF SONGS 6:3

*Y*ou are His, and He is yours! Jesus gave His life for you so you can live in perfect harmony with Him. You were created for His pleasure, destined to discover the joy of living without compromise diverting your heart. Nothing stands in the way of true devotion. Nothing can separate you from this love if you don't let it.

The dance of sacrificial love has never looked as beautiful as when you let Him take the lead. No longer are you focused on yourself but rather in pouring your life out to the Lord. Pure agape love never thinks about what it receives. It gives itself fully to the object of its affection. This is what Jesus has done for you—loved you without any reservation or concern for how you may or may not respond. If you love the Lord with all your heart, soul, mind, and strength, you'll experience freedom in new measure.

Father, I want to love you with purity and unselfishness. I give you all that I am and all that I'm not. You are my true love. May all that is within me bring you glory. Help me to never allow my light to grow dim, but if it does, blow upon my life and ignite my passion once again.

United

The Bridegroom-King
O my beloved, you are lovely.
When I see you in your beauty,
I see a radiant city where we will dwell as one.
—Song of Songs 6:4

*Y*ou are like a radiant city, shining brightly for the world to see. Filled with the brilliant splendor of God, you've been called to shine into the darkest places on earth. Evil cannot overwhelm the glory that lives inside of you. Desert seasons cannot suffocate what you carry.

When you immerse yourself in the radiant beams that stream from His heart, they burst out of all that you say and do. The light of love—and the revelation of all Jesus is—can be seen in you. People notice you, whether you realize it or not. Love has changed you, and they want to experience it too. Never doubt the tangible presence of God inside of you. Not only do you bring to others the light of Christ, you also bring to Him delight and pleasure like none other.

Lord, I want to live from the inside out. I want my faith to be uncompromising and true. You are the fire that floods my veins and the glory I love to share with others. Help me to remember I'm an example of your radiance in the earth. With all of my strength, I want to walk with uncompromising commitment and devotion to you. May others be drawn to the kindness of your touch.

More Than Any Other

More pleasing than any pleasure,
more delightful than any delight,
you have ravished my heart,
stealing away my strength to resist you.
—SONG OF SONGS 6:4

Imagine, if you will, a most beautiful sunset—striking colors of scarlet red and vivid orange that leave you awestruck. Captivated by the beauty of God's creation, you can scarcely look away. As it washes over you, both peace and delight soothe your soul. Even the birds of the air take note and rise to bask in its calming beauty.

The Master Artist, this perfect Creator who breathed the world's most exquisite sights into existence, says that *you* are His most beautiful creation. He admires your beauty the same way that you look at a sunset—you leave Him breathless. Nothing compares to the delight He feels when He gazes upon you.

Right now, take time to be still and allow Him a moment to enjoy you. He's gazing at you with love. Say no words, do nothing but be in this moment with Him. Let His love wash over you today. To Him, you are not just beautiful; you are beauty itself.

Father, come enjoy my offering of love today. I still my mind and turn my heart to you with total abandon. You have made me beautiful, and in you, I am whole. You love me purely. Come, and we will lavish each other with holy love.

You Ravish His Heart

More pleasing than any pleasure,
more delightful than any delight,
you have ravished my heart,
stealing away my strength to resist you.
Even hosts of angels stand in awe of you.

—Song of Songs 6:4

Every time you've worshipped the Lord amid questions and pain, each moment you've run to Him for help, remaining loyal when temptation raged—you have caught His attention. Your loyalty and love have made it impossible for Him to resist you.

Let this revelation sink deeply into your consciousness: you have ravished His heart. Your unrelenting passion fulfills a longing within the omnipotent and perfect God. Nothing touches Him more than your devotion, especially when everything around you feels unstable. What an honor it is to know that your worship—your ceaseless desire to live for Him—delights His heart. Never withhold it. He has no strength to resist you. You have conquered the Conqueror with your relentless devotion!

Father, I bow before you in humility. I long to bring you the love that touches your heart. I'm privileged to be the child that thrills you with true worship. This passion you have placed inside my chest beats to bless you forever.

Irresistible

Turn your eyes from me; I can't take it anymore!
I can't resist the passion of these eyes that I adore.
Overpowered by a glance, my ravished heart—undone.
Held captive by your love, I am truly overcome!

—Song of Songs 6:5

The most powerful One, who has no rival, is undone when you look at Him. You have the capacity to overwhelm the heart of God. Don't rush off without absorbing this truth. Let this revelation incubate within you: you are the object of God's desire. You, despite your weaknesses and with all your imperfections, are the one He adores. "Look away," He says to you. "I can't handle the passion that streams from your eyes."

You are the wonder that the angels cannot ignore. You are a vessel of His divinity that all of heaven and hell take note of. When the name above all names spills from your lips in wondrous songs of adoration, the presence of God fills the atmosphere. He's enamored with you. Blessed by the way you've built your life on the foundation of His love.

Be blessed by my love, Lord! You have welcomed me into your presence, and I stand before you in awe. I'm undone by you, that you would take the time to know me and to be blessed by my insufficient and insignificant words of praise. It seems that you deserve so much more, so I simply surrender it all and pray that hearts around the world would be awakened by your love.

Held by Love

Turn your eyes from me; I can't take it anymore!
I can't resist the passion of these eyes that I adore.
Overpowered by a glance, my ravished heart—undone.
Held captive by your love, I am truly overcome!

—SONG OF SONGS 6:5

It wasn't the power of the enemy that held your Lord to the cross. It would have been easy for Jesus to come down and walk away from such horrible torture. It was His love for you that left Him no other choice.

Even before you were born, He knew you. He already saw your eyes of passion that would one day become His inheritance. He longed to be your Bridegroom, even before the earth was established. Now, your passionate, love-filled worship has become the fulfillment of His desire. Never doubt how much power your worshipping words hold—He is eternally held captive by your love! This same passion has the power to silence the enemy and bring God rushing to your aid. What strength you have! You truly are more than a conqueror.

Lord, you have covered me with your glory, yet honor me as if this beauty were my own. Your ways are higher than I can grasp, yet I reach to hold your truth within me forever. Keep my heart before you always. Never let me stray. Your love for me has left me with no rebuttal. I want to love you and please you forever.

Devoted

For *your undying devotion to me*
is the most yielded sacrifice.
—Song of Songs 6:5

Nothing goes unnoticed by the Lord. He holds every tear, knows the times you've said yes to Him when it was difficult to do so, and understands the questions that cause your heart and mind to conflict. These moments of undying devotion to God are precious to Him.

Never doubt whether He's listening or watching—He always is. He sees every sacrifice you make. The things you've cast aside to follow Him have caught His attention. Your love touches His heart profoundly. Your devotion rises to Him as a pleasing offering. Jesus is cheering you on. He champions your cause and will bless all that you've laid at His feet. Don't give up! Lift your hands and raise your voice in songs of praise and shouts of victory! He is even more devoted to you than you are to Him.

What an honor it is to follow you, Lord. All that I am and hold dear, I submit to you. May my love bless you, like a costly and fragrant offering. May my worship be a pleasing sound to your ears. May my total devotion always be the guiding force of all that I say and do.

Shine

The shining of your spirit
shows how you have taken my truth
to become balanced and complete.

—Song of Songs 6:6

How amazing it is to know that the Spirit of God lives inside you. You are holy and righteous because of love's perfect sacrifice. You will always be radiant because of the most glorious One who abides inside of you. However, in this verse Jesus isn't talking about how beautiful *His* Spirit is within you. He's talking about the beauty of *your* spirit.

Your yielded will is your gift to Him. It is yours and yours alone. You shine with brilliance as you live before Him in full abandon. As you depend on Him and continually seek His presence, you're becoming the mature and glorious bride He knew you would be. You're learning who you are in Him and discovering your true identity. Your spirit, in fact your entire being, radiates with beauty.

Jesus, I want my life to be a gift of never-ending enjoyment to you. I desire to glow with the glory that streams from a grateful heart. Let my beauty be untainted by the lure of the world. I give you all that I am, forever.

Balanced

The shining of your spirit
shows how **you have taken my truth
to become balanced** and complete.

—SONG OF SONGS 6:6

*G*od's Word is perfect nourishment to your spirit. As we study the Scriptures and meditate upon the truth within, we become unshakeable in our faith. Diligently spending time in His Word is vital. It is the foundation of everything we believe. It isn't enough to hear good preaching; we must discover the depths of His Word for ourselves. We must personally wield its power in order to realize its strength.

There must be balance in our lives, and God's Word is the fulcrum on which we rest. Having balance means that we not only study our Bibles, but we are intimately acquainted with the God of the Bible. Not only are we at ease in His arms and enjoy His love, but we also eat His Word and strengthen our faith.

Father, thank you for your Word. It lights the path before me and anchors my soul. It is the truth that brings me comfort when the storms of life rage against my soul. Deliver me from any mind-sets that are contrary to your Word. Let my spirit and soul live in agreement with your promises, for they are faithful and true.

Complete

The shining of your spirit
shows how you have taken my truth
to become balanced **and complete.**
—Song of Songs 6:6

*G*od Himself is the answer to your every prayer. He pours out miracles, releases healing, strengthens the weary, and imparts perfect wisdom for every situation. His grace and mercy have no limit. His power is unstoppable. His hands, which formed time and space, have placed you in His heart, where you are safe and empowered. You are complete in Christ.

Breakthrough, hope, health, favor—anything you could possibly need—is found in Him. Your inadequacies only serve to drive you closer to Him and remind you of your continuous need for Him. He loves to fill the areas that we yield to His sovereignty. Surrender everything today. In your frailty, rejoice! He truly does equip, empower, and perfect you.

Father, you are my strength, my answer, and the wind that stirs up my faith. I lack nothing when I release everything to you. I am not defeated, insignificant, or forgotten. I have your ear and you know what I need. You are faithful to fulfill each promise you've made. Even now, I feel you refreshing my soul. You will never let me down. In you, I am complete.

Emotion

Your beautiful blushing cheeks
reveal how real your passion is for me,
even hidden behind your veil of humility.
—Song of Songs 6:7

Cheeks speak of your emotions. You should never be ashamed of your feelings or hide them from God. Frustration and sorrow need to be processed with the Lord. Anger should catapult you into victory against the enemy and stir righteousness inside you. Outrageous zeal and passion for the Lord's presence is meant to be embraced and expressed.

Be true to what you feel and don't ignore what is happening inside of you. Don't hold on to pain, fear, and unforgiveness. Learn healthy ways to walk through each situation with the Lord. The stirring you experience within should always lead you to Him. He is the best Counselor. How beautiful and honoring it is to the Lord when we take all that we feel and talk it through with Him.

Lord, you have created me with so many emotions. Sometimes they try to steal my attention away from you, but instead, I will embrace each one and bring it to you. Let each of my feelings propel me closer to you. Purify any tainted mind-set. Unlock my heart, so I don't bury or ignore my feelings and instead find the freedom they release to my soul.

Passion

Your beautiful blushing cheeks
reveal ***how real your passion is for me***,
even hidden behind your veil of humility.
—SONG OF SONGS 6:7

*G*od's presence is meant to be enjoyed. Release your inhibitions and don't try to make sense of something that is spiritual. His ways are higher than yours. Your mind cannot wrap itself around what you experience during blissful encounters with His glory. Simply embrace the mystery. The depths of His heart are calling out to yours.

Passion for the Lord is real. It's holy. It fuels your heart with motivation and boldness to pursue Him even when He feels distant. You were created for His presence. You were designed to experience love that cannot be defined by human interpretation. This passion is inside of you now, but its fires must be stirred and tended to. They are fanned by His nearness but must be ignited by your worship. Never let them go out.

Lord, my heart is overwhelmed with desire for your tangible touch. I reach to you with something much more profound than my words or actions. I reach with a passion that burns inside my chest. It cannot be denied. Engage my heart with holy encounters of your love. Fill me. Meet with me. Let me see you, face-to-face.

Humility

Your beautiful blushing cheeks
reveal how real your passion is for me,
even **hidden behind your veil of humility**.

—Song of Songs 6:7

*I*t is your hidden life, unknown to anyone but God, which makes you attractive to the Bridegroom. What you do in secret, where no one else can see, is precious to Him. The prayers, the tears, the crazy dances of uninhibited zeal, and the holy moments of dedication move His heart. Beneath the veil of His glory, He pulls you close and returns your affection with His own. Nothing compares to these divine encounters of His love.

These private times are meant to catapult us into a life of true greatness. We take the secrets of His heart that He reveals and pour them out to those in need. It is our life of humility, not bragging about our encounters or boasting about our gifts, which make us beautiful. We simply embrace what we receive in the chambers of His presence, then use it to help others.

Lord, you see through every intention. Fine-tune my motives, so that all I do is honorable and pure. Let every prayer be seasoned with humility and washed in the waters of holiness. Help me to grow in grace and tenderness, taking what I've received in your presence and faithfully releasing it to others, without seeking approval or endorsement from anyone but you.

Chosen

I could have chosen any from among the vast multitude
of royal ones who follow me.
—Song of Songs 6:8

You have been chosen by God, set apart for His glory and honor. You are one of a kind, created for a divine purpose. Nobody brings Him what you do. The love and devotion that stream from your heart are unique and exclusive. What you offer the Lord is beautiful.

When others overlook you, remember that God's desire is fixed on you. You don't have to wave your arms and shout for Him to hear. You already have His heart and His attention. Simply grasp the warmth of His love within you and love Him in return. He sees. He knows. Even when His presence feels clouded and obscured, He's there. Seasons of silence will only serve to sharpen your hearing and enable you to recognize His whisper. Never despise the seasons of waiting because they will soon reveal His faithfulness. Fasten your heart to His and hold on for the ride of your life!

Father, you always make me feel special. Thank you for choosing me—for placing your anointing and gifts within me. My life is not my own because you have set me apart and sealed me for your purpose. Help me to remember the great value you see in me. Your love has become the assurance of my victory.

Royalty

I could have chosen any from among the vast multitude
of *royal ones who follow me*.

—Song of Songs 6:8

*H*ave you ever thought of yourself as royalty? If not, it's time to start. You are the child of the Most High God and the bride of the King of kings. His glory outshines the brightest sun, and you were created in His image. You will reign with Him for all eternity, but He has called you to begin that journey now.

Now is the time when your words carry the power to transform lives. Right now, your faith matters. Now is the time to stand in your identity and release His power to those in need. At this very moment, your words, spoken in agreement with His, cause shifts in the atmosphere. As royalty, you must think differently. Align your thoughts with His. Let your speech agree with His, regardless of how outrageous it sounds. You are a royal bride, representing her majestic Bridegroom and His Kingdom.

Lord, I want to carry myself as your confident bride and represent you well. Rising within me is the truth that I am royalty and you are my Sovereign King. Your scepter is extended toward me, and you have invited me into your holy presence. You have clothed me in glory and together we will release it upon the earth.

October

Glorious Obsession

But one is my beloved dove—unrivaled in your beauty,
without equal, beyond compare,
the perfect one, the only one for me.
—Song of Songs 6:9

Over and over again, Jesus affirms you and boasts of His love for you. At times it may seem redundant, but He knows how quickly you forget. He doesn't just want you to get the message; He wants you to hear it enough to really believe it. Though His love may sound like a fairy tale, it's true—a perfect love story. The way He sees you is beyond human reasoning, so He tells you, again and again.

If it sounds like the Lord has an obsession, it's because He does! Jesus is totally obsessed with you in the most holy way. He reminds you repeatedly how beautiful and powerful you are, so that insecurity and fear won't cause you to forsake your calling. When you're secure in your identity, you walk with boldness and poise. Humility seasons your attitude when you know that it's only by His grace that you stand. The extravagant love of the Lord is the kiss of promise upon your life, and He will remind you for eternity.

Lord, your ways constantly astound me! To think that I move your heart, the same way you move mine, is a mystery that I willingly embrace. Thank you for reminding me of your love. Thank you for settling my heart with your empowering touch.

Perfect

But one is my beloved dove—unrivaled in your beauty,
without equal, beyond compare,
the perfect one, the only one for me.
—Song of Songs 6:9

The love of God and the way He sees us certainly is an enigma. It defies reason. It sees things that no one else does. It believes the very best about you. To top it off, this all-knowing God, who is the very definition of wisdom, calls you perfect. Perfect!

God views you through the eyes of love—not love that is blind, but love that sees clearly. He doesn't overlook the areas you need to overcome, or pretend they aren't there. Instead, He leads you into encounters with His truth until truth becomes the desire of your heart. He encourages you as a victorious conqueror and leads you on a journey to become that person, rather than focusing on your sin, weaknesses, or failure. You are not defined by your past or your mistakes. You are defined by what He says you are—perfect.

Lord, your mercy has lifted my burdens. Your grace has empowered me and given me eyes to see myself the way that you see me. Now I want to live in the light of this revelation towards others. Enable me to tap into your viewpoint and to see others through this lens of mercy and grace.

Above Reproach

Others see your beauty and sing of your joy.
Brides and queens chant your praise:
"How blessed is she!"
—Song of Songs 6:9

As you recognize your royal identity and become secure in who He says you are, you will see life differently. You will embrace your calling as His perfect partner. You will speak, act, and believe on a higher level than you have before. Suddenly, impossible situations don't scare you—they embolden you until a roar of faith explodes from your spirit.

When you step into your calling as His bride, people can't help but take notice. The grace of God shining through you is attractive, drawing men close. You aren't afraid to love others without exception, while standing firm in your convictions. This type of seasoned compassion is attractive, while legalistic tones push people away. Even those who don't share your beliefs will speak highly of you and trust you, all because of the way you speak the truth in love.

Father, I want to live above reproach. I want to roar with holy passion for your ways and to love others unconditionally. Help me to represent you well as I embrace your call upon my life. Bless me with the grace to shine your radiant splendor and tender compassion into the lives of those I meet.

Arise

Look at you now—
arising as the dayspring of the dawn,
fair as the shining moon.

—Song of Songs 6:10

Out of the darkness, a light is rising. It's chasing away the shadows and shining in brilliant splendor. This is a picture of you. You are like the dawn of a new day. His love and encouragement have permeated your beliefs, chased away the fears that held you back, and have transformed you. You've emerged as the morning light, releasing mercy, and bringing hope and refreshing everywhere you go.

You don't have to look outside of yourself for the answers you need because the answers are within. So often we pray for God to break through and shine His light into the darkness, forgetting that the power of His Spirit is within. You can illuminate your trials with hope, draw from the well of His wisdom, and replace lies with His truth. Take a deep breath, stand up tall, and agree with His Word. Agree with the anointing and glory of His Spirit that abides within *you*, radiant one!

God, the glory of your presence has illuminated my entire being. I am filled with hope, truth, and life. The anointing and power of your Spirit flows through my veins. When trouble raises its head, I will declare your Word and stand on its saving grace. I will rise out of every trial in victory because you're alive within me.

Fairer Than the Moon

Look at you now—
arising as the dayspring of the dawn,
fair as the shining moon.
Bright and brilliant as the sun in all its strength.
Astonishing to behold as a majestic army
waving banners of victory.

—Song of Songs 6:10

*L*ight always shines brightest in the darkness. During the gloomiest and most obscure times of your life, look for the light piercing through every crevice it can find. God's glory is always waiting to be discovered. It illuminates every situation, bringing wisdom, peace, joy, and hope. Nothing can stop it.

In this same way, *you* rule over the night. *You* are the breaker of darkness. As the bride of Christ, *you* are rising in beauty and reflecting His glory in the darkest hour. Fear cannot hold you back when love propels you forward. When hopelessness abounds, you become an ambassador of hope. Nothing deters you from releasing His presence into every situation when you believe that His light shines brightly within you.

Lord, for too long I sat back, waiting for you to breakthrough for me, as if what you imparted to me wasn't enough. Now, I choose to believe that your light within me has the power to eradicate darkness. I've already been equipped for victory, and I will embrace this truth with confidence and faith.

As Brilliant as the Sun

Bright and brilliant as the sun in all its strength.
Astonishing to behold as a majestic army
waving banners of victory.
—Song of Songs 6:10

Many argue that God would never give His glory to another, but as His child, you are not another. You are the temple of His Holy Spirit, fearfully and wonderfully made. You are mystically united—one with Christ. The same glory that Jesus exuded when He walked upon the earth abides inside of you. The power that raised Him from the grave is the power that surges through you! Now *you* shine as bright as the sun!

From glory to glory God takes you—each moment, transforming you into the image of Jesus with greater clarity. The enemy knows this and fears you. He doesn't want you to believe it. This is the time to be bold, love fervently, forgive quickly, and to let your light shine. Heal the sick, set the captives free, and believe the impossible is possible! You aren't called to hide; you were created to display His brilliance into every sector of society He has placed you in.

Father, infuse me with the courage and faith to fully embrace all that you say that I am. Help me to never hold back from sharing you, in all your brilliance, to the world. I will walk with you, and together, we will release your light. One day at a time, one person at a time.

Valleys

I decided to go down to the valley streams
where the orchards of the king grow and mature.
—Song of Songs 6:11

We love the mountaintop experiences with the Lord—the seasons when things are going right. We are content to rest in His arms and enjoy the view of victory. Then suddenly, and usually without warning, we go from mountaintop to valley-low. Nothing works out the way we want it to. We long for the heights of victory, rejuvenation, and celebration once again.

Yet, as we mature and become assured of the Lord's love, we recognize that the valleys are a place of incredible transformation. Our worship flows from a depth of surrender, otherwise unknown. Streams of refreshing are purposefully sought instead of expecting to simply receive them. We're refined and emerge as pure as gold. Before long, these seasons are appreciated and not despised. Ultimately, compassion overtakes selfishness, and we step into the valleys for the sole purpose of encouraging others. We have become His confident bride.

Lord, for so long, I despised the valley seasons. I wanted joy and comfort and nothing more. Now, I understand that when I'm weary and dry, I thirst for you even more. Abandoned devotion flows from wells that I didn't know I had. At last I see that whether mountain-high or valley-low, you are with me. For this, I am grateful and will bless others with the joy I've discovered.

Transforming Love

I decided to go down to the valley streams
where ***the orchards of the king grow and mature.
I longed to know if hearts were opening***.
—SONG OF SONGS 6:11

*T*he process of transformation always leads to wholeness, healing, and restoration. There was a time when the church wounded the Shulamite. Those she trusted treated her poorly, because in immaturity, they didn't understand how to love. It's an unpleasant fact that people will hurt and mistreat you, just as you will undoubtedly and often unintentionally hurt others. How you process that pain with the Lord and learn to forgive will determine the level of character that defines your life.

When you cry out for His heart and desire to see others through the eyes of mercy and understanding, He will not deny you. God's healing balm will mend your heart. Miraculously, you'll be able to face those who hurt you and experience no pain. In your prayer time, God's compassion will fill you with desire to pray for them. Regardless of what you've been through, open your heart to love again.

Lord, you've poured out love and mercy to me without measure, and I will do the same. Give me your heart for those who have hurt me. Take my pain as I choose to forgive. Free me and heal me so completely that I truly long to see them become all you've created them to be.

Maturing Love

And the budding vines blooming with new growth?
Has their springtime of passionate love arrived?
—Song of Songs 6:11

This is the mark of maturing love—when our hearts long to see others awakened in their intimacy with Jesus. With the same mercy and compassion that Jesus shows us, we reach out to those who are weak and frail in their faith. We remember that everyone needs encouragement and support, and we're moved to become that blessing for others.

The Lord's desires become ours, and the cries of His heart become important to us as we grow in our relationship with Him. Maturity shifts our focus away from us and concentrates on helping others. Our prayers no longer center on being blessed but instead become arrows of faith for others.

The next time you see someone who needs hope, encourage them. To those who feel rejected, a smile and a kind word may change their day. Look for ways to reach out. Don't despise those who are weary. Be the blessing you'd want someone to be for you.

Lord, fill me with your desire. Stir my heart for those who have never stirred my heart before. Ignite me with zeal to see others grow in their identity. Release your insights for those I encounter, so I can be a blessing to them and see them blossom in their relationship with you.

Unconditional Love

Then suddenly my longings transported me.
My divine desire brought me next to my beloved prince,
sitting with him in his royal chariot.
We were lifted up together!
—Song of Songs 6:12

*L*ove for Jesus will transport you from one level of glory to the next. As you gaze into His eyes, His love for you will stir your love for others. Your longing for more of Him catapults you into your destiny of caring for people.

The intense zeal of God to reach out and bless becomes yours. Unconditional love for the Lord grows into unconditional love for others. Strong desire and enthusiasm moves through your soul to serve His people. As you grow in His image, His love not only transforms you but also transforms those around you. This is the effect of perfect love upon your heart. And when you are no longer only focused on your needs, you can be trusted with deeper revelations of His truth.

Father, your love compels me to reach out to those around me. My mind-set is changing from selfishness to unconditional love for others. I want to be an example of your radiant bride upon the earth. I ask you for a compassionate heart that imparts hope, joy, and healing to those in need. May I be moved by the same things that move you.

Genuine

Zion Maidens, Brides-to-be
Come back! *Return to us, O maiden of his majesty.*
Dance for us as we gaze upon your beauty.
—Song of Songs 6:13

It's rare to encounter authenticity these days. People are so concerned about what others think that they lose themselves in the process. When you meet people who are confident and kind, who embrace their uniqueness, it rouses your own sense of individuality. We are drawn to people who are real and encouraged by those who see life through the lens of joyous expectation.

Positivity is contagious. Happy people attract friends. Hope and joy are infectious. More influential yet are those filled with the Spirit of Life! When God's beauty rests upon you and His joy streams from you, you become a drink of fresh water to those who are thirsty. People are tired of lifeless religion, but they want something powerful that will change their lives. Let them encounter this through you.

Lord, I want to be someone who isn't afraid of being myself. I never want to wear a mask that hides what I feel, just so someone will approve of me. I'm okay with being me. I have a beautiful life, and it's going to get even better. Let my attitude be a breath of fresh air to someone today. Let the fragrance of your love flow through me.

Power and Humility

Why would you seek a mere Shulamite like me?
Why would you want to see my dance of love?

—Song of Songs 6:13

We are continually confronted with our own imperfections. In a sense, this is a good thing. Though we shouldn't focus on our faults, remaining humble and dependent upon the Lord is key to success in His Kingdom. Yes, we are royalty and anointed to speak life in place of death, but it's only to the degree that we recognize our need for Him that we experience an unstoppable flow of power. And when true power flows, watch out!

The greater your anointing, the greater your need for a pure and untainted heart. When you're entrusted with life-changing revelation, it's undeniable; many will look at you with awe. Therefore, power and humility must go hand-in-hand. Every spiritual gift and each sign and wonder that flows through you must always point to Jesus, the One from whom this power flows.

Lord, I want your glory to surge through every prayer I pray. I believe your power is at work in my life and will change those who encounter it. I yield my heart and every motivation at your feet—purify me. May I remain humble and live before you and others with integrity, so your power will flow through me.

The Dance of Love

The Bridegroom-King
*Because you dance so gracefully,
as though you danced with angels!*
—Song of Songs 6:13

Your life of unrelenting devotion to God and your willingness to love others as you are loved causes the angels to dance. Go ahead and join them! Let your movements of unrestrained praise release you into new levels of joy and freedom. May your prayers flow in unison with the Spirit of God. May you dance upon His cloud of glory and sense the angels that surround you.

Your dance of love is beautiful to the Lord, even if you feel as if you have two left feet. Your unhindered passion, which flows from your heart, is a movement of grace unto the Lord. Your life is flowing in union with the heart and breath of God. Take some time today to let your dance of love and songs of praise rise to Him. Let them become a stairway straight into His presence.

Jesus, your love enables me to dance in the storms. Take my hand and let's dance away my cares. You are the joy that sets me free—the fire that ignites my soul with unquenchable passion for your presence. We will move with the grace of a beautiful pas de deux that causes the angels to stand in awe.

Go!

How beautiful on the mountains are
the sandaled feet of this one bringing such good news.
You are truly royalty!

—Song of Songs 7:1

*E*verything about your life must flow from intimacy with the Lord. The things you say and how you say them, the way you forgive, and your willingness to serve others are all signs that you've been with Jesus. When Christ is the center of your life, you become fearless—shining His light into the darkest, most sin-filled places and setting the captives free.

You don't have to be an ordained evangelist with an internationally recognized ministry or know every Scripture in the Bible to carry the gospel to those around you. You don't even need to be an extrovert! You only need to be willing to open your mouth and allow the compassion of Christ to flow out. Share a story of God's faithfulness with a co-worker, post something encouraging on social media, or simply start a conversation with a stranger and watch what happens. The world needs Jesus!

Jesus, I want you to be the basis for everything I do. Whether I'm home alone or out in a crowd, I want my thoughts to flow in unison with yours. Be the anchor that steadies me and the wisdom that guides me. Fill me with courage and kindness as we touch the world together.

Ushering In

**The way you walk so gracefully in my ways
displays such dignity.**
You are truly the poetry of God—his very handiwork.
—Song of Songs 7:1

The way you move upon the earth in justice, love, and mercy are a true demonstration of the reality of God. When you handle yourself wisely and with royal character, you honor the Lord. This doesn't mean that you're the boring one at every gathering; it simply means that your attitude reflects the One who abides within you.

Let your life be an example of His joy, compassion, generosity, and wisdom. When others complain and see a glass half empty, be the optimist. When people are discouraged and hopeless, be the voice of hope. Champion every good cause. Celebrate the victories of others! Be the breath of fresh air and let's usher in the presence of God into every situation.

Jesus, help me to live in a way that makes other people feel important. Let my words, thoughts, and actions be filled with Kingdom truth and seasoned with grace. May I demonstrate the joy and freedom that comes from living with you. May your glory within me resonate and draw others to you.

Masterpiece

The way you walk so gracefully in my ways
displays such dignity.
You are truly the poetry of God—his very handiwork.
—Song of Songs 7:1

Throughout the earth, God has arranged the expanse of His beautiful creation for all to see. Yet there is one work of art that stands above the rest—you. You are His masterpiece. Carefully woven together in your mother's womb, you were created in His image. He chose to manifest the reality of His brilliance through creation, but you alone reveal the magnificent expression of His love.

The intricacies of your body, soul, and spirit cannot be duplicated by human wisdom. Your creativity, your emotions, even the dreams that greet you in the night, are like poetry written upon your soul. The synergy of your cells and the beat of your heart are the intermingling of His wonder within you. Your spirit is breathed to life by the infilling of His Spirit. Everything about you points to the genius of His creativity and wisdom.

God, I stand in awe of your creation. The substance of your love is manifest all around me. Your brilliance is seen in each person I meet. Thank you for choosing humanity—for choosing me—to reflect your most magnificent splendor. I am your masterpiece.

The Fullness Within

Out of your innermost being
is flowing the fullness of my Spirit—
never failing to satisfy.

—Song of Songs 7:2

Everything you need has already been granted to you through Jesus. You are a well of God's presence. He lives and abides within you, streaming into every fiber of your being and flowing from you into every situation. His Spirit has qualified you to live in the same power that Jesus did when He walked the earth.

This ever-flowing fullness of His Spirit is often translated as "blended wine," which speaks of balance and nourishment. It delights your heart and stirs your desire to give to others. All that God is—all of His love, wisdom, and power—has found its home in you. Now it's up to you to release it. Let it flow like a fountain, quenching your deepest thirst and the thirsty hearts around you.

Lord, you are the hope that lives within me—the power that calms the storms. You've given me all that I need to live a happy and victorious life. Make me your goblet of blended wine for others to enjoy. Let my words refresh the souls of the weary, and my actions convey your significance. I will not hold back from sharing what you've given me.

Multiply

Within your womb there is a birthing of harvest wheat;
they are the sons and daughters
nurtured by the purity you impart.

—Song of Songs 7:2

As you partner with Jesus, you will become mature fathers and mothers to those who were once like you. When you eat from the manna of His presence, you become bread—substance for others to glean from. His presence in you has qualified you as a minister—a releaser of His Kingdom to those He brings to you. You are called to duplicate yourself.

Pay attention to the people who show up in your life. They aren't there by accident. Pour into those who are drawn to what you carry. Impart to them the wisdom and revelations God has given you. Pray with them, teach them, encourage them, and disciple them, so they in turn can nurture others. Live as an example for them to follow. Let them see the good and the bad and the path to God in every situation. He has prepared you to birth a harvest.

Father, you have filled me with your Spirit, now fill me with the confidence, wisdom, and insight that I need to lead others. Let my ceiling become their floor. May my revelations launch them into even greater revelations. May their passion for you be even deeper than mine. Give me your heart for those you've placed in my care. Help me to lead them well.

Gracious

How gracious you have become!
—Song of Songs 7:3

The more time you spend with Jesus, the more you will act like Him. This doesn't mean you lose your personality; it simply means that your personality becomes more refined. Graciousness becomes the earmark of your life. You find yourself thinking of ways to bless people. Circumstances that would normally cause you to become angry and impatient suddenly don't bother you. When you see people going through a hard time, your faith-filled outlook changes the atmosphere.

The fruit of the Spirit becomes evident in your life when you seek to honor the Lord and love others. People love being around those who are gracious and make them feel good about life. Aim to be known for your love, joy, peace, patience, kindness, generosity, faithfulness, gentleness, and self-control (Galatians 5:22). Seek to live with a giving heart.

Father, smooth out my rough edges. I want to be more like you. Strip me of selfishness and show me how to bless others. I want graciousness to define me. Let it be seen in the way I behave and heard in the words I speak. May the people in my life, even the strangers I meet, feel their lives are better for having known me.

Shining with Courage

Your life stands tall as a tower, like a shining light on a hill.
Your revelation eyes are pure, like pools of refreshing—
sparkling light for a multitude.
Such discernment surrounds you,
protecting you from the enemy's advance.
—Song of Songs 7:4

The light of the world lives inside of you. The river of God flows from within. Confident in His power that resides in your innermost being, you stand as a tower for all to see. Tenacity comes at a price. It's the result of going through the dark night of the soul and becoming assured of God's power and love.

Your life is a testimony of God's faithfulness that is meant to be shared. As you become resolute in your faith and renew your mind with the Word of God, you become a tower of refuge for others. Your passion for the Lord is contagious. Your wisdom helps to put things in perspective. Your unshakeable faith encourages them. Your positive attitude makes them feel good about life. The way you care for people and allow God's love to shine through you has made you like a city set on a hill.

Lord, I want my life to reflect the glory of your Spirit inside of me. I want to be known as a person filled with faith and hope and who inspires others to be their best. Cleanse any negative mind-sets that divert my focus from the truth. You have proven your faithfulness to me; now I will stand and share your love with confidence.

Revelation

Your life stands tall as a tower, like a shining light on a hill.
Your revelation eyes are pure, like pools of refreshing—
sparkling light for a multitude.
Such discernment surrounds you,
protecting you from the enemy's advance.

—Song of Songs 7:4

God has designed you with an innate desire to know Him. He wants to unveil to you the mysteries of His Kingdom and His ways because you're His child. When you pursue pure, God-given revelation, it will transform you. Spiritual insight will characterize your life as the eyes of your understanding become enlightened.

Heavenly realities are hidden, so you won't take them for granted. They are gifts the Lord wants to give you, if you're willing to seek them. Treasures of insight and revelation are worth the time it takes to discover them. Hunger and thirst for truth, and He will satisfy you. The Word will open in ways you never knew possible when you dive into it with an open heart. People will come to you for counsel, and you'll be surprised at the wisdom that streams from your lips—pure and refreshing.

Father, I hunger and thirst for truth, which can only be revealed by your Spirit. I'm not satisfied with what I know. Yesterday's encounters have left me unfulfilled. Breathe upon my spirit and open my soul to receive deeper revelation. I must have more of you!

Discernment

Your life stands tall as a tower, like a shining light on a hill.
Your revelation eyes are pure, like pools of refreshing—
sparkling light for a multitude.
Such discernment surrounds you,
protecting you from the enemy's advance.
—Song of Songs 7:4

Spiritual discernment is such a valuable gift. It's recognizing what is of God and what is not. Discernment often feels as if a simple knowing inside of you where you just *know* something by the Spirit. It isn't reserved for a select few; it's available to everyone through the Holy Spirit within you.

Pay attention to the gentle nudges, thoughts, and ideas because often it's the Holy Spirit speaking to you. Without much effort, you know how to pray for a specific situation, understand what someone is going through even when they haven't said a word, and sense when the enemy is about to attack. Discernment in spiritual warfare will protect you from the schemes of the enemy. Spiritual discernment is based on the Word of God and transcends logic. It is knowledge that defies human reasoning, and *you* were created to enjoy it.

Lord, speak to me. Give me ears to hear and a heart to perceive when you're trying to get my attention. Help me to stay tuned in to your Spirit and not to ignore even the slightest prodding. I want to live with my spirit continually aware of what you're revealing. Thank you for showing me how to pray in every situation.

Redeeming Love

Redeeming love crowns you as royalty.
Your thoughts are full of life, wisdom, and virtue.
Even a king is held captive by your beauty.
—Song of Songs 7:5

The longer you walk with the Lord, the more you will taste the fruit of His redemption. Not only has He redeemed you from spiritual captivity and seated you in heavenly places, but each day the reward of His suffering is evident in your life.

Jesus has paid a great price so you can have an enjoyable life. You are not held captive by fear, because His perfect love has set you free. So, shake off worry. Temptation gets easier to overcome when your desire is to honor Him. Sickness bows to the power of the cross. Confusion no longer plagues you because you have the mind of Christ. Poverty cannot hold royal children prisoner when they understand the riches that are truly theirs. Decide today to become more aware of His blessings and promises than anything else. These things are rightfully yours!

Jesus, today I choose to step into victory because defeat is not any option. Darkness cannot plague me because your light shines brightly within me and chases away the shadows. You have crowned me with the gift of perfect redemption and continually reveal its blessing in my life.

Thoughts

Redeeming love crowns you as royalty.
Your thoughts are full of life, wisdom, and virtue.
Even a king is held captive by your beauty.
—Song of Songs 7:5

*G*od wants you to live a life free from worry, fear, and stress. When you choose to set your mind on His promises, your thinking will come into alignment with truth. Peace and confidence will be your daily portion. Worry cannot exist where faith reigns. Fear cannot dominate your thoughts when you're saturated with the realization that God is truly faithful and absolutely in love with you.

Meditate on His promises for your situation. Call for wisdom, and you will have it. Declare His Word over every problem, and discouragement will melt away. Worry and stress feel horrible because they go against the very purposes of God for your life. Remember who you are, bride of the Most High King! You were created to live in victory. You are destined for greatness!

Jesus, you have given me all that I need to live in peace, joy, and godliness. I purpose today to focus on your goodness and faithfulness and to not let negative thinking litter my mind. You love me. You will take care of everything. Today is going to be a great day!

Captivating

Redeeming love crowns you as royalty.
Your thoughts are full of life, wisdom, and virtue.
Even a king is held captive by your beauty.

—Song of Songs 7:5

*J*esus enjoys you in every season of your soul. Even when you feel dry, weary, and your worship seems like lifeless words that crash to the ground, He is still blessed. Your devotion captivates Him.

Whether you can sense His presence or not, He is with you, and He's always watching. When your heart clings to the Bridegroom in undying love, it's only a matter of time before you sense His nearness. He cannot turn His eyes away from a heart that is inflamed with holy passion for Him, even if sometimes it feels as if your flame has been snuffed out. In the face of your resolve to do the will of God, regardless of cost, Jesus is filled with delight and affection. He is overcome—completely overjoyed to be imprisoned by your love.

Lord, I reach out to you with love that sometimes feels lifeless and dry. What an honor it is to know that you see how deep my love is for you, even when I can't find the words to express it. When I'm overwhelmed with life's demands and nothing seems to be going right, I will rest in your arms and offer you my heart.

Inexplicable Beauty

How delicious is your fair beauty;
it cannot be described
as I count the delights you bring to me.
Love has become the greatest.

—Song of Songs 7:6

*J*esus has placed His holiness inside of you and wrapped you with garments of glory. You are so beautiful that human words cannot describe you. The nature of God within you runs deeper than your skin. It springs up from the deepest well and floods every part of you, spirit, soul, and body.

Let yourself be wooed by the Lord's tender words. He is constantly speaking, continuously drawing you closer. Lean in as He pours His words of affirmation over your spirit and soul. At times, we can get so caught up with making sure activity (praying, reading, singing) fills our prayer time that we forget how important it is to simply enjoy the Lord as He enjoys us. His presence and the way He affirms us is like a healing balm to our soul. Let Him refresh you with His love today.

Father, I love the way you love me. Your words of tender affection and affirmation make me feel alive. Knowing how you think of me has filled me with confidence. As I come into your presence, I purpose to spend time letting us enjoy each other. You truly are the radiance that makes me shine with beauty.

Delight in Me

How delicious is your fair beauty;
it cannot be described
as *I count the delights you bring to me.*
Love has become the greatest.

—Song of Songs 7:6

*E*very sacrifice you've ever made for the Lord and the times you've chosen His will over an easier path have caught His attention. He's seen everything you've done in submission to Him, even when no one else did. Every worship-drenched tear you've cried is precious in His sight.

Jesus wants you to understand how significantly you have captured His heart. That's why He tells you over and over. He's thrilled with your desire to please Him, and He doesn't turn His nose up at your imperfect love. You aren't a surprise to the Lord. He knew exactly what He was getting when He chose you. God is pleased with you because He looks at you through blood-soaked lenses. You are made perfect because of the cross.

Jesus, thank you for the cross, for your mercy that accepts the offerings of my heart. Your love has become so real to me that sacrifices don't move me the way they once did. It's my joy to live in a way that brings you honor.

The Greatest Is Love

How delicious is your fair beauty;
it cannot be described
as I count the delights you bring to me.
Love has become the greatest.
—SONG OF SONGS 7:6

There is nothing greater in the whole world than love. No power in heaven or hell can compare. Love held Jesus to the cross. Love has set you free. Love has the power to change your life from now throughout eternity.

God Himself is the very definition of love. The depths of His unconditional love have saturated every crevice of your soul. His love is the breath of life; it's everything you need. The power of it topples the strongest of enemies yet soothes the surrendered soul. It makes you brave and fills you with expectancy. It heals. It is warm and inviting, yet outrageous and overwhelming. It is His love in you that gives you the ability to love purely and without restraint. Let your heart embrace His passion today. The treasures of love are priceless.

Father, your love steadies me. May I be so firmly rooted and grounded in your love that nothing can throw me off balance. Take me deeper and purify my heart, so I can handle more of this unrelenting glory. Your perfect love for me has left me with no other option than to surrender all.

Victorious

You stand in victory above the rest,
stately and secure as you share with me
your vineyard of love.

—Song of Songs 7:7

Others may appear to have it all together on the outside, but no one has more going for them than Spirit-filled Christians. Regardless of what you're going through, Jesus knows exactly how to lead you through to victory. The passage through the desert seasons may seem precarious, but you can trust Him.

Fear cannot hold you; cycles of failure do not define you; nor is anxiety your portion. Your trials cause your roots to grow deeper. The Spirit of the living God is inside of you, impregnating you with hope. Faith makes you stand tall and strong like a palm tree whose strength and beauty is witnessed in the fiercest of storms. Begin to thank Him for breakthrough, even before you see it manifest. This is what ignites your faith and awakens you to His presence. You are more than a conqueror; you are victorious.

Jesus, you are my victory and the assurance of all that remains unseen. You are with me everywhere I go. At times the path seems treacherous, but with you, I can conquer every opposition. Your love fills me with boldness, so I roar with faith in every storm I face.

Stately and Secure

You stand in victory above the rest,
stately and secure as you share with me
your vineyard of love.

—Song of Songs 7:7

Beloved, you are stately and secure because you are His. He knows how to supply your every need. Don't be moved by what you see. Don't turn away from your battles. Look them in the face with the confidence of an overcomer. Drive the sword of His Word straight into the enemy's plan and watch it crumble!

When you plant yourself deep within the soil of God's truth, the turbulent winds of opposition will not blow you over. Though you may hear the storm, feel the storm, and at times be shaken by it, you will not be destroyed. You are steadfast and immovable. Believe the promises that Jesus has given you. Use them as food to strengthen your spirit. Drink from the oasis of His love. Stand upon His Word—it is a steady foundation. Sink deeper into it and wield it to win every battle.

Father, your Word is alive and powerful. It steadies my fearful soul and fills me with the power to believe. It equips me and trains my hands for battle. It lifts my burdens and gives me hope. Your Word anchors my faith when the storms of life rage. I am steadfast and secure when I stand upon your truth.

Your Vineyard

You stand in victory above the rest,
stately and secure as you **share with me
your vineyard of love.**

—Song of Songs 7:7

You are not just a garden of fragrant beauty; you have become a nourishing and bountiful vineyard. Within you are the fruits of spiritual maturity: discernment, gifting, anointing, and grace to feed others. Clusters of sweet fruit now adorn your life.

The affections of your heart to bless others is pleasing in the Lord's sight. As you go about your day, listen—truly listen—to others as they open up and give you glimpses into their lives. The Holy Spirit will quicken to your spirit exactly how to help them. Release the testimony of His faithfulness and never doubt the abundance you have to offer. You are a reservoir of light and hope.

Lord, wrap me in your unending strength and favor, so that everywhere I go, others will see your goodness and be drawn to your love. Your presence within me is a fruitful vineyard that I long to share with others. May my testimony of your faithfulness spark hope in others and ignite passion for you that is inextinguishable.

November

Revival

Now I decree, *I will ascend and arise.*
I will take hold of you with my power,
possessing every part of my fruitful bride.
Your love I will drink as wine,
and your words will be mine.

—Song of Songs 7:8

Jesus is not going to leave the church the way it is. The Son of God will rise over us and anoint us with power, unlike anything we've ever experienced. United with Him, nothing will stop this end-time move of God. Signs and wonders will flood the nations—through us.

There is nothing man can do to duplicate true revival. When it comes, it will not be a series of hyped-up meetings set by someone's agenda. Never look for conferences or great preachers to spark your zeal. You are a vessel of God's glory! Jesus is the fire burning within you! You are the answer to the cry of those around you. As His bride, you will rise with passion, unable to contain the love that has empowered you.

Cry out for revival! Your heart is where it begins.

Lord, let revival begin in me. Rise within my spirit and ignite my heart with passion to see people set free. Flood our streets with glory that cannot be denied. Saturate the dry ground of every weary soul and reveal your love in undeniable ways. Heal through our hands. Let miracles flow. May your bride become a vessel of compassion that will not hold back its power.

Habitation

Now I decree, I will ascend and arise.
I will take hold of you with my power,
possessing every part of my fruitful bride.
Your love I will drink as wine,
and your words will be mine.

—Song of Songs 7:8

esus wants to fill every area of your life. Surrender everything. Yield every thought, hope, dream, question, and
fear to the Lord. Make your life a habitation for His glory. Hold
nothing back from Him.

Jesus isn't interested in spending time with you only when
you go to church or when you set aside time to pray. He wants
to live in continual communion with you. Expect Him to speak
to you while watching a movie, lean into His arms when you're
washing dishes, and listen for His whispers as you drive down
the street. Welcome Him into your conversations, work, and
time with family or friends. Begin to live in the awareness of
what you sense stirring inside of you. Live your life in tune with
Him.

Lord, I want to be a habitation for your presence. Teach me how to
become aware of you, regardless of what I'm doing. Fill my dreams
with your counsel and my thoughts with your desires. I want to live
in harmony with you as you possess every part of me.

Fine Wine

Now I decree, I will ascend and arise.
I will take hold of you with my power,
possessing every part of my fruitful bride.
Your love I will drink as wine,
and your words will be mine.

—Song of Songs 7:8

This fruitful vineyard that you're becoming is like intoxicating love to the Lord. He drinks it in. The most pleasurable thing outside of the Godhead is this love relationship between Christ and His bride. In the holy place, this secret garden of His presence, you're empowered to fulfill your destiny.

If it feels as if you've been sitting on a shelf, waiting for your dreams to come to pass, it isn't because Jesus has forgotten about you. He is simply letting you age to perfection. In other words, He's refining and preparing you. You're becoming mature and balanced, and He knows exactly when you're ready to be poured out to others. Be encouraged, you are the fine wine that Jesus has saved for last.

Jesus, your love overwhelms my soul so profoundly that at times I can barely stand in your holy presence. I'm like a person intoxicated with wine when you pour out your glory. Yet somehow, my love has this same effect on you. This is my desire—to bless you as you bless me and to become all you've purposed for me to be, even if I must wait for your perfect timing to be revealed in my life.

Speak

Now I decree, I will ascend and arise.
I will take hold of you with my power,
possessing every part of my fruitful bride.
Your love I will drink as wine,
and ***your words will be mine.***

—Song of Songs 7:8

The Hebrew text here is literally, "May the fragrance of your breath be like apples." Throughout the Song of Songs, the mouth speaks of intimacy with Jesus. Apples represent the promises of God. When you've been eating the Word of God and soaking in His presence, you will release the fragrance of His promises on every breath.

Oh, that every word we speak would be pleasing to those who hear. God wants us to encourage and call out the gold in others—in essence, to have "apple breath." Truth is always meant to lead people to their greatest potential in Him. It should always be spoken in love. Your speech has the power to change someone's life. Always aim to lavish people with words that build them up and never tear them down.

Father, may my words echo your heart. Let others recognize your voice when they hear what I have to say. Your promises will spill from my lips with the sweet fragrance of your love. May all that I say honor you and encourage those I meet.

Kisses

For your kisses of love are exhilarating,
more than any delight I've known before.
Your kisses of love awaken even the lips of sleeping ones.
—Song of Songs 7:9

*N*othing compares to His nearness. When Jesus meets with you, it is undeniably real. He longs to kiss you with His goodness. His kisses are His blessings upon your life and the reality of His divine love as it saturates your soul. It inspires, revives, and causes your heart to soar. His kiss is exhilarating! It sets your heart ablaze and fills you with contagious passion.

Now *you* have the ability to release the kiss of God into the life of another. Become the blessing of His love for others to experience. Share the good news of His presence with those who have not yet become familiar with it. Let the kisses of compassion be released through you and look for ways to lend a helping hand.

Father, your presence is like a kiss upon my soul. You bless me in so many different ways. Help me not to be selfish with this gift of love that you've given me. Show me how I can live as a tangible example of your love to those I meet. Reveal yourself to people through me as I live with compassion and holy fire guiding my life.

Taste and See

For your kisses of love are exhilarating,
more than any delight I've known before.
Your kisses of love awaken even the lips of sleeping ones.

—SONG OF SONGS 7:9

*J*esus' love is beyond compare. It's like taking everything you love and enjoy, combining it, then multiplying it by a million. The things that touch your heart—every beautiful thing you have ever seen and each life-giving word that's ever been spoken—is but a glimpse of His perfect love. Throughout the earth, God has given us samples of His love: the laugh of a baby, the colors of an evening sky, the joys of friendship, and the unity of family.

Take these things into account and it's no wonder our hearts are overwhelmed by Him. Each day, God's splendor is revealed as a gift in a multitude of ways. He enjoys lavishing us with surprising delight. Yet, the greatest mystery remains: how does this One, who paints the skies and plays a symphony upon the wind, find this same delight in us? I dare say it will take an eternity to understand, but this is the beauty of the God we serve.

Lord, you fill me with joy with the things you purposefully do to delight my heart. Sometimes it feels as if I need to try harder to please you, but then I remember that you're just as delighted in my love as I am in yours. That's when I'm undone by your love all over again.

Wake Up!

For your kisses of love are exhilarating,
more than any delight I've known before.
Your kisses of love awaken even the lips of sleeping ones.

—Song of Songs 7:9

God will never force Himself upon anyone, but He knows how to awaken those who are spiritually asleep. Never doubt His power or love for both unbelievers and those who have closed their ears to His voice. He has ways of reaching those who have become dull, and He loves them even more than we do.

Though it does happen, it's rare for unbelievers to have a sovereign encounter with Jesus where they meet Him face-to-face. Most of the time, Jesus gently woos hearts and then sends us to introduce them to the One they've unknowingly yearned for. It only takes one touch from the heart of the Savior to ignite a roaring fire, but usually the blaze is started through your hands. *You* may be the divine appointment that God has set to change someone else's life.

Father, help me to be sensitive to the leading of your Spirit everywhere I go. May dead hearts come alive as you release your love through me. May those who have become spiritually dull rise in greater passion for you than ever before. Stir my love for others, so I never resist you as you seek to reach people through me.

To Be One

The Shulamite Bride
Now I know that I am filled with my beloved
and all his desires are fulfilled in me.
—Song of Songs 7:10

When Jesus truly owns your heart, He is all you care about. Every aspect of your life revolves around living for Him and pleasing Him. It becomes a way of life, a joy that happens naturally, just as husbands and wives seek to love and honor each other.

What an incredible revelation to truly understand that you are one with Him. Being consumed with desire for the Lord actually makes your life more enjoyable. Fear and anxiety no longer dominate you because His perfect love chases them away. You're willing to live a life of radical faith, because you believe you're partnering and walking with Him. You can literally feel His presence as He guides you through the roughest waters. This is what we live for: to experience the joy of union with our Beloved.

Jesus, the purpose of my life, my very existence, is to be one with you. You are the joy that is set before me every day. I live to hear you, to feel your warm embrace, and to reveal your love to others. May I become aware of your presence within me, regardless of where I am or what I'm doing. Let all of me be consumed by all of you.

For Him

The Shulamite Bride
Now I know that I am filled with my beloved
and ***all his desires are fulfilled in me.***
—Song of Songs 7:10

*Y*ou are the fulfillment of God's desire. Before the foundation of the world, you were on His mind. Everything that the Father, Son, and Holy Spirit yearn for, the very reason Jesus came to the earth, is satisfied by you—His bride.

We spend our lives reaching for so many different things to satisfy our desires, but God reaches for one. Everything He does, ever has done, or ever will do is for the unity of His bride. He loves to be with you. Even when you forget about Him, He's thinking of you. His thoughts for you are more than can be numbered. He looks for ways to bless you. When you're misunderstood and rejected, He's for you. Let these thoughts overshadow all other thoughts. Understanding this awakens an even deeper abandonment to Him. This is why we love Him because He first loved us.

Father, I want to reach for you the way that you reach for me—without reservation or hesitation. Destroy any barriers, mental or otherwise, that would keep you out. I want to be fully yours and know you as you know me. Your love and mercy are my greatest reward.

Come

> ***Come away, my lover.***
> Come with me to the far away fields.
> We will run away together to the forgotten places
> and show them redeeming love.
> —SONG OF SONGS 7:11

First love intimacy with the Lord must continuously be cultivated. Holy zeal for the Lord doesn't burn brightly for a season, only to be snuffed out once we become mature. We don't forsake our relationship with Him in order to work *for* Him. Studying His Word, evangelizing, and all your godly duties are good. But there is nothing like stepping away from it all and enjoying Him.

Your entire life—all that you think, do, and say—must flow from a place of abundant overflow. Don't become so busy serving that you get dull and dry. The days of overwhelming encounter should never become a faint memory. It's your responsibility, not the church's, to pursue God's presence. You must stir your holy hunger and refuse to be satisfied by anything other than Him. Cry out for Him to come closer! God is always willing to manifest His love, but sometimes we're too distracted to notice when it's here.

Lord, so many things fight for my attention. At times I'm pulled in so many directions that I neglect my relationship with you. Forgive me. Even in seasons of extreme busyness, may you always be my soul's delight and profound passion. My days are so much brighter and filled with endless possibilities when I seek you first.

Let's Go!

Come away, my lover.
Come with me to the far away fields.
We will run away together to the forgotten places
and show them redeeming love.
—Song of Songs 7:11

Becoming one with the Lord means that His desires become yours. You don't need ten confirmations, hours of counsel, or a booming voice from heaven to know if what you want to do is okay with Him. God put His desires in you. God has anointed you to run with Him. He gets excited when you tell Him that you want to do something extreme for Him, and He's always ready for an adventure.

It's important to have dreams. Zeal must never be quenched, and though we must always heed sound wisdom and counsel, radical faith rarely makes sense. Too many have sat around doing nothing because they weren't completely sure they should act on what was in their hearts. If what is in your heart doesn't go against God's Word and truly burns within you, go for it! Seek the Lord for the correct timing, seek counsel, and be diligent to prepare, then go out and change the world!

Jesus, I want to burn with unquenchable zeal to run with you. Free me from indecisiveness, selfishness, doubt, and anything that may be resting like a wet blanket over my soul. Lead me by your Spirit and anoint my desires, so they explode with faith that doesn't make sense.

Not Forgotten

Come away, my lover.
Come with me to the far away fields.
*We will run away together to the forgotten places
and show them redeeming love.*
—Song of Songs 7:11

Someone has to reach those who have been forgotten. Someone must rescue children from the sex-slave trade, someone has to give answers to the druggie on the street corner, and someone needs to help the spiritually impoverished in this country and in faraway lands.

Often, we become so consumed with our own lives and the circles we're in that we forget there's a world in desperate need of help. Let me encourage you today that *you* can make a difference. Whether you're called to walk among the nations, feel the joyful burden to intercede, or to reach out to the forgotten ones in your own city, there's always a call to run with Jesus. Don't be discouraged or neglect to let your light shine in the darkest places, even if the task feels too big. Remember, you serve a big God!

Lord, the world looks different through your eyes. Give me your heart for the hurting and the broken. Show me what part I am to play in pouring your love out to people near and far. Strip me of selfish thinking that isn't willing to be uncomfortable. Be the fire that sets my soul ablaze to run with you.

The Vineyard in Others

Let us arise and run to the vineyards of your people
and see if the budding vines of love are now in full bloom.
We will discover if their passion is awakened.
There I will display my love for you.

—SONG OF SONGS 7:12

As we mature as His bride, our hearts for a united body of Christ begin to form. We sense His love and excitement over the many different denominations that reflect Him. Notice here that the Shulamite calls these places *vineyards*. She sees Christians, regardless of their differences, the way Jesus does.

When you encounter other denominations or churches, do you focus on what you don't agree with? Do you find fault with every little thing that isn't the way you think it should be? Every Christian denomination carries facets of truth. They may worship or pray differently from you, and they might interpret Scripture differently than you. But if their hearts are turned to Jesus, they've got the main thing right. You are called to pray for those who are in error and never to judge, condemn, or cause division. It's time to forsake the theology of criticism and embrace the doctrine of love.

Father, forgive me for thinking I've got it all together. There is so much about your Kingdom that I don't yet understand. Help me to embrace everyone, especially my brothers and sisters in you, with open arms. Let unity, passion, and acceptance begin to define those who make up your beautiful vineyard.

Maturing Desire

Let us arise and run to the vineyards of your people
and see if the budding vines of love are now in full bloom.
We will discover if their passion is awakened.
There I will display my love for you.
—Song of Songs 7:12

During your immature years, serving others may seem like a distraction from your enjoyment of God. Ministry can feel like a hindrance or painful duty. But as you mature in full union with Him, you become a vessel possessed by His life. The overflow of your relationship with Him creates a desire to cultivate the garden of God in others. You're fully aware you have something to offer, but wisdom anchors you in Him.

Running with Him in ministry, while maintaining first-love relationship with the Lord, changes your perspective. The immature don't stir frustration or criticism within you; instead, your heart is toward them. It becomes a joy to pour into those whose passion hasn't been awakened. The urgency to embrace your calling stems from a desire to honor Him but also from the compassion you have for others and a confidence in your identity.

Lord, your desire within me has stirred my heart toward others. It's an honor to see others through your eyes and feel your excitement for those newly growing in their faith. Let my passion ignite passion in others, my hope spark their hope, and my faith encourage those who are weary.

Love on Display

We will discover if their passion is awakened.
There I will display my love for you.
—Song of Songs 7:12

When people know you are a radical follower of Jesus, they watch. Whether you like it or not, your life is an advertisement for the Kingdom of God. The way you handle disappointment, honor and serve others, and view life will either attract or repel others.

The power and reality of your relationship with the Lord should create desire for Him in others. It's important not to hide behind a mask of pretense, trying to convince people that the Christian life is always enjoyable. They need to journey with you, hear your struggles and victories, and watch as you find strength in God. Your love for Him should be evident. Your hope should be contagious. Keep your spirit and soul healthy and saturated with His presence. When you're whole, you will shine and release His love every chance you get. Attract people to the realities of loving Him.

Lord, I want to display our love in a way that is contagious! I want others to feel as if they can relate to me because I'm genuine. I never want to come across as prideful, and I always want people to walk away from me feeling encouraged and heard. I want to be your chariot of fire that provokes people toward a journey of their own with you.

Royal Love

The love apples are in bloom,
sending forth their fragrance of spring.
The rarest of fruits are found at our doors—
the new as well as the old.

—Song of Songs 7:13

There is a fragrance of love that saturates the air around you. Others may sense it, but for you, the bride, it stirs up something deep and profound. This is royal love shared between you and your Bridegroom-King. This type of love fills you with desire to nurture others.

The divine relationship between you and Jesus is different from any other. It satisfies you in ways nothing else can. It fills you with the certainty of love, which you cannot keep to yourself. An overwhelming desire to pour into others and share what you've learned, and continue to experience, tugs at your heart. The Holy Spirit has created you to reproduce yourself. Practically speaking, this means staying sensitive to the needs of those around you, friends and strangers alike, and looking for ways to bring the reality of God's presence into their lives. We don't look at people as projects; we simply learn to love.

Jesus, you are the fragrance of love that has filled my life. You are the King who has won my unrestrained devotion. Now I want to share this love, to resurrect lifeless souls, and to spark hope in the hearts of the hopeless.

Rare

The love apples are in bloom,
sending forth their fragrance of spring.
The rarest of fruits are found at our doors—
the new as well as the old.

—Song of Songs 7:13

*G*race and glory have kissed your life. This substance of love swells within you like warm waves upon the shore. Though it cannot be touched with human hands, it is incredibly real and extremely rare. It is spiritual and mysterious, yet pure and holy. Unlike most valuable and extraordinary things, it is available to anyone who wants it.

This curious love is sampled by all when they taste the fruits of love, joy, peace, patience, kindness, goodness, faithfulness, gentleness and self-control, which you release. Your impassioned heart, which has surrendered all to follow the Lord, is uncommon and witnessed by those around you. This is the rarest of loves that must be accepted and savored to be understood. Yield continually to it and relish every moment. You were designed for a life of extravagant devotion that is hard to describe.

Jesus, I love embracing the mystery of our relationship. Nothing compares to what I feel when you're near. Everything else seems less real, less important, and less satisfying than the substance of your love. Pour yourself into me as I release myself to you without reservation. We will eat the rare delicacies of holy love, together.

Testimony

The rarest of fruits are found at our doors—
the new as well as the old.
I have stored them for you, my lover-friend!
—SONG OF SONGS 7:13

As you grow, the joys you share with the Lord are a combination of your history together, the revelation of today, and the excitement of things to come. When you look back at the pains of disappointment that have turned into some of your greatest victories, or you remember the many times He's answered your prayers, you cannot help but love Him more. It's the difficult times, when you held on, though you didn't think you could, which fuel your faith in the ever-present God.

Draw from your deep experiences of the past and lean into the ever-fresh revelation of today. Tap into God's desire for your future. Laugh with Him as you dream of things to come. You are a well of testimony—draw from the waters within and pour out the waters to those you know. Let your history, your peace in the present, and your faith for tomorrow stir the wells of hope in others.

Father, thank you for your faithfulness in times past, your ever-present help now, and the joys yet to come. I love doing life with you and walking with you every day. Help me to keep the wells within fresh and pure, so I can continually be a source of encouragement and support to others.

Your Friend

The love apples are in bloom,
sending forth their fragrance of spring.
The rarest of fruits are found at our doors—
the new as well as the old.
I have stored them for you, *my lover-friend!*

—SONG OF SONGS 7:13

esus is not only your Lord and King; He's also your Friend who loves you more than any other. You don't have to face life alone or stand on your own two feet. He is with you, and He wants to walk with you every day. His love is relevant and applicable to every situation.

Jesus loves you so much that He's tattooed your name in the palm of His hand. He longs to embrace you and pour the oil of His healing love over your heart. You were created to experience depths of this relationship in greater ways than you've ever known. As your Friend, He loves to laugh with you and talk about your day. He has secrets to share, ideas you've never considered, and perfect wisdom to guide you. He *gets you*, understanding your personality more than anyone else. Relax and enjoy Him as your Friend.

Jesus, you have won me over. You're the best friend I've ever had. You don't just listen; you wrap me in your arms and breathe encouragement into the depths of my soul. Flood my senses with the reality of your nearness and the sweetness of your touch. Let's laugh and play, plan and adventure. With you, life is so much fun!

Communicating Love

If only I could show everyone
this passionate desire I have for you.
If only I could express it fully,
no matter who was watching me,
without shame or embarrassment.
—Song of Songs 8:1

Walking the streets with our hands raised in praise, or through the grocery store with tears of devotion streaming from our faces, most likely won't cause people to fall on their knees and join in. In fact, they may stay far away. Our deepest devotion for the Lord isn't meant to be a badge of holiness that we flaunt before others. It is precious and personal. However, love has many ways of being communicated.

One of the simplest ways is by listening to people and then sharing what God has done for you in a way that encourages them in their situation. Your personal account of His faithfulness honors God and makes Him relatable. The Holy Spirit inside of you will gently nudge or carefully warn you, so that you know what to share or what not to share with each person. Live with a determined purpose to show your love for Him by the way you treat others.

Lord, I want to live in a way that expresses my love for you and stirs desire in others. Teach me how to be a good listener and to make people feel understood. Release your fragrance through me, and let my words of encouragement be sweet like honey.

Express Yourself

If only I could show everyone
this passionate desire I have for you.
If only I could express it fully,
no matter who was watching me,
without shame or embarrassment.

—Song of Songs 8:1

How do we express these deep movings of our hearts—this overwhelming love that stirs so profoundly within us? His love is so remarkable and intense that much of the time it seems impossible to give voice to how it makes us feel.

God has given us so many avenues to try to convey these rich emotions. Writers pen them, artists display them for all to see, and dancers use movement in an effort to articulate what cannot be put into words. Musicians, singers, and others give us a sliver of what they so desperately desire to communicate. No matter how *you* express it, express it! Give the world a taste.

Father, your love is so intense that I find it hard to describe. You've given me a unique and creative way to express what's in my heart, but still I wish I could somehow convey it more accurately. Your love is deeply spiritual yet touches every part of my soul and body. Anoint me with a greater ability to take what is in me and relay it to others.

You Are a Well

If only I could show everyone
this passionate desire I have for you.
If only I could express it fully,
no matter who was watching me,
without shame or embarrassment.

—Song of Songs 8:1

You were called to be the light of the world—the express image of God on this earth. Inside of you is a well, ready to overflow with truth, compassion, and hope for all. Often, Christians live in extremes: some walk around quoting Scriptures, hoping the fear of judgment will turn people's hearts. Others say nothing and live their Christian lives as if guarding an embarrassing secret.

Let me encourage you to live and love, boldly. Speak truth, expressed with love, never judgment. Be a well of refreshing and look for opportunities to encourage people. For example: Have you ever had complete strangers inexplicably open up to you? Maybe they tell you about their problems, fears, or illnesses. Don't ignore them, because they're drawn to the answer that you carry. Learn to love everyone you meet and let the well flow!

Lord, help me to never hide what I believe but to never force truth on anyone. Teach me how to bless others by the way I live, speak, and interact. I will not be ashamed of my relationship with you because you have never been ashamed of me.

Lead Him

I long to bring you to my innermost chamber—
this holy sanctuary you have formed within me.
O that I might carry you within me.
I would give you the spiced wine of my love,
this full cup of bliss that we share.
We would drink our fill until ...

—SONG OF SONGS 8:2

It is one thing to know that the Lord leads you; it is an entirely different idea to think He allows you to lead Him. The very blueprint and desire of God has been ingrained within you, inspiring you to fulfill His purposes for your life. He puts a desire in you, then waits for you to act on it and draw Him back into it, so the two of you can do it together.

As you reach for His presence and invite Him to fill the deepest part of your being, He responds with love. When you take the initiative to pray for someone who's sick, He comes on the scene with healing. You intercede for revival and realize that your heart beats with His desires. You are a vessel of the Holy Spirit, filled with godly desires and ideas. Never be afraid of what inspires you. It inspires Him as well!

Lord, I love doing life with you. I never have to be afraid of trying new things or taking risks, because if I fall, I fall right into your arms. Each day becomes an adventure as I learn to trust you more. Not only do you lead me, but when my heart is pure, you enjoy when I lead you.

Aware

I long to bring you to my innermost chamber—
this holy sanctuary you have formed within me.
O that I might carry you within me.
I would give you the spiced wine of my love,
this full cup of bliss that we share.
We would drink our fill until …

—Song of Songs 8:2

The presence of God inside of you can be felt tangibly. Much like the way the sun warms your body on a summer day, His presence bathes you with radiance from the inside. It can be felt from the moment you wake to the moment you go to sleep, if you choose to acknowledge it.

You carry the Spirit of God inside of you. Every fiber of your being is pulsating with glory—a spiritual reality that can be experienced physically. That doesn't change when you lose focus, but losing focus will affect your awareness of it. Though this internal encounter is always available to you, busyness and distraction will dull the sense of His presence. If the cry of your heart is to live in a state of continual mindfulness of God, desire alone will catapult you into a new and glorious way of life.

Father, hide me in the paradise of your presence, always. Overwhelm me with love that steals my attention away from everything else. I want to see you clearly with no shadow of sin to blur my vision. Your love is like a holy fire, burning away all desire for frivolous pursuits. Help me to be mindful of your love, always.

His Cup of Delight

I long to bring you to my innermost chamber—
this holy sanctuary you have formed within me.
O that I might carry you within me.
I would *give you the spiced wine of my love*,
this full cup of bliss that we share.
We would drink our fill until ...

—Song of Songs 8:2

Give Jesus your best and most unreserved worship. Lavish Him with songs of love and words of adoration, whether you sense His nearness or you're spiritually dry for a season. Never let your worship be determined by how you feel. Let distraction fall from you like a cumbersome restrictive shell as you lift your heart to Him.

What an honor it is to give Him your best and most costly adoration. You become His very own cup of delight as you pour out love to Him like sweet wine. In return, as you open your heart to Him, joy and gladness saturate your soul. For those who have learned the secret of divine romance, this holy exchange of love becomes a way of life.

Lord, I offer you my love, my life, my all. I bow before you, my heart on fire with a reality I have yet to see. You are worthy. Even when I'm still, my heart is filled with waves of adoration that transcend words. May my offering of holy love honor you, my King.

Step In

I long to bring you to my innermost chamber—
this holy sanctuary you have formed within me.
O that I might carry you within me.
I would give you the spiced wine of my love,
this full cup of bliss that we share.
We would drink our fill until ...

—SONG OF SONGS 8:2

There is a depth of prayer with the Lord that is so glorious, it's hard to describe. It is a place of bliss that goes far beyond words and touches the deepest part of who you are. It breathes life into even the deadest soul. It blazes its way through fear and unbelief. It is God Himself—the One whose majesty fills the earth with wonder.

You were created for this designed to share this cup of bliss with Him. Step into the mystery and wonder of His presence. Silence the running thoughts by being still and listening for His voice. If this is foreign to you, bring a Scripture into your thoughts and ponder it. Or, simply and quietly say, "Jesus." Then be still and wait for Him to pour His love all over you as peace and joy simultaneously flood your soul.

Father, I want to know you more. Touch my eyes, so I may see you more clearly. Whisper into my ears, so they awaken to your voice. Embrace every part of me with glory divine. It doesn't matter to me how you come, just come. Let me know you as you know me.

Thoughts

> *His left hand cradles my head*
> while his right hand holds me close.
> We are at rest in this love.
>
> —Song of Songs 8:3

Take a deep breath and lean back into His embrace. Stay there and rest a while. The Lord's left hand cradles your head—surrounding your thoughts with the power of His love and faithfulness. Release your anxiety and stress to Him. You weren't designed to live in constant worry or to be troubled by a myriad of disturbing thoughts.

God has invited you to dive into the waterfalls of peace, which tumble over every thought and smooth every jagged imagination. His refreshing presence flows, washes away stress, and stills your soul. He woos you into the posture of trust, where He can communicate with you and exchange fear for faith. He simply needs you to surrender to His embrace.

Father, hold me. I need you to chase away the stress with the truth of your faithfulness. My thoughts have become a whirling storm of dust, and I cannot seem to find my peace. Come, wash me in the cleansing waters of your presence, and I will see clearly again.

Close

His left hand cradles my head
while ***his right hand holds me close.***
We are at rest in this love.

—Song of Songs 8:3

The Lord desires to draw you close. As His left hand slides under your head, He becomes the Lord of your thoughts. With His right hand, He pulls you against His chest—so near that you smell the fragrance of His love. So close that you're aware of the sweetness of His breath. It is the most fulfilling and soothing hug you've ever felt.

In the Bible, the right hand is a symbol of strength and power. The most powerful One of all, the One who has beaten death, hell, and the grave, tenderly holds you. This same God, who created the heavens and the earth and everything that was made, has time to hold you. As a matter of fact, it thrills His heart to do so. Imagine Him smiling as He draws you near. Let the reality of His embrace give you a glimpse into the vastness of who He is.

Father, if there is any part of me that would oppose your love, strip it away. I don't want anything to separate me from you. You are magnificent and powerful. You tether the earth with the sound of your voice yet free my soul to experience your touch. Come, hold me now, and I will not resist.

His left hand cradles my head
while his right hand holds me close.
We are at rest in this love.

—SONG OF SONGS 8:3

There are seasons for everything. Seasons of abundance and joy, periods of rest, times of sorrow, stretches of busyness, and occasions of weariness. No matter where you find yourself, the peace and rest of God are always available. You don't have to be in a season of stillness to take time to bask in His love.

Most of the time, God won't interrupt your day to overwhelm you with His love. Though He does do that on occasion, usually you must first come by faith to receive it. He's always there, always ready to steady you and rejuvenate your soul. His arms will never push you away. Lean into Him now and rest in His love. Quiet your mind for a moment, and let Him breathe life into every season of your soul.

God, your arms embrace me and draw me into a place of perfect peace. Let the posture of my heart find you now and in every moment. In your presence, I am content. I fix my heart on you and ask you to take care of everything else. There is nothing like resting in the comfort of your love.

Awake

Promise me, brides-to-be,
by the gentle gazelles and delicate deer,
that *you'll not disturb my love until he is ready to arise.*

—SONG OF SONGS 8:4

Do you remember the moment when the Lord greeted you with His love for the first time? The occasions of encountering His presence are life changing. He knows exactly how to reach into the deepest caverns of our souls and illuminate them. He longs to awaken our spirits with His triumphant love.

We often pray for God to reveal Himself to those who are spiritually asleep, expecting to see the fruit of our prayers instantly. When we don't, it's easy to become disillusioned, wondering if He will ever unveil their spirits to the greatness of His love. However, God always hears our prayers, and since we know it's His will to draw others to Himself, we need only believe and trust Him. His timing is perfect, and while He won't force Himself on anyone, He knows exactly how to awaken sleeping hearts.

Thank you, Lord, for your perfect love that awakens even the dullest spirit. Nothing is too hard for you. No one is beyond your reach. You know exactly what every sleeping one needs in order to be rejuvenated. Breathe your breath of life into every weary one. Make yourself known with the reality of your love.

December

Transformed

The Bridegroom-King
Who is this one? Look at her now!
She arises out of her desert, clinging to her beloved.
—Song of Songs 8:5

The longer you walk with the Lord, the less you resemble the person you used to be. The Holy Spirit has made you His dwelling place; your heart has become the chamber room of His glory. Continuously transforming from glory to glory, you are changing from the inside out.

Like a caterpillar encapsulated in a cocoon, God will tuck you into Himself until you emerge as a new creation—dazzling and remarkable to behold. These are seasons of hiddenness— the years when you mature and grow closer to Him, learning lessons that refine motives and attitudes. God is patient, and He doesn't grow tired of smoothing out your rough edges. He will finish the beautiful work He has begun in you!

❧

Father, strengthen me with your presence. Polish me with your glory, so I shine like you. Let every motive of my heart be fine-tuned, flowing in unison with you. May every part of me be transformed into your image. I want to become more like you and will not despise the lessons you teach.

Cling to Him

The Bridegroom-King
Who is this one? Look at her now!
She arises out of her desert, clinging to her beloved.
—SONG OF SONGS 8:5

Difficult times create character, greater devotion, and a firm foundation upon which to build our lives if our hearts remain tender toward the Lord. The way we cling to Him during trials is vitally important. The enemy seeks to destroy our faith, but the heart of the impassioned believer can never be fully quenched. Desert seasons, when we feel disillusioned, weary, and often confused, are inescapable. Sometimes we're left with questions and occasionally anger toward the very One who so graciously got us through.

This is when we must take every thought that contradicts His goodness and lay it at His feet, as an offering of love and surrender. Never be afraid of brokenness. Some of your deepest revelations and encounters with the Lord are there. He is there to mend and restore as you cling tightly to Him. Remember, Jesus' greatest victory came out of His harshest pain. Before long, your desert will become a flowing fountain.

❧

Father, don't let the desert seasons destroy me. Though sometimes it feels as if I'm barely holding on to you, I know you've got me. Soon, I will rise and run with you, but for now, I will rest in your love. You won't let me go.

Under the Apple Tree

When I awakened you under the apple tree,
as you were feasting upon me,
I awakened your innermost being with the travail of birth
as you longed for more of me.

—Song of Songs 8:5

*I*f Jesus had not stirred our hearts and roused us to seek Him, we would be lost. We owe it all to Him. Under the shadow of His eternal love, He awakened us to see the cross. It was the sovereign work of the Spirit that initiated our salvation, and it is He who continues to work in us.

The apple tree is a picture of Christ in the fullness of His love. When He unveiled our hearts and roused our desire for Him, we truly came alive. This is first-love passion, which must be continually summoned. It is a flame of desire that must be constantly tended, so the fire within does not grow dim. As we bring our hearts closer to Him, He deepens our love and conquers our doubts and fears. Our life has become His garden where the fruit of His love grows.

❧

Jesus, you're my magnificent salvation—the One who took away my sin. The substance of your love has triumphed over everything that could separate me from you. You're my life, my love, and the reason I sing. The power of your resurrection surges through every part of me, and I am yours—completely.

Travail

When I awakened you under the apple tree,
as you were feasting upon me,
I awakened your innermost being with the travail of birth
as you longed for more of me.

—SONG OF SONGS 8:5

The very depths of God's heart beckon us with intensity and purpose. We walk with Him, listening as He talks about His love for humankind, and we cannot help but be moved by these same longings. No longer do we only think about what He can do for us; our maturing and unselfish love drives us to share His heart with others.

As we grow in Him and become spiritually, emotionally, and physically whole, we want to see others experience equal wholeness. We're motivated by an intense longing to see more of Christ birthed in the earth. We labor in intercession and in sharing the gospel, in order to see others captured by these same holy affections and begin their own glorious Shulamite journey.

Father, give me your heart for those around me who don't yet know you. Fill me with desire that propels me to run with you as together we reach the lost. Kindle my spirit with fiery love that bows in intercession. Breathe life into their dry bones and heal the wounds of their shattered hearts.

Sealed

Fasten me upon your heart as a seal of fire forevermore.
This living, consuming flame
will seal you as my prisoner of love.

—Song of Songs 8:6

We started this journey with a longing for God's kisses, but it culminates with the fiery seal of divine love encasing our hearts. It's better than we ever dreamed it could be! His love is more mysterious and majestic than we could have ever conceived. He awakens us to secrets and treasures of life that are so profound that they must be experienced in order to understand them.

God's ways are higher than our own. He offers us love to love Him with. He woos our hearts to know Him; He imparts zeal to discover the treasures of heaven. He seals us with passion, promise, protection, approval, and favor. It isn't our devotion, past victories, or the way we discipline our flesh that fastens us to His heart; it is His grace alone. We gratefully yield our lives to the King, and He seals us as His very own.

Father, possess my soul, my spirit, and my life. May your divine love be the seal that irrevocably fastens me to you. Your indescribable mercy has won my heart, and I praise you with joy that bubbles from the wells within. You have sealed me with a holy kiss, and your love has empowered me to live in victory.

Stronger

My passion is stronger
than the chains of death and the grave,
all consuming as the very flashes of fire
from the burning heart of God.
Place this fierce, unrelenting fire over your entire being.

—Song of Songs 8:6

God's love is inescapable. It seems odd that He would compare His love to something like death, but He does. Nobody escapes the grave. Death is a prevailing, comprehensive power. Once it holds you, it will not let go. This is what God's love is like—just as the grave will not release its victims, so Jesus' love will not surrender you or ever let you go. The power of His love will claim all of you—forever.

You cannot escape His love. In weak and weary faith, when doubts and questions cast a muddy film over your heart, Jesus still reaches for you. He will draw you into His loving arms, continuously, for your entire life. He will rain down mercy and extend His hand into the deepest darkest pit. There's no hiding from Him. He is not content with a partial ownership of your heart. His is a jealous love. Relentless, omnipotent love will eventually win.

❧

Father, I'm humbled by your endless mercy, amazed by the way you relentlessly pursue me. Life is colorless and dreary when I lose sight of you, but your love still holds on tight. You never give up on me. Fan the flame of love in my heart and burn within me forever.

All of Me

My passion is stronger
than the chains of death and the grave,
***all consuming as the very flashes of fire
from the burning heart of God.***
Place this fierce, unrelenting fire over your entire being.

—Song of Songs 8:6

To fully experience the flames of holy passion, you must embrace them. Love must consume every aspect of your life. If you desire to be fully His, it's essential that you open yourself to God's cleansing fire. Each desire, every temptation, all fears, all relationships, and the greatest and smallest things that pertain to you—spirit, soul, and body—must be yielded to Him.

Invite Jesus to be Lord of everything. Allow His fire to burn away the things that aren't pleasing to Him. As you continue on this journey, He will tenderly reveal areas that are not fully His. Letting go of habits, mind-sets, and incorrect theology can be painful at first, but surrendering always results in joyous freedom. Accept and be thankful for these times—only a loving Father cares so deeply for His child.

❧

Lord, I surrender all. I want nothing in me that contradicts the glorious ways of your Kingdom. You can have every part of me—I will not hold back. I may not like some of the areas you want to change in me, but I know your ways are good and right. Pour out your grace as I unconditionally open my heart to you.

Unquenchable Fire

Rivers of pain and persecution
will never extinguish this flame.
Endless floods will be unable
to quench this raging fire that burns within you.

—Song of Songs 8:7

This divine love, shared between you and the Lord, has sealed you. Your yielded heart has become the fuel for God's sacred and eternal flame that burns within. The many waters of difficulties, trials, and pain cannot quench this fire. Though at times your passion for Him may feel like nothing more than a flickering ember, His mercy and grace will spark a blazing fire once again.

His flaming heart abides inside of you, and though it's unstoppable, it's important to tend it. Rivers of misunderstanding, heartache, or disappointment cannot quench His love, but the choice to embrace healing is yours. Likewise, neither can floods of accusation, condemnation, or rejection snuff out the sacred flame. His love will always burn within you, but you must choose to accept it. Joseph felt temptation, Peter denied our Lord Jesus, Saul of Tarsus persecuted the saints—but nothing could extinguish Love's jealous flames for them.

Jesus, the fire of your love has enflamed my being. I will not resist its roaring flame. I invite your fiery gaze to search my soul and burn away the debris. May your love burn brightly within me, kindling fires of love everywhere we go.

Consumed

Everything will be consumed.
It will stop at nothing
as you yield everything to this furious fire
until it won't even seem to you like a sacrifice anymore.

—Song of Songs 8:7

Sometimes we experience God's love so intensely, we feel as if we might spontaneously explode! A cry in our hearts arises from a zealous desire to be fully His. Then there are times when we feel as if we're stuck on a spiritual plateau. It seems nothing we do will ever *truly* change us. We get caught in cycles of frustration, highlighting our own lack of strength instead of leaning upon His.

Allow gratefulness to flood your soul today. Your magnificent, merciful, loving, and powerful God sees your weaknesses and knows exactly how to help. All He's looking for is the *yes* that streams from your heart. Once He sees that, He comes running with such power that it cannot be stopped. It's His delight to answer the cries of your heart for Christlikeness. Rest in this truth today and release yourself from perfectionism. Simply be His. He will never give up on you.

❦

Jesus, stop at nothing to make me wholly yours. No matter how hard I try, I can't do everything right, and I need your grace. You know my weaknesses and struggles—I won't try to hide. Without you I'd be a mess, so I'll run into your arms over and over again.

Worth It All

Everything will be consumed.
It will stop at nothing
as you yield everything to this furious fire
until *it won't even seem to you like a sacrifice anymore.*

—Song of Songs 8:7

What an honor and delight it is to give everything for the sake of love. Jesus is a perfect example of unselfish love. He gave all He had for you. That is how love is—it doesn't think twice about laying everything on the line. It has no price tag. When you truly love someone, you would pay anything to save that person's life. Homes, savings, and cars—you'd give them all in exchange for the lives of those you love.

As passionate lovers of Jesus, we've thrown caution to the wind and embraced life with Him without regard to what it costs us. Love has prompted us to lay aside the foolish, sinful desires that once darkened and littered our paths. We've decided to go anywhere and do anything He asks with no strings in our souls other than the chord of His love. This selfless love makes you beautiful to the King.

❦

Jesus, I pray that my life would honor you. Unmask any areas where I'm selfish and stubborn. I want to look, sound, and be just like you. I want to radiate with selfless abandon that's willing to lay it all down for the sake of love. May the beauty of my surrendered heart be pleasing in your sight. You are worth it all.

December 11

It's Time

The Shulamite Bride
My brothers said to me when I was young,
"Our sister is so immature.
What will we do to guard her for her wedding day?"
—SONG OF SONGS 8:8

There's a time in every young Christian's life when others teach him or her about Jesus. Those more mature in the Lord introduced you to Jesus, then taught, encouraged, and helped you as you embarked upon this journey. Now it's time for you to do the same.

Those who don't yet know the depths of His love need someone to unlock their soul. You hold the key. You don't have to understand every Scripture or have a fancy title before your name to free those who are spiritually imprisoned. All you need is to have feasted on His love for yourself and be willing to share your experience. It doesn't take much—He is already wooing most hearts. They just need to taste and see He is good. Your testimonies of His faithfulness, your encounters with His glory, and your joy are things the world longs for.

❧

Lord, I want my passion to be contagious. Let me shine with the substance of your reality. When people are around me, may they be drawn to the truth that lives within me. You've given me so much to share; you've blessed me with so many people to help me along the way. Now help me to do the same—to reach out to others with your love.

Wedding Day

The Shulamite Bride
My brothers said to me when I was young,
"Our sister is so immature.
What will we do to guard her for her wedding day?"
—SONG OF SONGS 8:8

We are the gift God will give to His Son on His wedding day. Those eyes of flaming love have pierced our soul, but one day we will gaze into them with unveiled vision. For now, we cultivate this love and surrender ourselves as never before. We are a part of the body of Christ, the true bride, and must help beautify her as a whole.

Let's live with purity and zeal for Jesus that ignites desire in others. Let's make passion for Him an epidemic that cannot be cured. Love well. Heal the sick. Adorn yourself with faith. Carry yourself with respect. Comfort the hurting and lonely. Be a voice of hope. Make a change in your society. Pray without ceasing by carrying the awareness of His love always. You are beautiful—a bride readying herself for her wedding day.

❧

Jesus, I want to be radiant and beautiful in the deepest part of my being when I meet you face-to-face. Thank you for your grace that adorns and enhances me in every way. May I come before you with a pure heart, carrying crowns to lay at your feet and bringing you the gifts of other souls.

Walls of Protection

The Bridegroom-King
"We will build a tower of redemption to protect her.
Since she is vulnerable,
we will enclose her with a wall of cedar boards."
—SONG OF SONGS 8:9

Jesus will not carry out His purposes of grace without the bride. You are His partner and His helper, His hands and His voice upon the earth. You are called to labor in love with Jesus. You are filled with the grace, anointing, and power to set the captives free.

From the towering heights of His presence, God will give you an eagle-eye view on the approaching enemies. Through your intercession, you can protect and fight for others. You are not just a bride resting in the King's chambers; you are one who knows her place by His side. You have made yourself ready to sit with Him on the throne. You are His queen and His co-ruler over all things. You will lead others to victory.

✦

God, you have surrounded me with yourself. You are my protection from the power of the enemy. You have lifted me up and anointed me to serve others from a seat of power and majesty. In you, I am complete. In you, I will arise and shine, and set the captives free.

Enclose Me

The Bridegroom-King
"We will build a tower of redemption to protect her.
Since she is vulnerable,
we will enclose her with a wall of cedar boards."
—SONG OF SONGS 8:9

*Y*ou are enclosed and protected by the fragrant sacrifice of Jesus. His love and the victory of the cross are compared to the fragrant cedars of Lebanon. Cedars, which are strong, expensive, and pleasantly scented, often speak of humanity. He has surrounded humanity with the victory of Calvary, and nothing can penetrate it!

The cedars in the temple were overlaid with gold. You are a holy temple of God, clothed with the golden glory of Jesus Christ. You are set apart—royal and beautiful. Protected by God's holy angels and chosen for an incredible purpose. Never belittle your calling. Whether you're pouring out love to a houseful of children, doing business with the elite, or encouraging those around you, you are important. You are enclosed in Him.

❧

Jesus, thank you for the way you protect me. You've surrounded me with love that shields me from evil. Your angels guard the anointing you've entrusted to me. May I live with the grace, power, and determination to fulfill my call and bring you the glory you deserve.

I Am a Bride

The Shulamite Bride
But *now I have grown and become a bride,*
and my love for him has made me
a tower of passion and contentment for my beloved.
—Song of Songs 8:10

How do you see yourself? By now, there is no denying that you bring joy to the Lord. He's made it clear to you the value that you have, and that He unmistakably chose you to partner with Him now and throughout eternity.

Perhaps you haven't quite grown into the crown that He's placed upon your head. Oh, but you will! You've been adorned with the glorious treasures of redemption, wisdom, peace, joy, hope, righteousness, and majesty. You are His, and He is yours. It doesn't matter if anyone else knows your name because He does. You aren't a nobody; you're a radiant bride who delights the heart of the Maker of heaven and earth. Always remember who you are and whose you are.

❧

Jesus, I bow before you, undone by the glory that shines from me. I look a lot like you. Your beauty is like an ornament of grace upon my life. I am royalty. I am fearfully and wonderfully made. I will fulfill your purpose for my life. I am yours. I am your bride.

December 16

Bliss

I am now a firm wall of protection for others,
guarding them from harm.
This is how he sees me—*I am the one who brings him bliss,*
finding favor in his eyes.

—SONG OF SONGS 8:10

Think about this: you bring the Father, Son, and Holy Spirit sheer bliss. Before you continue to read, give that truth a moment to sink in. You delight God's heart, and He is not disappointed with you. When He thinks of you, He is stirred with joy.

God doesn't mark you by your failures. He sees you through the sacrifice of perfect love. Even when you're displeased with yourself, He's standing with His arms wide open, ready to flood you with grace. We are our own worst critics. We judge ourselves much more harshly than the Lord does. Remember, He sees you with the finished product in mind. He doesn't look at you and wonder how He'll ever mature you to the point of perfection. Even when He corrects you, it's done with the conviction of tender love. It is with pleasure that He knows you. And He truly knows you—more than anyone else in the world, and you still bring Him joy.

Father, if I truly bring you bliss, and I know I do, then come close. Let's spend the day together. All that's good and pleasing in your sight is a gift from you. I can't even take credit for the love I love you with! Thank you for loving me so completely and giving me the honor of living with you.

Favor

I am now a firm wall of protection for others,
guarding them from harm.
This is how he sees me—I am the one who brings him bliss,
finding favor in his eyes.
—Song of Songs 8:10

*N*othing will stand in the way of the purposes of God for you when He is the center of your life. There may be many different paths that lead you forth in your destiny, but as you fix your eyes on Him, He will guide each step. His favor will open doors of opportunity that surprise you.

Be confident! Expect to see the promises of God come to pass in your life. His favor will demolish walls that try to withstand you. It will draw people to you who normally wouldn't give you the time of day. They will be like keys, unlocking doors that you couldn't go through before. Shake off discouragement and unbelief because your day of favor has come! You have found favor with God and those around you, and it's better than all the riches in the world. God's hand of blessing is upon your life.

Father, I sense your favor surrounding me. Thank you for these amazing doors of opportunity that are opening. They always come at the perfect time, and you love to surprise me. Give me wisdom to navigate them well. I'm excited to see where this path of blessing will lead. I expect to live under the covering of your favor, forever.

Vineyard of Love

My bridegroom-king has a vineyard of love
made from a multitude of followers.
His caretakers of this vineyard
have given my beloved their best.

—Song of Songs 8:11

God's intentions are always for your good and are motivated by His great compassion. His vineyard of love is bursting with ripened fruit, and He's invited you to eat your fill. Health, favor, joy, wisdom, and peace are ready to be plucked from the vine of His eternal blessing.

You were created to enjoy Him and to enjoy life. He wants the best for you. That doesn't mean that you won't go through hard times. It does mean, however, that when you go through hard times, He will be with you. He will draw you into the provision of His love and the faithfulness of His promises. He will heal every wound with the kisses of a good Father. His love will cause you to overcome.

❧

Father, your love satisfies my greatest needs. It's intoxicating and delightful. Life with you is vibrant and enjoyable—a vineyard of the choicest fruit. Even when the darkest clouds sit like shadows upon my soul, your love bursts through with joy that sets me free.

Chosen

> My bridegroom-king has a vineyard of love
> made from a multitude of followers.
> ***His caretakers of this vineyard***
> have given my beloved their best.
> —Song of Songs 8:11

The king's vineyard is a picture of the church. The Creator of the universe, the One who breathed form and substance into every living thing, trusts you to take care of those He loves. Redeemed by His fiery love, *you* have been put in charge of tending His vineyard.

As His bride, you have been chosen to be a mother or father to those He's placed in your care. Mentor them, encourage them, champion them in their calling, dreams, and anointing. Inspire them to grow closer to the Lord than you are and to become all that their hearts' desire. Never pull people to you for what they can do for you, but rather to help them fulfill their destiny. Treat everyone with love and respect. Carry yourself with honor and integrity. Remember, not only are *you* royalty, but those you serve are as well.

❦

Jesus, you inspire me, and I want to inspire others the same way. Give me grace and wisdom to lead others in their pursuit of you. Help me to represent you well and to equip others the best that I can with no thought for what I will get out of it. Thank you for choosing me to tend your vineyard of love.

Forever

> But as for **my own vineyard of love,**
> **I give it all to you forever.**
> And I will give double honor
> to those who serve my beloved
> and have watched over my soul.
>
> —Song of Songs 8:12

Nothing pleases the Lord more than when you invite Him into every moment. Whether it's spending time with Him in prayer, acknowledging Him throughout the day, thanking Him when things go well, or offering comfort to the hurting, He loves doing life with you. Your vineyard—your very life—encases everything you do and think.

This is a relationship that will last forever. This tangible reality starts right now. Invite Him today to enjoy you, in every thought, word, and action. Share every aspect of your life with Him, so that everything is impacted by His holy power. Offer Him your best by living in a way that beckons His presence and displays His love for others.

❧

Father, I want to be an example of one who loves you wholeheartedly, so all your lovers will follow me as I follow you. Fill every hour of my day with the reality of your nearness. I want every thought to lead to you and every action to reflect this love that has pierced my soul.

Honor

But as for my own vineyard of love,
I give it all to you forever.
And *I will give double honor*
to those who serve my beloved
and have watched over my soul.

—Song of Songs 8:12

O h, how it pleases the Lord's heart when you honor His servants. Those who labor in ministry—pastors, missionaries, those who reach the homeless, the ones who rescue children from the sex trade, or the parent who's raising a child in the ways of the Lord—all deserve to be treated with dignity and respect. You may not agree with everyone's doctrine. They may even be misusing their power, but you are called to honor and never criticize.

No matter what people do, regardless of how terrible their attitudes or actions may be at times, always look for the good in them. If you can't seem to find anything, ask the Lord how *He* sees them. This is how we honor and represent His Kingdom well. Always be willing to shower mercy, grace, and compassion on others, the same way God does to you.

❧

Father, I want to be a vessel of honor. I want to be known as a person who can find the good in anyone. May I always treat your servants with the respect they deserve. I want to see everyone through your eyes. Help me to represent your Kingdom well and make people feel honored and appreciated.

Reward

And I will give double honor
to those who serve my beloved
and have watched over my soul.

—Song of Songs 8:12

*L*iving by this standard of honoring others means remembering to recognize those who have helped you on your journey. When you stand before God in heaven, He'll not only reward you for what you have done on this earth, but He'll also honor those who have poured into your life through prayer, counsel, and friendship. In His eyes, they have a part in all you accomplish for Him, and they will be rewarded for it.

Those who have cared for you, supported you, and taught you deserve to be honored. Think back to different seasons of your life and the people God brought to help you through. Whether you're still in contact with them or not, perhaps you could reach out and thank them. If the relationship has been damaged, maybe this is your nudge to restore. Find a way to show appreciation to those who have walked side by side with you. This simple act of honoring doesn't only bless them; it blesses the Lord.

Lord, when I think of all the people you've brought into my life to help me at different times, I feel so loved. Whether they've only helped me once or have stuck with me through thick and thin, I still remember their kindness and support. Bless them all, Lord! I'm so grateful for the way you have loved me through them.

One

My beloved, one with me in my garden,
how marvelous that my friends, the brides-to-be,
now hear your voice and song.
Let me now hear it again.

—SONG OF SONGS 8:13

It may not always feel like it, but you are one with the Lord. You were created to hear what's on His heart, to see things the way He sees them, and to believe what He believes. He is the God who turns impossibility into possibility. He holds the answer to every problem. He never worries or succumbs to temptation. He is righteous and holy, filled with joy and faith for every situation.

You can live in full awareness of His presence in you, every single day. Let your faith soar to new heights. Everything that He is, you are. Release your cares and take on His thoughts. Make His attitude your attitude. It's time for a shift into hope that never disappoints. This is your portion and your inheritance. God is for you, and He will make a way even if there seems to be no way.

Father, I want to think like you—to always expect the best outcome in every situation. I want to always hear the voice of hope and faith rising within me, when doubt, fear, or worry try to raise their ugly heads. You are the God of victory, peace, and joy, and you are one with me!

Finding Your Tribe

My beloved, one with me *in my garden,*
how marvelous that my friends, the brides-to-be,
now hear your voice and song.
Let me now hear it again.
—SONG OF SONGS 8:13

One of the important ways of tending to the garden of our soul is by finding like-minded believers to surround ourselves with. I like to call it "finding your tribe." This means finding people you feel comfortable around—people you can open up to and be real with. People who mutually encourage and support each other.

There are different levels of friendship, but some of the most impacting may come from those who aren't close friends yet always know the right thing to say. Finding friends who you're willing to invite into the garden of your life takes time. Perhaps you don't fit in where you are, or you can't find like-minded people. Don't give up! Ask the Lord to help you find your tribe, and get ready! God is faithful to bring people into your life both to bless you and to be blessed by you.

❧

Father, surround me with people who make me feel known and loved and who will be blessed by what I have to offer. Regardless of the package they come in, whether they're young, old, or slightly different from what I'm used to, I know you will help me to find my tribe—the place where I fit in.

Listen

My beloved, one with me in my garden,
how marvelous that my friends, the brides-to-be,
now hear your voice and song.
Let me now hear it again.

—Song of Songs 8:13

*L*ean in and incline your ear to your Father's voice. God fashioned you with the ability to hear Him and to know when He speaks. Discovering the many different ways He conveys His heart is a process. The longer we walk with the Lord, the more exciting it is to realize how often He's actually speaking.

His voice is frequently a quiet small thought that rises within and gives you hope and wisdom. Sometimes it's an unsettling feeling, warning you not to do something. Many times, it comes through the things you read or watch. It encourages you through the words of a worship song, imparts wisdom through a book, is heard through the counsel of a friend, or countless other ways. It never contradicts His Word, and it always settles well within you, even if it's challenging. Pay attention. God is speaking to you today.

❧

I'm listening, Lord. I know I'll be learning to discern your voice for my entire life, but that's okay—it creates desire to hear you more. I love the many ways you get my attention. It doesn't matter how you speak to me; I just want to know when you do. Help me discover your voice in unexpected ways today.

Arise

The Bridegroom and the Bride in Divine Duet
Arise, my darling!
Come quickly, my beloved.
Come and be the graceful gazelle with me.
Come be like a dancing deer with me.

—SONG OF SONGS 8:14

*J*esus is calling you closer. He never tires of you and no matter how close you are to Him; you can always draw closer. This is the life of the bride—to spend your life becoming more acquainted with His love, growing in His grace, and ascending from glory to glory.

Jesus is cheering you on, calling you to arise and shine—to know Him intimately and to release this love to others. This is your purpose! Now is your time. You don't need to wait until things are exactly as you think they should be before you can pour out to others. You only need to have confidence in the One who is in you and with you. Arise and leave complacency behind. Go and be His hands, His compassion, and His voice. The world is waiting.

❦

Jesus, when I say your name, my heart comes alive. Excitement wells within as I realize all you've done inside me. With joy, I come closer every day. Let the fragrance of your presence be released by the way I live and love. May your glory shine forth from me, even when I don't say a word.

Come Quickly

The Bridegroom and the Bride in Divine Duet
Arise, my darling!
Come quickly, my beloved.
Come and be the graceful gazelle with me.
Come be like a dancing deer with me.

—Song of Songs 8:14

Oh, how He loves you! Deep within your spirit, a cry is erupting—it thunders in unison with the desire of God. United in urgency, His will mingling with yours, the longing for continual communion, and the desire to run together are overwhelming. The more you know Him, the greater your motivation to know Him more.

No one touches your spirit and revives your soul like Jesus does. Each morning, when you open your eyes, let your heart reach for Him. Expect Him to rush to meet with you. Get excited about the ideas that stir your heart when He is near. He is ready and willing to run with you as you invite Him to guide you each day. Let your yearning for Him lead you to His heart for others.

Lord, faith is exploding within me. The details of my purpose will fall into place as I set my heart on these two things: to love you and share this love with others. Your presence, stirring within, is impossible to ignore, so I will rise with you, shake off procrastination, and go.

You Were Made for This!

The Bridegroom and the Bride in Divine Duet
Arise, my darling!
Come quickly, my beloved.
Come and be the graceful gazelle with me.
Come be like a dancing deer with me.

—SONG OF SONGS 8:14

*L*et you heart soar with freedom as you realize that everything is possible with the Lord. What once scared you—those mountains you once were afraid to climb—have become your playground. Insurmountable walls of opposition have become dust under your feet.

It's time to become confident in who you are so you don't give a second thought to God's invitation to reach greater heights. Soon, with the agility of a gazelle, you will frolic in situations that once caused you to cower and hide. Instead of dreading the attacks of the enemy, courage and boldness become weapons that destroy him. You know that nothing can stop the power of God within you. You were made for the mountains. God will not let you fall. You were made for freedom!

❧

Father, I feel faith rising in me like never before. Some of the situations I'm facing seem like insurmountable mountains, but fear has no place in me. You are my Champion, and with you, I always win. I will stand on your Word and see your victory come to pass.

Dance with Him

We will dance in the high place of the sky,
yes, on the mountains of fragrant spice.
Forever we shall be united as one!

—Song of Songs 8:14

The fears that once held you captive have been obliterated. Inhibitions have turned into dances of freedom. Forever you will dance in the highest realms of glory, rejoicing over your glorious union with Him.

Jesus is the Lord of the dance, and He ever so skillfully leads you into the most beautiful pas-de-deux of all time. You cannot stumble when He holds you in His arms. You are beautiful and graceful, powerful in every move you execute. Even the angels stand in awe of this effortless dance you share with the Lord. You are destined to move in perfect unity with Him, and you don't have to wait until you get to heaven—you can dance with Him now. Jesus is extending His hand to you today and saying, "May I have this dance?"

❧

Jesus, take my hand and lead me. May every movement of my spirit, soul, and body flow in harmony with you. Let your grace refine me and your power transform me into the most glorious bride of all.

Victorious

We will dance in the high place of the sky,
yes, **on the mountains of fragrant spice.**
Forever we shall be united as one!
—Song of Songs 8:14

*N*othing can stop you if you just believe. In every season of the soul, victory runs deeper than what you see. Difficulties only serve to strengthen you. Mountains that once separated you from the Lord are now easy to climb. God has become the strength of your life.

The same mountain of spices that once caused you to cower in fear now excites your sense of adventure. Trials that tried to destroy you have become foundations for you to dance upon. They now serve as memorials for some of God's greatest manifestations of love in your life. You can look at the past and laugh because you are more than a conqueror! Jesus has proven His love for you. Now go! Enjoy life as His conquering bride. You are victorious!

❧

Jesus, you empower me to do things I never thought I could. I'm not afraid of the mountains anymore because you've proved your faithfulness so many times. I look forward to each day and every season of my soul because you are with me. In you, I am victorious!

One

We will dance in the high place of the sky,
yes, on the mountains of fragrant spice.
Forever we shall be united as one!

—Song of Songs 8:14

Lift your voice and rejoice! In heaven, you will forever be united with the Lord. Dancing together in unbroken communion in the high places of the sky, you will one day skip with Him, never to be separated again. You will receive your full inheritance and see Him face-to-face with nothing to obscure your view. All of your questions will find their answer and all of your pain will disappear.

The best part is that eternity starts now. The joy you'll experience in heaven, the nearness of the Lord, the peace and the wholeness—all were designed to begin while you're still here on earth. Life with the Lord *now* should be a taste of heaven. Unspeakable happiness awaits you there, but it is available to you today. Tap into the joys of heaven that surpass your natural circumstances. Receive all that God has for you! You were created to be one with Him. You are destined for joy!

Jesus, when I think about the joys of heaven, I can hardly contain myself. Though I already see you in part, it thrills my heart to imagine what it will be like to see you face-to-face. Take my hand and lead me into your eternal joys that begin right now. I am one with you—yours forever.

About the Authors

Dr. Brian Simmons is known as a passionate lover of God and the lead translator of The Passion Translation, a new heart-level Bible translation that conveys God's passion for people and His world by translating the original, life-changing message of God's Word for modern readers. Brian and his wife, Candice, travel full-time as speakers and Bible teachers.

Gretchen Rodriguez is a writer and author of award-winning fiction. Her heart burns with one main message: intimacy with Jesus and discovering the reality of His presence. She is also a dancer and ballet teacher. Gretchen, her husband, and their three daughters invested nine years as missionaries in Puerto Rico and now make Redding, California, their home.